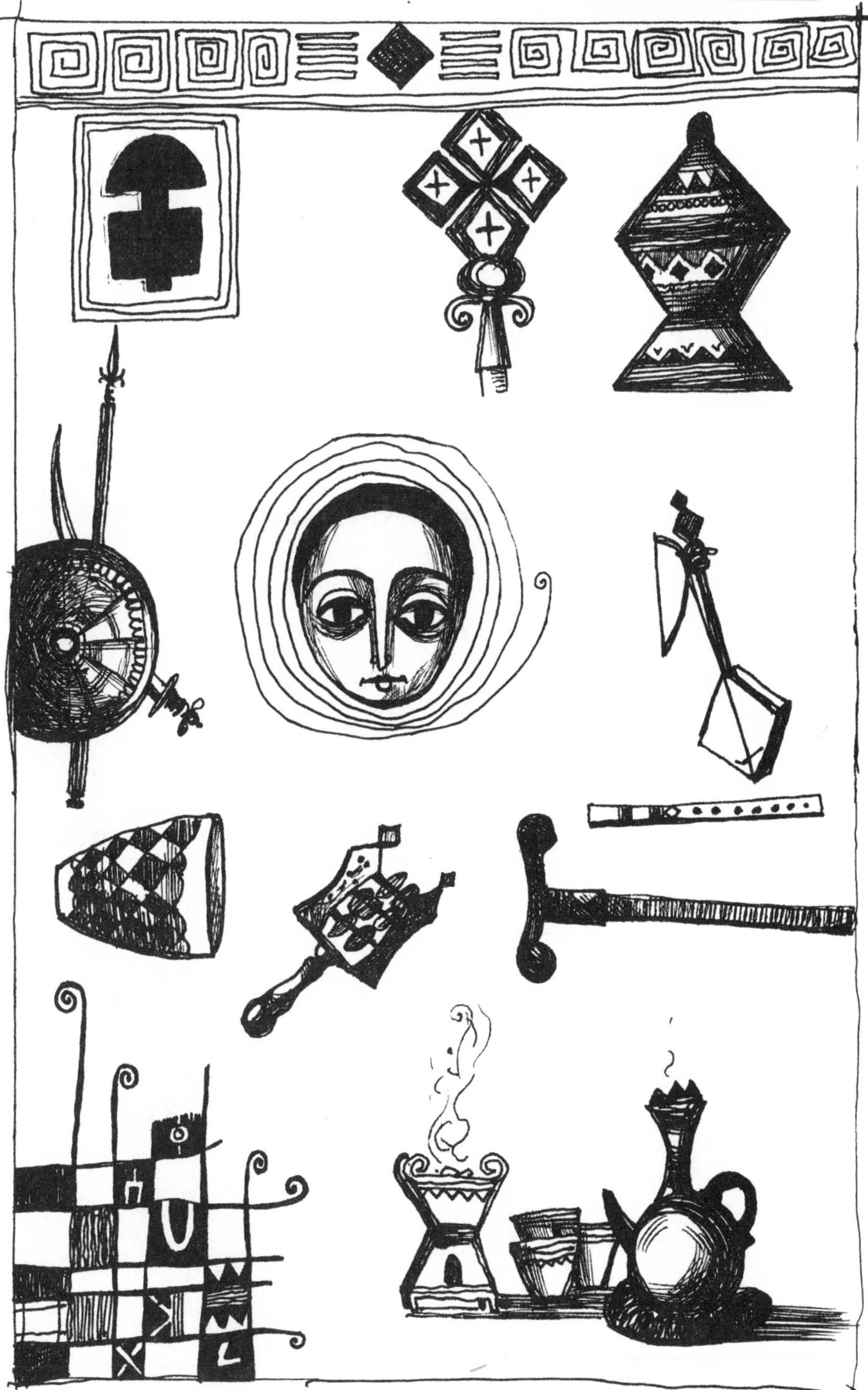

1 PERSONAL IDENTIFICATION

How to give and ask information about ...
1. Name
2. Home address
3. Telephone number
4. Age
5. Nationality
6. Likes and dislikes

A. **QUESTIONS**	B. **ANSWERS**
1.1 What's [What is] your name?	1.2 (My name is) Charles. 1.3 (My name is) Mary.
2.1 What's your address?	2.2 (My address is) 5, Market Street.
3.1 What's your telephone number?	3.2 (My telephone number is) 340 1256.

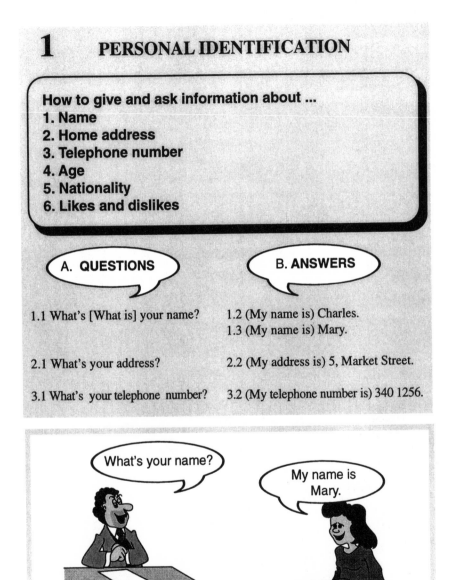

የግል መረጃ

እንዴት መረጃ እንደምትሰጥና እንደምትጠይቅ
1. ስም
2. አድራሻ
3. የስልክ ቊጥር
4. ዕድሜ
5. ዜግነት
6. የምትወደውና የምትጠላው

1.1 ስምህ ማን ነው? (m)
ስምሽ ማን ነው? (f)

1.2 ስሜ ቻርለስ ነው
1.3 ስሜ ሚርያም ነው

2.1 አድራሻህ የት ነው? (m)
አድራሻሽ የት ነው? (f)

2.2 ገበያ ጎዳና ቊ. 5 ነው

3.1 የስልክ ቊጥርህ ስንት ነው? (m)
የስልክ ቊጥርሽ ስንት ነው? (f)

3.2 የስልክ ቊጥሬ 340 1256 ነው

IDENTIFICAZIONE PERSONALE

Come dare e chiedere informazioni su ...
1. il nome
2. l'indirizzo
3. il numero di telefono
4. l'età
5. la nazionalità
6. le preferenze

1.1 Come ti chiami?

1.2 (Mi chiamo) Carlo.
1.3 (Mi chiamo) Maria.

2.1 Qual è il tuo indirizzo?

2.2 (Il mio indirizzo è) Via del Mercato, n. 5.

3.1 Qual è il tuo numero di telefono?

3.2 (Il mio numero di telefono è) 340 12 56.

4.1 How old are you?	4.2 I'm fourteen. 4.3 I'm fifteen. 4.4 I'm sixteen.
4.5 When were you born ?	4.6 (I was born) on the 2nd of January 1974.
4.7 When is your birthday?	4.8The 3rd of February. 4.9 The 4th of March.
5.1 What nationality are you?	5.2 I'm English. 5.3 I'm Italian. 5.4 I'm American. 5.5 I'm Ethiopian.
5.6 Are you Italian? 5.8 Is he/she English? 5.10 Are you Italian? 5.12 Are they English?	5.7 No, I'm Spanish. 5.9 No, he/she is American. 5.11 No, we are Spanish. 5.13 No, they are American.

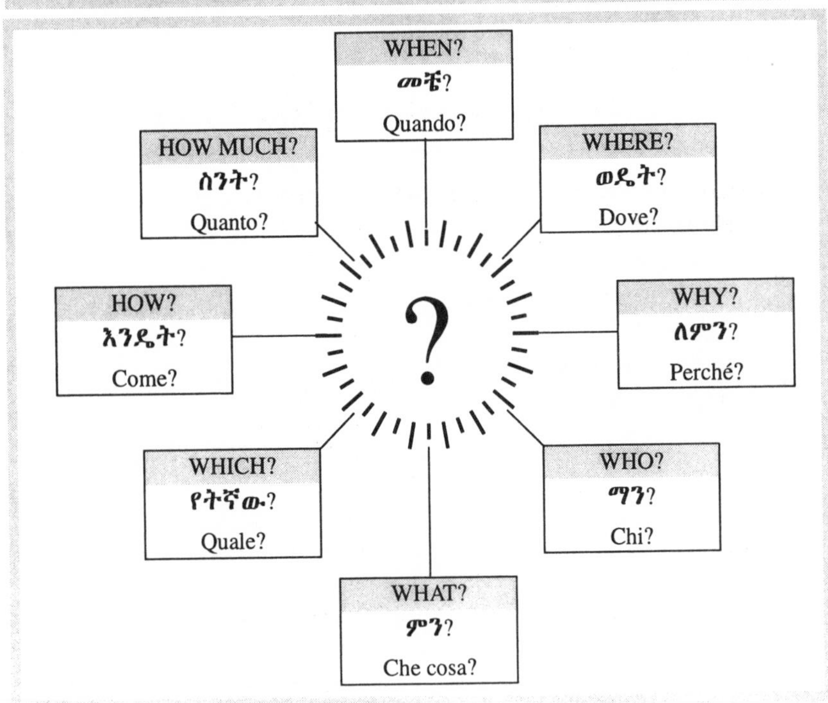

4.1 ዕድሜህ ስንት ነው? (m) 4.1 ዕድሜሽ ስንት ነው? (f)	4.2 ዕድሜዬ 14 ነው 4.3 ዕድሜዬ 15 ነው 4.4 ዕድሜዬ 16 ነው
4.5 መቼ ተወለድክ/ሽ?	4.6 ጥር 2/1974
4.7 የተወለድክበት ዕለት መቼ ነው? (m) የተወለድሽበት ዕለት መቼ ነው? (f)	4.8 የካቲት 3 4.9 መጋቢት 4
5.1 ዜግነትህ/ሽ ምንድ ነው?	5.2 እንግሊዛዊ/ት ነኝ 5.3 ኢጣልያዊ/ት ነኝ 5.4 አመሪካዊ/ት ነኝ 5.5 ኢትዮጵያዊ/ት ነኝ
5.6 ኢጣልያዊ/ት ነህ/ነሽ?	5.7 አይደለሁም፡ እስፓኛዊ/ት ነኝ
5.8 እንግሊዛዊ/ት ነው/ናት?	5.9 አይደለም/አይደለችም፡ አመሪካዊ/ት ነው/ናት
5.10 ኢጣልያውያን ናችሁ?	5.11 አይደለንም፡ እስፓኛውያን ነን
5.12 እንግሊዛውያን ናቸው?	5.13 አይደሉም፡ አመሪካውያን ናቸው

4.1 Quanti anni hai?	4.2 Ho quattordici anni. 4.3 Ho quindici anni. 4.4 Ho sedici anni.
4.5 Quando sei nato? (m) Quando sei nata? (f)	4.6 (Sono nato) il 2 gennaio 1974. (Sono nata) il 2 gennaio 1974.
4.7 Quando è il tuo compleanno?	4.8 Il 3 febbraio. 4.9 Il 4 marzo.
5.1 Di che nazionalità sei?	5.2 Sono inglese. 5.3 Sono italiano/a. 5.4 Sono americano/a. 5.5 Sono etiope.
5.6 Sei italiano/a?	5.7 No, sono spagnolo/a.
5.8 È inglese?	5.9 No, è americano/a.
5.10 Siete italiani/e?	5.11 No, siamo spagnoli/e.
5.12Sono inglesi?	5.13 No, sono americani/e.

5.14 Where were you born?

5.15 (I was born) in Gondar.
5.16 (I was born) in Addis Ababa.
5.17 (I was born) in Italy.
5.18 (I was born) in England.

5.19 Where are you from?

5.20 I'm from England.
5.21 I'm from Italy.
5.22 I'm from the United States.
5.23 I'm from Ethiopia.

6.1 Do you like Italian?
6.3 Do you like this book?
6.4 Do you like this pen?

6.2 Yes, I do [I like it].

6.5 Do you like these books?
6.7 Do you like these pens?

6.6 Yes, I do [I like them].
6.8 No, I prefer these (pens).

5.14 የት ነው የተወለድከው? (m)
የት ነው የተወለድሽው? (f)

5.15 ጎንደር ነው የተወለድኩት
5.16 አዲስ አበባ ነው የተወለድኩት
5.17 ጣልያን አገር ነው የተወለድኩት
5.18 እንግሊዝ አገር ነው የተወለድኩት

5.19 ከየት ነው የመጣሃው? (m)
ከየት ነው የመጣሽው? (f)

5.20 ከእንግሊዝ አገር
5,21 ከጣልያን አገር
5.22 ከተባበሩት የአመሪካ መንግስታት
5.23 ከኢትዮጵያ

6.1 ጣልያንኛ ትወዳለህ/ትወጅያለሽ ወይ?
6.3 ይቺ መጽሐፍ ደስ ትልሃለች/
ትልሻለች ወይ?
6.4 ይቺ እስክሪፕቶ ደስ ትልሃለች/
ትልሻለች ወይ?

6.2 አዎ፡ እወዳለሁኝ
አዎ፡ ደስ ትለኛለች

6.5 እነኚህ መጻሕፍት ደስ ይሉሃል/
ይሉሻል ወይ?
6.7 እነኚህ እስክሪፕቶዎች ደስ ይሉሃል/
ይሉሻል ወይ?

6.6 አዎ፡ ደስ ይሉኛል
6.8 አይሉኝም፡ እነኚህን እስክሪፕቶች
እመርጣለሁ

INFORMALE (tu)	**FORMALE (Lei)**
Ciao!	Buongiorno!
Come ti chiami?	Come si chiama?
Ti presento Franco.	Le presento il signor Marconi.
Di che nazionalità sei?	Di che nazionalità è?
Di dove sei?	Di dove è?
Parli italiano?	Parla italiano?
Come stai?	Come sta?
Non c'è male. E tu?	Non c'è male. E lei?
Qual è il tuo indirizzo?	Qual è il suo indirizzo?
Quando è il tuo compleanno?	Quando è il suo compleanno?
Quanti anni hai?	Quanti anni ha?
Sei sposato?	E' sposato?
Ti piace l'italiano?	Le piace l'italiano?

5.14 Dove sei nato?
Dove sei nata?

5.15 Sono nato/a a Gondar.
5.16 Sono nato/a ad Addis Abeba.
5.17 Sono nato/a in Italia.
5.18 Sono nato/a in Inghilterra.

5.19 Da dove vieni?

5.20 (Vengo) dall'Inghilterra.
5.21 (Vengo) dall'Italia.
5.22 (Vengo) dagli Stati Uniti.
5.23 (Vengo) dall'Etiopia.

6.1 Ti piace l'italiano?
6.3 Ti piace questo libro?
6.4 Ti piace questa penna?

6.2 Sì, (mi piace).

6.5 Ti piacciono questi libri?
6.7 Ti piacciono queste penne?

6.6 Sì, (mi piacciono).
6.8 No, (preferisco queste penne).

Numbers
አሃዞች
Numeri

0 zero			
1 one	11 eleven	21 twenty-one	40 forty
2 two	12 twelve	22 twenty-two	50 fifty
3 three	13 thirteen	23 twenty-three	60 sixty
4 four	14 fourteen	24 twenty-four	70 seventy
5 five	15 fifteen	25 twenty-five	80 eighty
6 six	16 sixteen	26 twenty-six	90 ninety
7 seven	17 seventeen	27 twenty-seven	100 a/one hundred
8 eight	18 eighteen	28 twenty-eight	200 two hundred
9 nine	19 nineteen	29 twenty-nine	1,000 a/one thousand
10 ten	20 twenty	30 thirty	1,000,000 a/one million

0 ዜሮ			
1 አንድ	11 አስራ አንድ	21 ሀያ አንድ	40 አርባ
2 ሁለት	12 አስራ ሁለት	22 ሀያ ሁለት	50 ሃምሳ (አምሳ)
3 ሦስት	13 አስራ ሦስት	23 ሀያ ሦስት	60 ስልሳ
4 አራት	14 አስራ አራት	24 ሀያ አራት	70 ሰባ
5 አምስት	15 አስራ አምስት	25 ሀያ አምስት	80 ሰማንያ
6 ስድስት	16 አስራ ስድስት	26 ሀያ ስድስት	90 ዘጠና
7 ሰባት	17 አስራ ሰባት	27 ሀያ ሰባት	100 መቶ
8 ስምንት	18 አስራ ስምንት	28 ሀያ ስምንት	200 ሁለት መቶ
9 ዘጠኝ	19 አስራ ዘጠኝ	29 ሀያ ዘጥኝ	1,000 አንድ ሺ
10 አስር	20 ሀያ	30 ሰላሳ	1,000,000 አንድ ሚልዮን

0 zero			
1 uno	11 undici	21 ventuno	40 quaranta
2 due	12 dodici	22 ventidue	50 cinquanta
3 tre	13 tredici	23 ventitré	60 sessanta
4 quattro	14 quattordici	24 ventiquattro	70 settanta
5 cinque	15 quindici	25 venticinque	80 ottanta
6 sei	16 sedici	26 ventisei	90 novanta
7 sette	17 diciassette	27 ventisette	100 cento
8 otto	18 diciotto	28 ventotto	200 duecento
9 nove	19 diciannove	29 ventinove	1.000 mille
10 dieci	20 venti	30 trenta	1.000.000 un milione

How to describe a person
ሰውን እንዴት ትገልጸዋለህ
Come descrivere una persona

1. Who?	Charles, Mary, David, ...
2. Age	He/She is ... (years old).
3. Height	Tall, short, medium height, ...
4. Build	Thin, fat, robust/strong, slim, ...
5. Hair	• Long, short, ... • Brown, black/dark, blonde/fair, ... • Straight hair, curly hair, ...
6. Eyes	Hazel, light blue, green, ...
7. Dress	Sporty/casual (wear), elegant/smart, ...
8. Character	Cheerful, good, calm, amusing, happy, kind, intelligent, nervous, honest, lazy, strict, lively, unpleasant, nice, ...
9. Occupation	Driver, waiter, housewife, shop-assistant, dentist, manager, unemployed, butcher, teacher (primary), mechanic, doctor, policeman, teacher, secretary, student, ...

1. ማን	ካርሎ፡ ሚርያም፡ ዳዊት
2. ዕድሜ	... ነው
3. ቁመት	ረጂም፡ አጭር፡ መካከለኛ
4. ቁመና	ቀጭን፡ ወፍራም፡ ጠንካራ፡ ሸንቃጣ
5. የራስ ጠጉር	ረጅም፡ አጭር፡ ቡናማ፡ ጥቁር፡ ቢጫ፡ ሉጫ ጠጉር፡ጥቅልል
6. አይኖች	ቡናማ፡ ሰማያዊ፡ አረንጓዴ
7. አለባበስ	ስፖርታዊ፡ ቄንጤኛ
8. ጸባይ	ደስተኛ፡ ጐበዝ፡ ዝምተኛ፡ ቀልደኛ፡ ደስታ የተሞላው፡ ተጫዋች፡ ብልህ፡ ቍጡ፡ ቅን፡ ሰነፍ፡ ጠንካራ፡ ተናዳጅ አስቀያሚ፡ ተወዳጅ
9. ሞያ	ሹፌር፡ አሳላፊ፡ ባለትዳር፡ የሱቅቤት ሰራተኛ፡ የጥርስ ሓኪም፡ ዲረክተር፡ ስራፈት፡ ስጋ ሻጭ፡ አስተማሪ፡ መካኒክ፡ ሓኪም፡ ፖሊስ፡ አስተማሪ፡ ጸሓፊ፡ ተማሪ

---

1. Chi?	Carlo, Maria, David, ...
2. Età	Ha ... anni.
3. Altezza	Alto, basso, di statura media, ...
4. Corporatura	Magro, grasso, robusto, snello, ...
5. Capelli	• Lunghi, corti, ... • Castani, neri, biondi, ... • Lisci, ricci, ...
6. Occhi	Castani, azzurri, verdi, ...
7. Abbigliamento	Sportivo, elegante, ...
8. Carattere	Allegro, bravo, calmo, divertente, felice, gentile, intelligente, nervoso, onesto, pigro, severo, vivace, antipatico, simpatico, ...
9. Mestieri e professioni	Autista, cameriere, casalinga, commesso, dentista, direttore, disoccupato, macellaio, maestro, meccanico, medico, poliziotto, professore, segretario, studente, ...

AMHARIC ALPHABET

1° Gï‘ïz	2° Ka‘ïb	3° Salïs	4° Rabï‘	5° Hamïs	6° Sadïs	7° Sabï‘
ሀ	ሁ	ሂ	ሃ	ሄ	ህ	ሆ
ለ	ሉ	ሊ	ላ	ሌ	ል	ሎ
ሐ	ሑ	ሒ	ሓ	ሔ	ሕ	ሖ
መ	ሙ	ሚ	ማ	ሜ	ም	ሞ
ሠ	ሡ	ሢ	ሣ	ሤ	ሥ	ሦ
ረ	ሩ	ሪ	ራ	ሬ	ር	ሮ
ሰ	ሱ	ሲ	ሳ	ሴ	ስ	ሶ
ሸ	ሹ	ሺ	ሻ	ሼ	ሽ	ሾ
ቀ	ቁ	ቂ	ቃ	ቄ	ቅ	ቆ
በ	ቡ	ቢ	ባ	ቤ	ብ	ቦ
ተ	ቱ	ቲ	ታ	ቴ	ት	ቶ
ቸ	ቹ	ቺ	ቻ	ቼ	ች	ቾ
ኀ	ኁ	ኂ	ኃ	ኄ	ኅ	ኆ
ነ	ኑ	ኒ	ና	ኔ	ን	ኖ
ኘ	ኙ	ኚ	ኛ	ኜ	ኝ	ኞ
አ	ኡ	ኢ	ኣ	ኤ	እ	ኦ
ከ	ኩ	ኪ	ካ	ኬ	ክ	ኮ
ኸ	ኹ	ኺ	ኻ	ኼ	ኽ	ኾ
ወ	ዉ	ዊ	ዋ	ዌ	ው	ዎ
ዐ	ዑ	ዒ	ዓ	ዔ	ዕ	ዖ
ዘ	ዙ	ዚ	ዛ	ዜ	ዝ	ዞ
ዠ	ዡ	ዢ	ዣ	ዤ	ዥ	ዦ
የ	ዩ	ዪ	ያ	ዬ	ይ	ዮ
ደ	ዱ	ዲ	ዳ	ዴ	ድ	ዶ
ጀ	ጁ	ጂ	ጃ	ጄ	ጅ	ጆ
ገ	ጉ	ጊ	ጋ	ጌ	ግ	ጎ
ጠ	ጡ	ጢ	ጣ	ጤ	ጥ	ጦ
ጨ	ጩ	ጪ	ጫ	ጬ	ጭ	ጮ
ጰ	ጱ	ጲ	ጳ	ጴ	ጵ	ጶ
ጸ	ጹ	ጺ	ጻ	ጼ	ጽ	ጾ
ፀ	ፁ	ፂ	ፃ	ፄ	ፅ	ፆ
ፈ	ፉ	ፊ	ፋ	ፌ	ፍ	ፎ
ፐ	ፑ	ፒ	ፓ	ፔ	ፕ	ፖ
ቨ	ቩ	ቪ	ቫ	ቬ	ቭ	ቮ
ኈ		ኊ	ኋ	ኌ	ኍ	
ኰ		ኲ	ኳ	ኴ	ኵ	
ቈ		ቊ	ቋ	ቌ	ቍ	
ጐ		ጒ	ጓ	ጔ	ጕ	

• See **Phonetic Transcriptions** p. 191

ENGLISH ALPHABET

A B C D E F G H I J K L M N O P Q R S T U V W X Y Z

ALFABETO ITALIANO

A B C D E F G H I L M N O P Q R S T U V Z (J K W X Y)

Key phrases ቍልፍ ቃላት Fraseologia essenziale

Key phrases	ቍልፍ ቃላት	Fraseologia essenziale
1. Do you speak English?	1. እንግሊዝኛ ትናገራለህ ወይ?	1. Parli inglese? Parla inglese? *
2. Not very well.	2. እስከዚህም አይደለም	2. Non molto bene.
3. Can you repeat, please?	3. እባክዎን ይድገሙልኝ	3. Potrebbe ripetere?
4. I don't understand.	4. አልገባኝም	4. Non capisco.
5. How do you say ...?	5. ምን ይባላል?	5. Come si dice ...?
6. How do you write ...?	6. እንዴት ይጻፋል?	6. Come si scrive ...?
7. What does ... mean?	7. ምን ማለትነው?	7. Che cosa vuol dire ...?
8. Excuse me!	8. ይቅርታ አድርግልኝ	8. Scusi?
9. I'm sorry.	9. አዝናለሁ	9. Mi dispiace.
10. Please.	10. እባክህን/ሽን	10. Per piacere.
11. Thank you.	11. አመሰግናለሁ	11. Grazie!
12. You're welcome.	12. ምንም አይደል	12. Prego!
13. How are you?	13. እንደምን ነህ/ነሽ?	13. Come stai? Come sta? *
14. Not bad.	14. ደህና	14. Non c'è male.
15. Very well, thank you. And you?	15. መልካም፥ እርስዎስ?	15. Bene grazie e tu/Lei?
16. Not too good ...	16. ብዙ አልተመቸኝም	16. Non molto bene ...
17. Good morning.	17. እንደምን አደሩ	17. Buongiorno.
18. Good evening.	18. እንደምን አመሹ	18. Buonasera.
19. Good night.	19. መልካም ሌሊት	19. Buonanotte.
20. Good-bye.	20. ደህና ሁኑ	20. Arrivederci.
21. Hello/Bye/See you!	21, ጤና ይስጥልኝ፥ ደህና ሁኑ፥ በደህና ያገናኘን	21. Ciao!
22. See you tomorrow.	22. ነገ እንገናኝ	22. A domani.
23. This is Mary.	23. ይቺ ሚርያም ናት	23. Questa è Maria.
24. May I introduce Mr. Keith Willis?	24. ከአቶ ከይዝ ዊልስ ጋር ላስተዋውቅህ ወይ?	24. Le presento il signor Marconi.
25. How do you do?	25. እንደምን ነዎት?	25. Piacere.
26. Pleased to meet you.	26.መልካም ትውውቅ ያድርግልን	26. Molto lieto (m) Molto lieta (f)

* Formale

2 FAMILY

HOW TO ...
Ask information about members of the family

1.1 How many are you in your family?

1.2 There are four of us.

1.3 Are there many of you in your family?

1.4 What's your father's name?

1.5 (His name is) Charles.
He's [He is] called Charles.

1.6 What is your grandfather's name?
1.7 What is your brother's name?
1.8 What is your uncle's name?
1.9 What is your cousin's name?
1.10 What is your son's name?
1.11 What is your husband's name?
1.12 What is your brother-in-law's name?
1.13 What is your nephew's name?
1.14 What is your father-in-law called?

ቤተ ሰብ

እንዴት ...
ስለ ቤተ ሰብ አባሎች መረጃ እንደምትጠይቅ

1.1 የቤተ ሰባችሁ አባላት ስንት ናቸው? 1.2 አራት ነን
1.3 በቤተ ሰባችሁ ስንት ናችሁ?

1.4 የአባትህ/ሽ ስም ማን ይባላል? (m/f) 1.5 ቻርለስ ይባላል
1.6 የአያትህ/ሽ ስም ማን ይባላል?
1.7 የወንድምህ/ሽ ስም ማን ይባላል?
1.8 የአጎትህ/ሽ ስም ማን ይባላል?
1.9 ያጎትህ/ሽ ልጅ ማን ይባላል?
የአክስትህ ልጅ ማን ይባላል?
1.10 የልጅህ/ሽ ስም ማን ይባላል?
1.11 የባለቤትሽ ስም ማን ይባላል?
1.12 የእህትህ/ሽ ባል ማን ይባላል?
1.13 የእህትህ/ሽ ልጅ ማን ይባላል?
የወንድምህ/ሽ ልጅ ማን ይባላል?
1.14 የአማችህ/ሽ ስም ማን ይባላል?

FAMIGLIA

Come ...
chiedere informazioni sui componenti della famiglia

1.1 Quanti siete in famiglia? 1.2 Siamo in quattro.
1.3 Siete tanti in famiglia?

1.4 Come si chiama tuo padre ? 1.5 (Si chiama) Carlo.
1.6 Come si chiama tuo nonno?
1.7 Come si chiama tuo fratello?
1.8 Come si chiama tuo zio?
1.9 Come si chiama tuo cugino?
1.10 Come si chiama tuo figlio?
1.11 Come si chiama tuo marito?
1.12 Come si chiama tuo cognato?
1.13 Come si chiama tuo nipote?
1.14 Come si chiama tuo suocero?

1.15 What's your mother's name?
1.17 What is your grandmother's name?
1.18 What is your sister's name?
1.19 What is your aunt's name?
1.20 What is your cousin's name?
1.21 What is your daughter's name?
1.22 What is your wife's name?
1.23 What is your sister-in-law's name?
1.24 What is your niece's name?
1.25 What is your mother-in-law called?

1.16 (Her name is) Mary.
She's [She is] called Mary.

1.26 Are you an only child?

1.27 No, I have two sisters.
1.28 No, I have an older brother.
1.29 No, I have a twin sister.

1.30 What job does your father do?
1.32 What job does your mother do?

1.31 He/She works in an office.
1.33 He/She works in a factory.
1.34 He/She works in a shop.
1.35 He/She is an office worker.
1.36 He/She is a labourer.
1.37 He/She is a (primary) teacher.
1.38 He/She is unemployed.

1.15 እናትህ/ሽ ማን ይባላሉ?
1.16 ሚርያም ይባላሉ
1.17 አያትህ/ሽ ማን ይባላሉ?
1.18 እህትህ/ሽ ማን ትባላለች?
1.19 አክስትህ/ሽ ማን ይባላሉ?
1.20 የወንድምህ/ሽ ልጅ ማን ይባላል?
የእህትህ/ሽ ልጅ ማን ይባላል?
1.21 ልጅህ/ሽ ማን ትባላለች?
1.22 ባለቤትህ ማን ትባላለች?
1.23 የወንድምህ/ሽ ሚስት ማን ትባላለች?
1.24 የአጎትህ/ሽ ልጅ ማን ትባላለች?
የአክስትህ/ሽ ልጅ ማን ትባላለች?
1.25 አማችህ/ሽ ማን ይባላሉ?

1.26 ለናትህ/ሽ አንድ ነህ/ሽ ወይ?
1.27 አይደለሁም፡ ሁለት እህቶች አሉኝ
1.28 አይደለሁም፡ ታላቅ ወንድም አለኝ
1.29 አይደለሁም፡ መንታያ እህት አለችኝ

1.30 አባትህ/ሽ ምን ይሰራሉ?
1.32 እናትህ/ሽ ምን ይሰራሉ?
1.31 ቢሮ ውስጥ ይሰራል/ትሰራለች
1.33 ፋብሪካ ውስጥ ይሰራል/ትሰራለች
1.34 ሱቅ ውስጥ ይሰራል/ትሰራለች
1.35 የቢሮ ሰራተኛ ነው/ናት
1.36 የቀን ሰራተኛ ነው/ናት
1.37 አስተማሪ ነው/ናት
1.38 ስራ የለውም/የላትም

1.15 Come si chiama tua madre?
1.16 Si chiama Maria.
1.17 Come si chiama tua nonna?
1.18 Come si chiama tua sorella?
1.19 Come si chiama tua zia?
1.20 Come si chiama tua cugina?
1.21 Come si chiama tua figlia?
1.22 Come si chiama tua moglie?
1.23 Come si chiama tua cognata?
1.24 Come si chiama tua nipote?
1.25 Come si chiama tua suocera?

1.26 Sei figlio unico?
Sei figlia unica?
1.27 No, ho due sorelle.
1.28 No, ho un fratello maggiore.
1.29 No, ho una sorella gemella.

1.30 Che lavoro fa tuo padre?
1.32 Che lavoro fa tua madre?
1.31 Lavora in un ufficio.
1.33 Lavora in una fabbrica.
1.34 Lavora in un negozio.
1.35 E' impiegato/impiegata.
1.36 E' operaio/operaia.
1.37 E' maestro/maestra.
1.38 E' disoccupato/disoccupata.

3 HOUSE AND HOME

HOW TO ...
1. **Say whether you live in a house, flat, etc., and ask others the same**
2. **Find out about garage, garden, etc.**
3. **Offer to help**
4. **Ask where places and things are in a house**
5. **Ask if another person needs soap, a towel, etc.**
6. **Invite someone to come in, to sit down**
7. **Thank someone for hospitality**

1.1 Where do you live?

1.2 I live in the town-centre.
1.3 I live in the suburbs.
1.4 I live in a flat.
1.5 I live in a block of flats.
1.6 I live in a villa.

መኖሪያ ቤት

እንዴት ...
1. በቪላ ወይም በአፓርታማ ወዘተ ውስጥ እንደምትኖር እንደምትገልጽና፣እንዲሁም ሌሎቹንም እንደምትጠይቅ
2. የመኪና ማቆምያ፣ የአትክልት ቦታዎች፣ወዘተ እንዳሉ እንደምትጠይቅ
3. እርዳታ እንደምትሰጥ
4. ክፍሎችና ዕቃዎች የት እንደሚገኙ እንደምትጠይቅ
5. ላንድ ሰው ፎጣና ሳሙና የሚያስፈልጉት መሆኑን እንደምትጠይቅ
6. ሰው እንዲገባና እንዲቀመጥ እንደምትጋብዝ
7. አንድ ሰው ላደረገልህ አቀባበል እንደምታመሰግን

1.1 የት ትኖራለህ/ትኖርያለሽ?

1.2 ከተማ ውስጥ እኖራለሁ
1.3 ከከተማ ውጭ እኖራለሁ
1.4 አፓርታማ ውስጥ እኖራለሁ
1.5 ባንድ ፎቅ ውስጥ እኖራለሁ
1.6 ባንድ ቪላ ውስጥ እኖራለሁ

CASA

Come ...
1. **dire se si abita in una villa, in un appartamento, ecc., e chiedere lo stesso ad altri**
2. **chiedere se ci sono un garage, un giardino, ecc.**
3. **offrire il proprio aiuto**
4. **chiedere dove si trovano le stanze e gli oggetti in una casa**
5. **chiedere a qualcuno se ha bisogno del sapone, di un asciugamano, ecc.**
6. **invitare qualcuno ad entrare, ad accomodarsi**
7. **ringraziare qualcuno per l'ospitalità**

1.1 Dove abiti?

1.2 Abito in centro.
1.3 Abito in periferia.
1.4 Abito in un appartamento.
1.5 Abito in un palazzo.
1.6 Abito in una villa.

2.1 Is there a garage?	2.2 Yes, (there is).
2.3 Is there a garden?	2.4 No, (there isn't).
2.5 Is there central heating?	
2.6 Is there a lift ?	
3.1 Can I give you a hand ?	3.2 No thank you, there is no need.
3.3 Can I be of any help?	3.4 (No, leave it!) I can manage.
3.5 Can I do something?	3.6 Yes, thank you ...
3.7 Can I lay the table ?	
3.8 Can I clear the table ?	
3.9 Can I wash the dishes?	
3.10 Can I make something to eat?	
3.11 Can I do the dusting?	
3.12 Can I do the ironing?	
4.1 Where's [Where is] the bathroom?	4.2 It's opposite ...
4.3 Where's the toilet?	4.4 It's at the end of ...
4.5 Where's the fridge?	4.6 It's next to ...
4.7 Where's the garage?	4.8 It's in front of ...

2.1 የመኪና ማቆምያ አለው ወይ?
2.3 የአትክልት ቦታ አለው ወይ?
2.5 የውኃ ማሞቅያ አለው ወይ?
2.6 ሊፍት አለው ወይ?

2.2 አዎ፡ አለው
2.4 የለውም

3.1 ልርዳህ/ሽ ወይ?
3.3 ልተባበር ወይ?
3.5 አንድ ነገር ልስራ ወይ?
3.7 ምግብ ላቅርብ ወይ?
3.8 ምግቡን ላንሳው ወይ?
3.9 እቃዎቹን ልጠባቸው ወይ?
3.10 የሚበላ ነገር ላቅርብ ወይ?
3.11 ቤቱን ላጸዳዳው ወይ?
3.12 ልተኩስ ወይ?

3.2 ደህና፡ አመሰግናለሁ፡ አያስፈልግም
3.4 ተወው/ተዪው፡ እኔ ራሴ አደርገዋለሁ
3.6 እሺ፡ አመሰግናለሁ

4.1 የገላ መታጠብያው የት ነው?
4.3 ሽንት ቤት የት ነው?
4.5 ማቀዝቀዣ የት ነው?
4.7 የመኪና ማቆምያ የት ነው?

4.2 ከ ... ፊት ለፊት
4.4 ከ ... መጨረሻ
4.6 ከ ... ቀጥሎ
4.8 ከ ... ፊት ለፊት

2.1 C’è il garage?
2.3 C’è il giardino?
2.5 C’è il riscaldamento centrale?
2.6 C’è l’ascensore?

2.2 Sì, (c’è).
2.4 No, (non c’è).

3.1 Posso darti una mano ?
3.3 Posso esserti utile?
3.5 Posso fare qualcosa?
3.7 Posso apparecchiare?
3.8 Posso sparecchiare?
3.9 Posso lavare i piatti?
3.10 Posso preparare da mangiare?
3.11 Posso spolverare?
3.12 Posso stirare?

3.2 No, grazie! Non c’è bisogno.
3.4 (No, lascia stare!) Faccio da solo/a.
3.6 Sì, grazie...

4.1 Dov’è il bagno?
4.3 Dov’è il gabinetto?
4.5 Dov’è il frigorifero?
4.7 Dov’è il garage?

4.2 E’ davanti a...
4.4 E’ in fondo a...
4.6 E’ accanto a...
4.8 E’ di fronte a...

5.1 Where's the pillow? 5.2 Here it is.
5.3 Where's the blanket? 5.4 Here it is.
5.5 Where's the cutlery? 5.6 Here they are.
5.7 Where are the plates? 5.8 Here they are.

6.1 Do you need any soap? 6.2 Yes, I need some ...
6.3 Do you need any toothpaste? 6.4 Yes, I need a ...
6.5 Do you need a towel?
6.6 Do you need an alarm clock?
6.7 Do you need anything?

7.1 May I come in? 7.2 Come in!
7.3 May I? 7.4 Make yourself comfortable!
7.5 Am I interrupting? 7.6 Not at all/(Please) come in!

8.1 Thank you for your hospitality!
8.2 You have (all) been so kind!
8.3 I hope I can do the same for you soon!

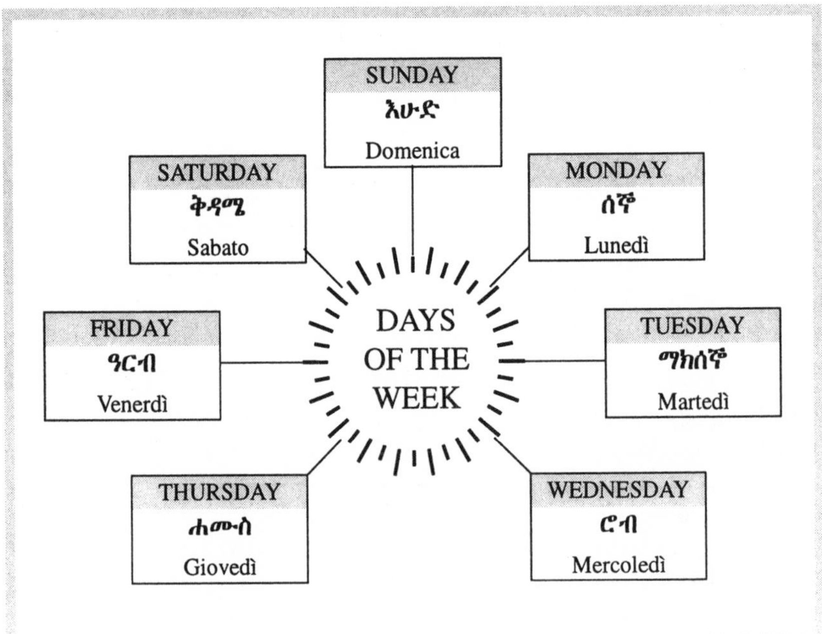

5.1 ትራስ የት አለ?
5.2 ይኸው
5.3 ብርድ ልብስ የት አለ?
5.4 ይኸው
5.5 ማንኪያዎችና ቢላዎች የት አሉ?
5.6 እኚውልህ (pl.)
5.7 ሰሃኖች የት አሉ?
5.8 ይኸው

6.1 ሳሙና ያስፈልግሃል/ሻል ወይ?
6.2 አዎ፥... ያስፈልገኛል
6.3 የጥርስ ሳሙና ያስፈልግሃል/ሻል ወይ?
6.4 አዎ፥... ያስፈልገኛል
6.5 ፎጣ ያስፈልግሃል/ሻል ወይ?
6.6 የሚቀሰቅስ ሰዓት ያስፈልግሃል/ሻል ወይ?
6.7 ሌላ የሚያስፈልግህ/ሽ ነገር አለ ወይ?

7.1 ልግባ?
7.2 ግባ/ግቢ
7.3 ይፈቀዳል ወይ?
7.4 ቍጭ በል/በይ
7.5 ረበሽኳችሁ ወይ?
7.6 ይግቡ

8.1 ለተደረገልኝ አቀባበል አመሰግናለሁ
8.2 ምስጋና ይገባችኋል
8.3 ውለታ መላሽ ያድርገኝ

5.1 Dove è il cuscino ?
5.2 Eccolo.
5.3 Dove è la coperta?
5.4 Eccola.
5.5 Dove sono le posate?
5.6 Eccole.
5.7 Dove sono i piatti?
5.8 Eccoli.

6.1 Hai bisogno del sapone ?
6.2 Sì, avrei bisogno di ...
6.3 Hai bisogno del dentifricio?
6.4 Sì, mi servirebbe ...
6.5 Hai bisogno dell'asciugamano?
6.6 Hai bisogno della sveglia?
6.7 Hai bisogno di qualcosa ?

7.1 Posso entrare?
7.2 Avanti!
7.3 Permesso?
7.4 Accomodati!
7.5 Disturbo?
7.6 (Prego), entra!

8.1 Grazie per l'ospitalità!
8.2 Siete stati molto gentili!
8.3 Spero di poter ricambiare presto!

DAILY ROUTINE

HOW TO ...

1. **State at what time you usually get up, go to bed and have meals**
2. **Say whether you have a job. If so, what job, what working hours, how much you earn**

1.1 What time do you wake up?	1.2 I wake up at ...
1.3 What time do you get up?	1.4 I get up at ...
1.5 What time do you have breakfast?	1.6 I have breakfast at ...
1.7 What time do you have lunch?	1.8 I have lunch at ...
1.9 What time do you have dinner?	1.10 I have dinner at ...
1.11 What time do you go to bed?	1.12 I go to bed at ...
1.13 What time do (you go to) sleep?	1.14 I (go to) sleep at ...

በየቀኑ የሚሰሩ ስራዎች

እንዴት ...
1. የምትነሳበትና የምትተኛበት እንዲሁም የምትበላበትን ሰዓት እንደምትገልጽ
2. ስራ እንዳለህና ካለህ ምን ዓይነት ስራ እንደምትሰራ ስንት ሰዓት እንደምትሰራና ስንትእንደምታገኝ እንደምትገልጽ

1.1 በስንት ሰዓት ትነቃለህ/ትነቅያለሽ? 1.2 በ ... ሰዓት እነቃለሁ
1.3 በስንት ሰዓት ትነሳለህ/ትነሽያለሽ? 1.4 በ ... ሰዓት እነሳለሁ
1.5 በስንት ሰዓት ቍርስህን ትበላለህ/ትበያለሽ? 1.6 በ ... ሰዓት ቍርሴን እበላለሁ
1.7 በስንት ሰዓት ምሳህን ትበላለህ/ትበያለሽ? 1.8 በ ... ሰዓት ምሳየን እበላለሁ
1.9 በስንት ሰዓት እራትህን ትበላለህ/ትበያለሽ? 1.10 በ ... ሰዓት እራቴን እበላለሁ
1.11 በስንት ሰዓት ትጋደማለህ/ትጋደምያለሽ? 1.12 በ ... ሰዓት እጋደማለሁ
1.13 በስንት ሰዓት ትተኛለህ/ትተኚያለሽ? 1.14 በ ... ሰዓት እተኛለሁ

ABITUDINI GIORNALIERE

Come ...
1. **dire a che ora di solito ci si alza, si va a dormire e si mangia**
2. **dire se si ha un lavoro, di che lavoro si tratta, quante ore si lavora, quanto si guadagna**

1.1 A che ora ti svegli? 1.2 Mi sveglio alle ...
1.3 A che ora ti alzi? 1.4 Mi alzo alle ...
1.5 A che ora fai colazione ? 1.6 Faccio colazione alle ...
1.7 A che ora pranzi? 1.8 Pranzo alle ...
1.9 A che ora ceni? 1.10 Ceno alle ...
1.11 A che ora vai a letto ? 1.12 Vado a letto alle ...
1.13 A che ora vai a dormire ? 1.14 Vado a dormire alle ...

1.15 Have you found a job?

1.16 Yes, I work in a bar.
1.17 I give English lessons.

1.18 Is it tiring?
1.20 Is it demanding?

1.19 No, not really.
1.21 Yes, but I like it.

1.22 How many hours do you work?

1.23 I work 8 hours a day.

1.24 How much do you earn?
1.26 Do you earn a lot?

1.25 I earn ... an hour.
1.27 I earn ... a month.

1.15 ስራ አገኘህ/ሽ ወይ?

1.16 አዎ፡ አንድ ቡና ቤት ውስጥ እሰራለሁ.
1.17 እንግሊዝኛ አስተምራለሁ

1.18 አድካሚ ነው ወይ?
1.20 ጉልበት ይጠይቃል ወይ?

1.19 እስከዚህም አይደለም
1.21 አዎ፡ ነገር ግን እወደዋለሁ

1.22 ስንት ሰዓት ትሰራለህ/ትሰርያለሽ?

1.23 በቀን 8 ሰዓት እሰራለሁ

1.24 ስንት ታገኛለህ/ታገኚያለሽ?
1.26 ብዙ ታገኛለህ/ታገኚያለሽ ወይ?

1.25 በሰዓት ... ብር አገኛለሁ
1.27 በወር ... ብር አገኛለሁ

1.15 Hai trovato un lavoro?

1.16 Sì, lavoro in un bar.
1.17 Do lezioni di inglese.

1.18 E' faticoso?
1.20 E' impegnativo?

1.19 No, non molto.
1.21 Sì, ma mi piace.

1.22 Quante ore lavori?

1.23 Lavoro 8 ore al giorno.

1.24 Quanto guadagni?
1.26 Guadagni molto?

1.25 Guadagno ... lire all'ora.
1.27 Guadagno ... lire al mese.

How to describe your house, flat, etc.
የምትኖርበትን ቦታ እንዴት እንደምትገልጽ
Come descrivere la propria abitazione ...

Key Words	**ቍልፍ ቃላት**	**Parole chiave**
there is, there are	አለ ... አሉ	c'è, ci sono
on the right	በስተቀኝ	a destra
on the left	በስተግራ	a sinistra
up	ከላይ	in alto
down	ከታች	in basso
in the middle of	በ ... መካከል	in mezzo a
at the bottom of	ከ ... ስር	in fondo a
on top of	ከ ... ላይ	in cima a
above	እላይ	sopra
below	እታች	sotto
near	አጠገብ ፡ ጋ	vicino a
next to	ቀጥሎ ያለው	accanto a
opposite/in front of	ከ ... ፊት ለፊት	di fronte a
inside	... ውስጥ	dentro
around	... አከባቢ	intorno
Vocabulary	**መዝገበ ቃላት**	**Vocabolario**
1 lift	1 ሊፍት	1 l'ascensore
2 bathroom	2 የገላ መታጠብያ	2 il bagno
3 balcony	3 ቨራንዳ	3 il balcone
4 bedroom	4 መኝታ ቤት	4 la camera da letto
5 cellar	5 ግምጃ ቤት	5 la cantina
6 corridor	6 ኮሪዶር/መተላለፊያ	6 il corridoio
7 kitchen	7 ማድ ቤት/ኩሽና	7 la cucina
8 entrance hall	8 መግቢያ	8 l'entrata
9 window	9 መስኮት	9 la finestra
10 wall	10 ግድግዳ	10 la parete
11 floor	11 ወለል	11 il pavimento
12 door	12 በር	12 la porta
13 main door	13 ደጃፍ	13 il portone
14 first/second floor	14 አንደኛ/ሁለተኛ ፎቅ	14 il primo/secondo piano
15 dining-room	15 የመመገብያ ክፍል	15 la sala da pranzo
16 stairs	16 ደረጃ	16 le scale
17 roof	17 ጣራ	17 il tetto

4 GEOGRAPHICAL SURROUNDINGS

HOW TO ...

1. **Give information about your home town or village and surrounding area**
2. **Describe the weather conditions (see p. 128)**
3. **Describe the climate of your own country and enquire about the climate in another country (see p. 128)**

1.1 Where do you live?

1.2 I live in Ethiopia.
1.3 I live in Italy.
1.4 I live in England.
1.5 I live in Rome.
1.6 I live in London.
1.7 I live in Chicago.

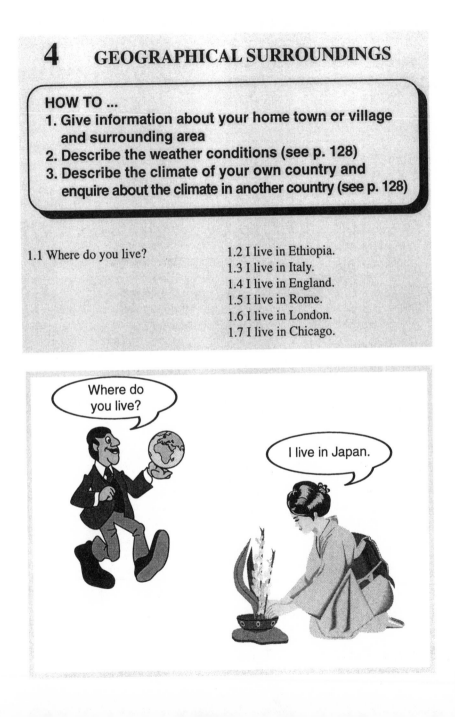

ጂኦግራፊያዊ አቀማመጥና የአየር ሁኔታ

እንዴት ...
ስለ ከተማህ ያገር ቤትህና አከባቢህ መረጃ እንደምትሰጥ

1.1 የት አገር ነው የምትኖረው/ የምትኖሪው?

1.2 ኢትዮጵያ ውስጥ እኖራለሁ
1.3 ጣልያን አገር እኖራለሁ
1.4 እንግሊዝ አገር እኖራለሁ
1.5 ሮማ ውስጥ እኖራለሁ
1.6 ለንደን ውስጥ እኖራለሁ
1.7 ቺካጎ ውስጥ እኖራለሁ

AMBIENTE GEOGRAFICO

Come ...
1. **dare informazioni sulla propria città o villaggio e sulla zona circostante**
2. **descrivere le condizioni meteorologiche (vedi p. 129)**
3. **descrivere il clima del proprio paese e porre domande su quello di un altro paese (vedi p. 129)**

1.1 Dove vivi?

1.2 Vivo in Etiopia.
1.3 Vivo in Italia.
1.4 Vivo in Inghilterra.
1.5 Vivo a Roma.
1.6 Vivo a Londra.
1.7 Vivo a Chicago.

1.8 Where are you from?	1.9 I'm [I am] from Addis Ababa. 1.10 I'm from Turin.
1.11 Where is it?	1.12 It's [It is] in northern Italy. 1.13 It's in central Italy. 1.14 It's in southern Italy. 1.15 It's in the north of Italy. 1.16 It's in the south of Italy.
1.17 Is it a large city?	1.18 No, it is a village in the mountains. 1.19 No, it is a village on a hill. 1.20 No, it is a village by the sea. 1.21 No, it is a village on a river. 1.22 No, it is a village on a lake.
1.23 Which is the nearest city?	1.24 (It's near) Turin. 1.25 (It's near) Naples. 1.26 (It's near) Addis Ababa.

1.8 ከየት አከባቢ ነህ/ነሽ?	1.9 የአዲስ አበባ ልጅ ነኝ 1.10 የቶሪኖ ልጅ ነኝ
1.11 የት ይገኛል/ትገኛለች?	1.12 በሰሜናዊ የጣልያን አገር ክፍል ይገኛል/ትገኛለች 1.13 ማሐል ጣልያን አገር ይገኛል/ትገኛለች 1.14 በደቡባዊ የጣልያን አገር ክፍል ይገኛል/ትገኛለች 1.15 በሰሜን ጣልያን አገር ይገኛል/ትገኛለች 1.16 በደቡብ ጣልያን አገር ይገኛል/ትገኛለች
1.17 ከተማው ትልቅ ነውን?	1.18 በኰረብታ ላይ የምትገኝ ትንሽ መንደር ናት 1.19 አይደለም አምባ ላይ የተቈረቈረች ትንሽ መንደር ናት 1.20 ባሕር ዳር የምትገኝ ትንሽ መንደር ናት 1.21 ወንዝ ዳር የምትገኝ ትንሽ መንደር ናት 1.22 ሃይቅ ዳር የምትገኝ ትንሽ መንደር ናት
1.23 በአቅራቢያ የምትገኘው ከተማ የትኛዋ ናት?	1.24 ቶሪኖ ናት 1.25 ናፖሊ ናት 1.26 አዲስ አበባ ናት

1.8 Di dove sei?	1.9 Sono di Addis Abeba. 1.10 Sono di Torino.
1.11 Dove si trova?	1.12 Si trova nell'Italia settentrionale. 1.13 Si trova nell'Italia centrale. 1.14 Si trova nell'Italia meridionale. 1.15 Si trova nel nord Italia. 1.16 Si trova nel sud Italia.
1.17 E' una grande città?	1.18 No, è un villaggio in montagna. 1.19 No, è un piccolo paese in collina. 1.20 No, è un piccolo paese sul mare. 1.21 No, è un piccolo paese su un fiume. 1.22 No, è un piccolo paese su un lago.
1.23 Qual è la città più vicina?	1.24 (E' vicino/a a) Torino. 1.25 (E' vicino/a a) Napoli. 1.26 (E' vicino/a ad) Addis Abeba.

1.27 What's the country-side like?

1.28 It's hilly.
1.29 It's enchanting.
1.30 It's monotonous.
1.31 It's picturesque.
1.32 It's wonderful.

1.33 Where do you live?

1.34 I live in the old part of town.
1.35 I live in the suburbs.

1.36 Is there an airport?
1.38 Is there a sports centre?
1.40 Is there a shopping centre?
1.41 Is there a castle?
1.42 Is there a cathedral?

1.37 Yes, (there is) ...
1.39 No, (there isn't) ...

1.27 የመንደሩ አከባቢ ምን ይመስላል?

1.28 በተራራ የተከበበ ነው
1.29 ማራኪ ነው
1.30 አሰልቺ ነው
1.31 አስደናቂ ነው
1.32 አስገራሚ ነው

1.33 የት ነው የምትኖረው/የምትኖሪው?

1.34 አሮጌው ከተማ አከባቢ እኖራለሁ
1.35 ከተማው ዳር አከባቢ እኖራለሁ

1.36 ኤርፖርት አለው ወይ?
1.38 የስፖርት ማእከል አለው ወይ?
1.40 የገበያ አዳራሽ አለው ወይ?
1.41 ታሪካዊ ግንብ አለው ወይ?
1.42 ቤተክርስትያን አለው ወይ?

1.37 አዎ፤ ... አለው
1.39 ... የለውም

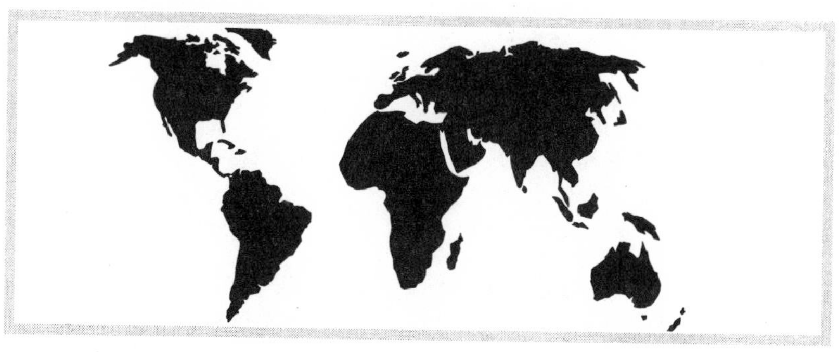

1.27 Com'è il paesaggio?

1.28 E' collinare.
1.29 E' incantevole.
1.30 E' monotono.
1.31 E' pittoresco.
1.32 E' stupendo.

1.33 Dove abiti?

1.34 Abito nel centro storico.
1.35 Abito in periferia.

1.36 C'è un aeroporto?
1.38 C'è un centro sportivo?
1.40 C'è un centro commerciale?
1.41 C'è un castello?
1.42 C'è una cattedrale?

1.37 Sì, (c'è) ...
1.39 No, (non c'è) ...

1.43 Are there many monuments?
1.45 Are there many shops?
1.47 Are there many gardens?
1.48 Are there many theatres?
1.49 Are there many avenues?
1.50 Are there many discotheques?
1.51 Are there many fountains?
1.52 Are there many industries?
1.53 Are there many factories?

1.44 Yes, (there are) ...
1.46 No, (there aren't) ...

1.43 ብዙ ሓውልቶች አሉ ወይ?
1.45 ብዙ ሱቆች አሉ ወይ?
1.47 ብዙ የአትክልት ቦታዎች አሉ ወይ?
1.48 ብዙ ትያትሮች ቤቶች አሉ ወይ?
1.49 ብዙ መንገዶች አሉ ወይ?
1.50 ብዙ ዲስኮቴኮች አሉ ወይ?
1.51 ብዙ የውሃ ምንጮች አሉ ወይ?
1.52 ብዙ ኢንዱስትሪዎች አሉ ወይ?
1.53 ብዙ ፋብሪካዎች አሉ ወይ?

1.44 አዎ፡ ... አሉ
1.46 ... የሉም

1.43 Ci sono molti monumenti?
1.45 Ci sono molti negozi?
1.47 Ci sono molti giardini?
1.48 Ci sono molti teatri?
1.49 Ci sono molti viali?
1.50 Ci sono molte discoteche?
1.51 Ci sono molte fontane?
1.52 Ci sono molte industrie?
1.53 Ci sono molte fabbriche?

1.44 Sì, (ci sono) ...
1.46 No, (non ci sono) ...

INFORMALE (tu)	**FORMALE (Lei)**
Di dove sei?	Di dov'è?
Dov'è la tua scuola?	Dov'è la sua scuola?
Che cosa fai di solito il week end?	Che cosa fa di solito il week end?
Ti piace vivere in Gran Bretagna?	Le piace vivere in Gran Bretagna?
Ti piacerebbe vivere in Italia?	Le piacerebbe vivere in Italia?

United Kingdom (Great Britain and Northern Ireland)

Borders:	The Atlantic Ocean, the North Sea, the English Channel
Area:	244,761 square km.
Population:	58,422,000
Density:	238 inhabitants per square km
Language:	English
Monetary Unit:	Pound Sterling
Capital:	London (6,904,600 inhabitants)
Flag:	The flag's colours are blue, white and red

Ethiopia

Borders:	Eritrea, Sudan, Kenya, Somalia, Djibouti
Area:	1,133,882 square km.
Population:	58,039,000
Density:	51 inhabitants per square km
Language:	Amharic, Oromo, Tigrinya (English is widely spoken)
Monetary Unit:	Birr
Capital:	Addis Ababa (1,912,500 inhabitants)
Flag:	The flag's colours are green, yellow and red with the national emblem in the centre.

Italy

Borders:	France, Switzerland, Austria and Slovenia
Area:	301,277 square km.
Population:	57,313,000
Density:	190 inhabitants per square km
Language:	Italian
Monetary Unit:	Italian Lira
Capital:	Rome (2,773,889 inhabitants)
Flag:	The flag's colours are green, white and red

5 TRAVEL AND TRANSPORT

HOW TO ...

1. Say how you get to school or place of work
2. Attract the attention of a passer-by
3. Ask the way to a place
4. Ask if there is a place nearby
5. Say you do not understand
6. Ask someone to repeat what they have said
7. Thank someone

1.1 How do you get to school?
1.3 How do you get to work?

1.2 By bus.
1.4 By car.
1.5 By train.
1.6 By bicycle.
1.7 By coach.
1.8 On foot.

ጉዞና መጓጓዣ

እንዴት ...
1. ወደ ትምህርት ቤት ወይም ወደ ስራ እንደምትሔድ እንደምትገልጽ
2. የመንገደኛው ፍላጐት እንደምትስብ
3. ወደ አንድ የተወሰነ ቦታ ለመድረስ እንደምትጠይቅ
4. የአንድ ቦታ ርቀት እንደምትጠይቅ
5. አልገባኝም እንደምትል
6. የተባለውን ይደገምልኝ እንደምትል
7. እንደምታመሰግን

1.1 ወደ ትምህርት ቤት በምን ትሔዳለህ?
1.2 በአውቶቡስ
1.3 ወደ ስራ በምን ትሔዳለህ?
1.4 በመኪና
1.5 በባቡር
1.6 በቢሲክለት
1.7 በአውቶቡስ
1.8 በእግር

TRASPORTI

Come ...
1. dire con quali mezzi si raggiunge la scuola o il posto di lavoro
2. attirare l'attenzione di un passante
3. chiedere informazioni per raggiungere un determinato luogo
4. chiedere se un determinato luogo è vicino
5. dire che non si è capito
6. chiedere a qualcuno di ripetere

1.1 Come vai a scuola?
1.2 In autobus.
1.3 Come vai al lavoro?
1.4 In macchina.
1.5 In treno.
1.6 In bicicletta.
1.7 In corriera.
1.8 A piedi.

1.9 How long does it take?	1.10 (About) 10 minutes. 1.11 (About) an hour ...
2.1 Excuse me!	2.2 Yes!
3.1 Where's [Where is] the museum?	3.2 Take the first on the right.
3.3 Where's the castle?	3.4 Take the second on the right.
3.5 Where's the post office?	3.6 Take the third on the right.
3.7 Where's the information centre?	3.8 Turn left.
3.9 Where's the church ?	3.10 (Go) straight on.
3.11 Where's the chemist?	3.12 Go as far as the traffic lights.
3.13 Where's the swimming pool?	3.14 Go as far as the cross-road.
3.15 Can you tell me the way to the police station?	3.16 Cross the road.
3.17 Can you tell me the way to the bus stop?	3.18 Cross the pedestrian crossing.
3.19 Can you tell me the way to the station?	3.20 It's there, on your right.

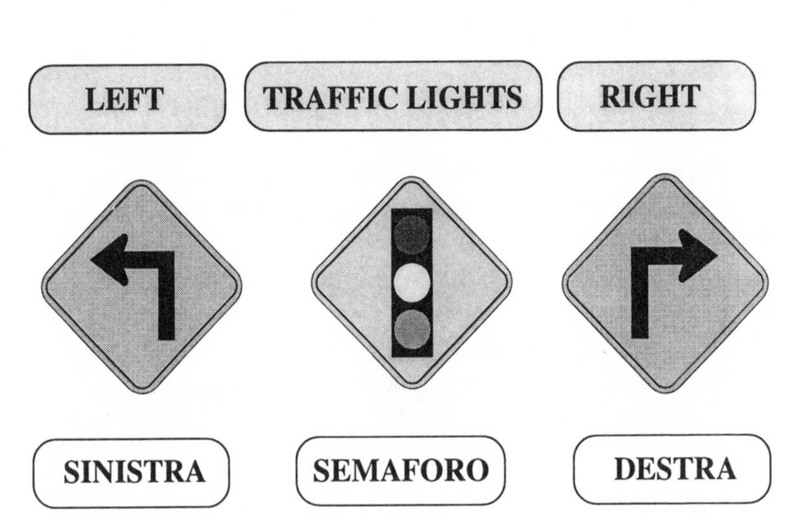

1.9 ስንት ሰዓት ይፈጃል?

1.10 አስር ደቂቃ ያህል
1.11 አንድ ሰዓት ያህል

2.1 ይቅርታ

2.2 እሺ ምን ነበር?

3.1 ቤተ መዘክሩ የት እንደሆነ ልትነግረኝ ትችላለህ ወይ?
3.2 ከመጀመርያው መጠምዘዣ ወደ ቀኝ ታጠፍ/ፊ
3.3 የጥንቱ ግንብ የት እንደሆነ ልትነግረኝ ትችላለህ ወይ?
3.4 ከሁለተኛው መጠምዘዣ ወደ ግራ ታጠፍ/ፊ
3.5 ፖስታ ቤቱ የት እንደሚገኝ ልትነግረኝ ትችላለህ ወይ?
3.6 ከሦስተኛው መጠምዘዣ ወደ ቀኝ ታጠፍ/ፊ
3.7 የማስታወቅያ ጽሕፈት ቤት የት እንደሆነ ልትነግረኝ ትችላለህ ወይ?
3.8 ወደ ግራ ታጠፍ/ፊ
3.9 ቤተ ክርስትያኑ የት እንደሆነ ልትነግረኝ ትችላለህ ወይ?
3.10 ወደ ፊት ቀጥል/ይ
3.11 መድኃኒት ቤቱ የት እንደሆነ ልትነግረኝ ትችላለህ ወይ?
3.12 እስከ ትራፊክ መብራቱ ቀጥል/ይ
3.13 መዋኛው የት እንደሆነ ልትነግረኝ ትችላለህ ወይ?
3.14 እስከ መስቀለኛው መንገድ ቀጥል/ይ
3.15 ፖሊስ ጣብያው የት እንደሆነ ልትነግረኝ ትችላለህ ወይ?
3.16 መንገዱን ተሻገር/ሪ
3.17 ፌርማታው የት እንደሆነ ልትነግረኝ ትችላለህ ወይ?
3.18 በነጩ መስመር ተሻገር/ሪ
3.19 የባቡር ጣብያው የት እንደሆነ ልትነግረኝ ትችላለህ ወይ?
3.20 እዚያ ነው በቀኝ በኩል

1.9 Quanto ci metti? / Quanto impieghi?

1.10 (Circa) 10 minuti.
1.11 (Circa) un'ora.

2.1 (Senta), scusi!

2.2 Sì, (dica)!

3.1 (Mi sa dire) dov'è il museo?
3.2 Prenda la prima a destra.
3.3 (Mi sa dire) dov'è il castello?
3.4 Prenda la seconda a destra.
3.5 (Mi sa dire) dov'è l'ufficio postale?
3.6 Prenda la terza a destra.
3.7 (Mi sa dire) dov'è l'ufficio informazioni?
3.8 Volti a sinistra.
3.9 (Mi sa dire) dov'è la chiesa?
3.10 Continui (sempre) dritto.
3.11 (Mi sa dire) dov'è la farmacia?
3.12 Vada fino al semaforo.
3.13 (Mi sa dire) dov'è la piscina?
3.14 Vada fino all'incrocio.
3.15 (Mi sa dire) dov'è la questura?
3.16 Attraversi la strada.
3.17 (Mi sa dire) dov'è la fermata dell'autobus?
3.18 Attraversi il passaggio pedonale.
3.19 (Mi sa dire) dov'è la stazione?
3.20 E' lì, sulla destra.

4.1 Excuse me, is there a bank near here?

4.2 20 metres, on the left.

4.3 Excuse me, is there a restaurant near here?

4.4 Opposite...

4.5 Next to...

4.6 Near...

4.7 On the road parallel to this one.

4.8 Is it very far from here?

4.9 No, (it's about) ten minutes walk.

4.10 Yes, you'll have to take a taxi.

5.1 Excuse me, what did you say?

5.2 I don't understand.

6.1 Could you say it again, please?

6.2 Could you speak more slowly, please?

7.1 Thank you!

7.2 Thank you very much!

7.3 Very kind of you!

4.1 ይቅርታ እዚህ አካባቢ ባንክ አለ ወይ?
4.2 ሀያ ሜትር ወደ ግራ
4.3 ይቅርታ እዚህ አካባቢ ምግብ ቤት አለ ወይ?
4.4 ፊት ለፊት
4.5 አጠገብ፡ በጐን
4.6 ... አጠገብ፡ ጋ
4.7 በዚህ መንገድ አኳያ

4.8 ከዚህ በጣም ይርቃል ወይ?
4.9 አይርቅም፡ በእግር አሥር ደቂቃ ያህል ይፈጃል
4.10 አዎ፡ ታክሲ መውሰድ ያስፈልገሃል

5.1 ይቅርታ፡ ምንድ ነው ያልከው?
5.2 አልገባኝም

6.1 ሊደግሙልኝ ይችላሉ ወይ?
6.2 ቀስ ብለው ሊናገሩ ይችላሉ ወይ?

7.1 አመሰግናለሁ
7.2 በጣም አመሰግናለሁ
7.3 በጣም ተደስቻለሁ

4.1 Scusi, c’è una banca qui vicino ?
4.2 A 20 metri, sulla sinistra.
4.3 Scusi, c’è un ristorante qui vicino ?
4.4 Di fronte a ...
4.5 Accanto a ...
4.6 Vicino a ...
4.7 Nella via parallela a questa.

4.8 E’ molto lontano da qui?
4.9 No, (circa) 10 minuti a piedi.
4.10 Sì, deve prendere un taxi.

5.1 Come, scusi?
5.2 Non capisco.

6.1 Può ripetere, per favore?
6.2 Può parlare più piano, per favore?

7.1 Grazie!
7.2 Mille grazie!
7.3 E’ molto gentile!

TRAVEL BY PUBLIC TRANSPORT

HOW TO ...

1. **Ask if there is a bus, train or coach to a particular place**
2. **Buy tickets specifying: single or return and class**
3. **Ask about the times of departure and arrival**
4. **Ask and check whether it is: the right platform, bus, coach or stop**
5. **Reserve a seat**
6. **Ask the time**

1.1 Is there a coach to Florence?

1.2 I'm [I am] sorry, I don't know.

1.3 Is there a bus to the station?

1.4 (Yes,) number 20.

1.5 Is there an express train for Bologna?

1.6 Yes, there's [There is] one in half an hour.

1.7 Yes, there's one at ten past seven.

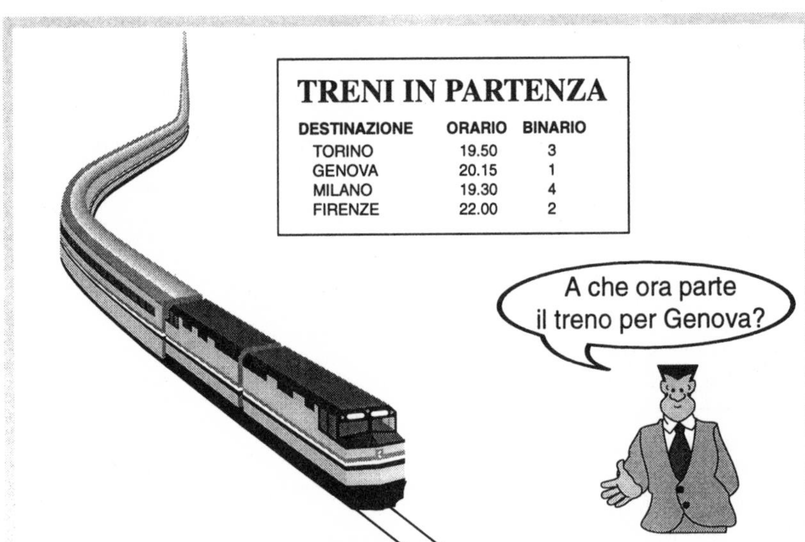

TRENI IN PARTENZA
DESTINAZIONE ORARIO BINARIO
TORINO 19.50 3
GENOVA 20.15 1
MILANO 19.30 4
FIRENZE 22.00 2
A che ora parte il treno per Genova?

በህዝብ መጓጓዣ መጓዝ

እንዴት ...
1. **ወደ አንድ የተወሰነ ቦታ የሚሔዱ አውቶቡሶች ወይም ባቡሮች እንዳሉ እንደምትጠይቅ**
2. **ደርሶ መልስ ቲኬት ለይተህ እንደምትገዛ**
3. **የመነሻና የመድረሻ ሰዓቶች እንደምትጠይቅ**
4. **ሓዲዱ የአውቶቡሱ ፌርማታ ትክክል መሆኑን እንደምታረጋግጥ**
5. **አስቀድመህ ቦታ እንደምትይዝ**
6. **ሰዓት እንደምትጠይቅ**

1.1 ወደ ፍሎረንስ የሚሔድ አውቶቡስ አለ ወይ?
1.2 ይቅርታ፡ አላወቅኩም
1.3 ወደ ለግሀር (ባቡር ጣብያ) የሚሔድ አውቶቡስ አለ ወይ?
1.4 አዎ፡ ሀያ ቍጥር

1.5 ወደ ቦሎኛ የሚሔድ ፈጣን አውቶቡስ አለ ወይ?
1.6 አዎ፡ ከግማሽ ሰዓት በኋላ የሚመጣ አለ
1.7 አዎ፡ በሰባት ሰዓት ካሥር የሚመጣ አለ

TRASPORTO PUBBLICO

Come ...
1. **chiedere se c'è un autobus, un treno o una corriera per un determinato luogo**
2. **comprare biglietti specificando se di sola andata o di andata e ritorno e la classe**
3. **chiedere gli orari di partenza e di arrivo**
4. **chiedere e verificare se il binario, l'autobus, la corriera o la fermata sono quelli giusti**
5. **prenotare un posto**
6. **chiedere l'ora**

1.1 C'è una corriera per Firenze?
1.2 Mi dispiace, non lo so.
1.3 C'è un autobus per la stazione?
1.4 Sì, il numero 20.

1.5 C'è un treno espresso per Bologna?
1.6 Sì, ce n'è uno tra mezz'ora.
1.7 Sì, ce n'è uno alle sette e dieci.

2.1 I'd like a single ticket. 2.3 I'd like a return ticket.	2.2 First class? 2.4 Second class?
3.1 What time is the next train for Rome? 3.3 What time is the next coach for Rome?	3.2 It leaves at 4.30 p.m.
3.4 What time does it leave Naples? 3.6 What time does it get to London?	3.5 It leaves at 3.00 p.m. 3.7 It gets in at 3.00 p.m.
4.1 Excuse me, is this platform 3? 4.3 Excuse me, is this the coach for ...? 4.5 Excuse me, is this the stop for ...?	4.2 Yes. 4.4 No, it's that one over there.
4.6 Which platform does the train for Genoa leave from?	4.7 It leaves from platform 3.
5.1 I'd like to reserve a seat. 5.2 I'd like to reserve a couchette.	

2.1 መሔጃ ቲኬት እፈልጋለሁ
2.2 አንደኛ ማዕረግ
2.3 መመለሻ ቲኬት እፈልጋለሁ
2.4 ሁለተኛ ማዕረግ

3.1 ባቡሩ በስንት ሰዓት ነው ወደ ሮማ የሚሔደው?
3.2 በ10:30 ነው የሚነሳው
3.3 አውቶቡሱ በስንት ሰዓት ነው ወደ ሮማ የሚሔደው?

3.4 በስንት ሰዓት ነው ከናፖሊ የሚነሳው?
3.5 በ 9 ሰዓት ነው የሚነሳው
3.6 በስንት ሰዓት ነው ወደ ሎንዶን የሚደርሰው?
3.7 በ 9 ሰዓት ነው የሚደርሰው

4.1 ይቅርታ፡ ሐዲዱ 3 ቍጥር ነው ወይ?
4.2 አዎ
4.3 ይቅርታ፡ ይህ ወደ ... የሚሔድ አውቶቡስ ነው ወይ?
4.4 አይደለም፡ እዚያው ነው
4.5 ይቅርታ፡ ... እዚህ ነው የሚቆመው?

4.6 ጀኖቫ የሚሔደው ባቡር ከየትኛው ሐዲድ ነው የሚነሳው?
4.7 ከሐዲድ 3 ቍጥር ነው የሚነሳው

5.1 አስቀድሜ ወንበር ለመያዝ እፈልጋለሁ
5.2 አስቀድሜ አልጋ ለመያዝ እፈልጋለሁ

2.1 Vorrei un biglietto di andata.
2.2 Di prima classe?
2.3 Vorrei un biglietto di andata e ritorno.
2.4 Di seconda classe?

3.1 A che ora parte il treno per Roma?
3.2 Parte alle 16.30.
3.3 A che ora parte la corriera per Roma?

3.4A che ora parte da Napoli?
3.5 Parte alle 15.00.
3.6 Quando arriva a Londra?
3.7 Arriva alle 15.00.

4.1 Scusi, è il binario n. 3?
4.2 Sì!
4.3 Scusi, è la corriera per ...?
4.4 No, è quella (laggiù).
4.5 Scusi, è la fermata per ... ?

4.6 Da che binario parte il treno per Genova?
4.7 Parte dal binario numero 3.

5.1 Vorrei prenotare un posto.
5.2 Vorrei prenotare una cuccetta.

Ask the time

What's the time?
What time is it?

1. It's [It is] midnight. (24.00)
2. It's midday/twelve o'clock. (12.00)
3. It's one (o'clock)/one p.m. (13.00)

4. It's two (o'clock)/two a.m. (2.00)
5. It's three (o'clock)/three a.m. (3.00)
6. It's four (o'clock)/four a.m. (4.00)
7. It's five (o'clock)/five a.m. (5.00)
8. It's six (o'clock)/six a.m. (6.00)
9. It's seven (o'clock)/seven a.m. (7.00)
10. It's eight (o'clock)/eight a.m. (8.00)
11. It's nine (o'clock)/nine a.m. (9.00)
12. It's ten (o'clock)/ten a.m. (10.00)
13. It's eleven (o'clock)/eleven a.m. (11.00)
14. It's twelve (o'clock)/twelve a.m. (12.00)
15. It's one (o'clock)/one p.m. (13.00)
16. It's two (o'clock)/two p.m. (14.00)
17. It's three (o'clock)/three p.m. (15.00)
18. It's four (o'clock)/four p.m. (16.00)
19. It's five (o'clock)/five p.m. (17.00)

...

20. It's five (minutes) past two. (2.05)
21. It's ten (minutes) past two. (2.10)
22. It's a quarter past two/two fifteen. (2.15)
23. It's twenty (minutes) past two/two twenty. (2.20)
24. It's half past two/two thirty. (2.30)
25. It's twenty-five (minutes) to three. (2.35)

26. It's twenty (minutes) to three. (2.40)
27. It's a quarter to three/two forty-five. (2.45)

ሰዓት መጠየቅ	Chiedere l’ora
ስንት ሰዓት ነው?	Che ora è? Che ore sono?
1. እኩለ ሌሊት ነው (6.00 - nightime)	1. E’ mezzanotte.
2. እኩለ ቀን ነው (6.00 - daytime)	2. E’ mezzogiorno.
3. ሰባት ሰዓት ነው (7.00 - daytime)	3. E’ l’una.
4. ስምንት ሰዓት ነው (8.00)	4. Sono le due.
5. ዘጠኝ ሰዓት ነው (9.00)	5. Sono le tre.
6. አሥር ሰዓት ነው (10.00)	6. Sono le quattro.
7 አሥራ አንድ ሰዓት ነው (11.00)	7. Sono le cinque.
8. አሥራ ሁለት ሰዓት ነው (12.00)	8. Sono le sei.
9. አንድ ሰዓት ነው (1.00)	9. Sono le sette.
10. ሁለት ሰዓት ነው (2.00)	10. Sono le otto.
11. ሦስት ሰዓት ነው (3.00)	11. Sono le nove.
12. አራት ሰዓት ነው (4.00)	12. Sono le dieci.
13. አምስት ሰዓት ነው (5.00)	13. Sono le undici.
14. ስድስት ሰዓት ነው (6.00)	14. Sono le dodici.
15. ከምሽቱ ሰባት ሰዓት ነው (7.00)	15. Sono le tredici.
16. ከምሽቱ ስምንት ሰዓት ነው (8.00)	16. Sono le quattordici.
17. ከምሽቱ ዘጠኝ ሰዓት ነው (9.00)	17. Sono le quindici.
18. ከምሽቱ አሥር ሰዓት ነው (10.00)	18. Sono le sedici.
19. ከምሽቱ አስራ አንድ ሰዓት ነው (11.00)	19. Sono le diciassette.
...	...
20. ስምንት ካምስት (8.05)	20. Sono le due e cinque.
21. ስምንት ካሥር (8.10)	21. Sono le due e dieci.
22. ስምንት ከሩብ (8.15)	22. Sono le due e quindici/un quarto.
23. ስምንት ከሀያ (8.20)	23. Sono le due e venti.
24. ስምንት ሰዓት ተኩል (8.30)	24. Sono le due e trenta/mezzo.
25. ለዘጠኝ ሰዓት ሀያ አምስት ጉዳይ (8.35)	25. Sono le due e trentacinque.
26. ለዘጠኝ ሰዓት ሀያ ጉዳይ (8.40)	26. Sono le tre meno venti.
27. ለዘጠኝ ሰዓት ሩብ ጉዳይ (8.45)	27. Sono le tre meno quindici/un quarto.

• Ethiopians calculate time in units of 12 hours, from 6.00 a.m. to 6.00 p.m.

TRAVEL BY AIR OR SEA

HOW TO ...

1. **Ask about times of departure and arrival**
2. **Buy tickets specifying: destination, single or return and class**
3. **Say where you would like to sit**
4. **Inform someone about your proposed times of arrival and departure**

1.1 What time is the a flight for Venice?
1.2 What time does the boat leave for Genoa?
1.3 What time does the ferry leave for Messina?
1.4 What time does the ferry arrive in Messina?

2.1 I'd [I would] like a single ticket to Rome.
2.2 I'd like a return ticket.
2.3 In tourist class.
2.4 In first class.

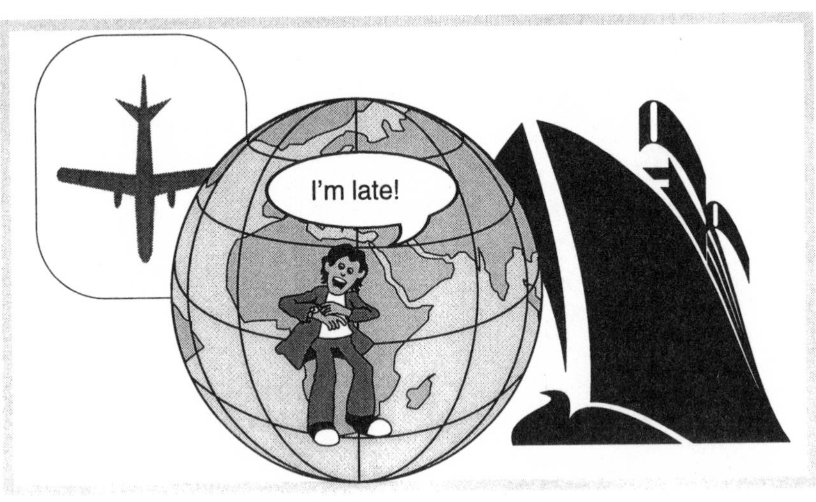

የአየርና የባሕር ጉዞ

እንዴት ...
1. የመነሻና የመድረሻ ሰዓቶች እንደምትጠይቅ
2. የምትደርስበት ቦታና የቲኬት ዓይነት ለይተህ እንደምትገልጽ
3. የት መቀመጥ እንደምትፈልግ እንደምትጠይቅ
4. ላንድ ሰው ሰዓትን በሚመለከት መረጃ እንደምትሰጥ

1.1 ወደ ቨነስያ በረራ በስንት ሰዓት ነው?
1.2 ወደ ጀኖዋ የሚሔድ መርከብ በስንት ሰዓት ነው የሚነሳው?
1.3 ወደ መሲና የሚሔደው መርከብ በስንት ሰዓት ነው የሚነሳው?
1.4 መርከቡ በስንት ሰዓት ነው ወደ መሲና የሚደርሰው?

2.1 ወደ ሮማ መሔጃ ቲኬት እፈልጋለሁ
2.2 የደርሶ መልስ ቲኬት ያስፈልገኛል
2.3 በቱሪስት ማዕረግ
2.4 በአንደኛ ማዕረግ

VIAGGIARE IN AEREO O VIA NAVE

Come ...
1. **chiedere gli orari di partenza e di arrivo**
2. **comprare biglietti specificando la destinazione, se di sola andata o di andata e ritorno e la classe**
3. **dire dove si desidera sedersi**
4. **informare qualcuno sull'orario di partenza e di arrivo**

1.1 A che ora c'è un volo per Venezia?
1.2 A che ora parte la nave per Genova?
1.3 A che ora parte il traghetto per Messina?
1.4 A che ora arriva a Messina?

2.1 Vorrei un biglietto di andata per Roma.
2.2 Vorrei un biglietto di andata e ritorno.
2.3 In classe turistica.
2.4 In prima classe.

3.1 I'd like a seat next to the window.
3.2 I'd like a seat near the corridor.
3.3 I'd like a seat in a (smoking) non-smoking compartment.

4.1 (At) what time are you leaving?
4.3 (At) what time is he/she leaving?
4.5 (At) what time are you leaving?
4.7 (At) what time are they leaving?
4.9 (At) what time are you arriving?

4.2 I'm leaving at six (o'clock).
4.4 He/she is leaving at seven.
4.6 We're [We are] leaving at eight.
4.8 They're leaving at nine.
4.10 I'm arriving at ten.

3.1 መስኮት አጠገብ መቀመጥ እፈልጋለሁ
3.2 ኮሪዶር አጠገብ መቀመጥ እፈልጋለሁ
3.3 ሲጋራ (በሚጨስበት) በማይጨስበት ክፍል ለመቀመጥ እፈልጋለሁ

4.1 በስንት ሰዓት ትነሳለህ?
4.3 በስንት ሰዓት ይነሳል/ትነሳለች? (m/f)
4.5 በስንት ሰዓት ትነሳላችሁ?
4.7 በስንት ሰዓት ይነሳሉ?
4.9 በስንት ሰዓት ትደርሳለህ?

4.2 በ 12 ሰዓት እነሳለሁ
4.4 በ 1 ሰዓት ይነሳል/ትነሳለች
4.6 በ 2 ሰዓት እንነሳለን
4.8 በ 3 ሰዓት ይነሳሉ
4.10 በ 4 ሰዓት እደርሳለሁ

3.1 Vorrei un posto accanto al finestrino.
3.2 Vorrei un posto vicino al corridoio.
3.3 Vorrei un posto tra i (non) fumatori.

4.1 A che ora partirai?
4.3 A che ora partirà?
4.5 A che ora partirete ?
4.7 A che ora partiranno?
4.9 A che ora arriverai?

4.2 Partirò alle sei.
4.4 Partirà alle sette.
4.6 Partiremo alle otto.
4.8 Partiranno alle nove.
4.10 Arriverò alle dieci.

PRIVATE TRANSPORT

HOW TO ...
1. Buy petrol by grade, volume or price
2. Ask someone to check oil, water and tyres
3. Ask if there is a place nearby
4. Ask for technical help
5. Ask for a receipt

1.1 I'd like 20 pounds worth of (unleaded) petrol.
1.2 I'd like 60 pounds worth of diesel.
1.3 I'd like 20 litres of four star.
1.4 Fill it up, please.

2.1 Can you check the oil, please?
2.2 Can you check the water, please?
2.3 Can you check the tyres, please?
2.4 Can you check the tyre pressure, please?

የግል መጓጓዣ

እንዴት ...
1. በዓይነት፣በብዛት፣በዋጋ ነዳጅ እንደምትገዛ
2. ዘይት፣ውኃ፣ጐማ ወዘተ እንዲያዩልህ እንደምትጠይቅ
3. የአንድ የተወሰነ ቦታ ርቀት እንደምትጠይቅ
4. ቴክኒካዊ እርዳታ እንደምትጠይቅ
5. ፋክቱር እንደምትጠይቅ

1.1 ለድ የሌለበት የ240 ብር ነዳጅ እፈልጋለሁ
1.2 የ 200 ብር ናፍታ እፈልጋለሁ
1.3 ሀያ ሊትር ፎረስታር እፈልጋለሁ
1.4 በንዚን ሊሞሉልኝ ይችላሉ ወይ?
2.1 እባክዎን ዘይት ይዩልኝ
2.2 እባክዎን ውኃዉን ይዩልኝ
2.3 እባክዎን ጐማዉን ይዩልኝ
2.4 እባክዎን የጐማዉን ያየር ግፊት ይዩልኝ

TRASPORTO PRIVATO

Come ...
1. comprare la benzina (tipo, qualità e prezzo)
2. chiedere di controllare l'olio, l'acqua, le gomme, ecc.
3. chiedere se un determinato luogo è vicino
4. chiedere l'aiuto di un tecnico
5. chiedere la ricevuta

1.1 (Vorrei) 60.000 lire di benzina (senza piombo).
1.2 (Vorrei) 50.000 lire di diesel.
1.3 (Vorrei) 20 litri di super.
1.4 (Mi faccia) il pieno, per favore.
2.1 Mi controlli l'olio, per favore.
2.2 Mi controlli l'acqua, per favore.
2.3 Mi controlli le gomme, per favore.
2.4 Mi controlli la pressione delle gomme, per favore.

3.1 Is there a garage near here?
3.2 Is there a motorway near here?
3.3 Is there a car park near here?
3.4 Is there a car wash near here?

4.1 I need a mechanic.
4.2 My car has broken down.
4.3 I've [I have] got engine trouble.
4.4 My battery is flat.
4.5 I've run out of petrol.

5.1 Can you give me a receipt, please? 5.2 Here you are. Have a good journey!

3.1 እዚህ አከባቢ ጋራዥ አለ ወይ?
3..2 እዚህ አከባቢ የመኪና መንገድ አለ ወይ?
3.3 እዚህ አከባቢ የመኪና ማቆምያ አለ ወይ?
3.4 እዚህ አከባቢ መኪና የሚታጠብበት ጋራዥ
አለ ወይ?

4.1 መካኒክ ያስፈልገኛል
4.2 መኪና ተበላሸብኝ
4.3 ሞተሬ አልሰራም አለ
4.4 ባትሪው ሞተ
4.5 በንዚን ጨረስኩኝ (አለቀብኝ)

5.1 ፋክቱር ሊሰጡኝ ይችላሉ ወይ? 5.2 ይኸው፡ መልካም መንገድ/ጉዞ

3.1 C'è un'officina qui vicino?
3.2 C'è un'autostrada qui vicino?
3.3 C'è un parcheggio qui vicino?
3.4 C'è un lavaggio qui vicino?

4.1 Ho bisogno di un meccanico.
4.2 Ho un guasto alla macchina.
4.3 Ho la macchina in panne.
4.4 Ho la batteria scarica.
4.5 Sono rimasta senza benzina.

5.1 Mi può dare la ricevuta, per favore? 5.2 Ecco a lei. Buon viaggio!

6 HOLIDAYS

HOW TO ...

1. **Say and enquire about where you and others normally spend your holidays and how long they last**
2. **Say how you spend your holidays and with whom**

1.1 Where do you usually go on holiday ?

1.2 Usually I go to Italy.

1.3 Where do you usually spend your holidays?

1.4 Usually I go to the mountains.

1.5 Sometimes I go to the seaside.

1.6 Often I go abroad.

1.7 Where are you going on holiday this year?

1.8 I'm going to Florence.

1.9 Where is he/she going on holiday this summer?

1.10 He/she is going to Florence.

1.11 Where are you going on holiday this summer?

1.12 We're going to Florence.

1.13 Where are they going on holiday this summer?

1.14 They're going to Florence.

1.15 I'm staying in England.

የዕረፍት ግዜና በዓላት

እንዴት ...

1. የዕረፍት ግዜህን ባጠቃላይ የት እንድምታሳልፈውና ምን ያህል እንደሚወስድብህ እንደምትገልጥና ሌሎቹንም እንዴት እንደምትጠይቅ
2. የዕረፍት ግዜህን እንዴትና ከማን ጋር እንደምታሳልፈው እንደምትገልጽ

1.1 አብዛኛውን ግዜ ለዕረፍት የት ትሔዳለህ/ትሔጂያለሽ?

1.2 አብዛኛውን ግዜ ወደ ጣልያን አገር እሔዳለሁ

1.3 አብዛኛውን ግዜ የዕረፍት ግዜህን/ ግዜሽን የት ታሳልፈዋለህ/ ታሳልፊዋለሽ?

1.4 አብዛኛውን ግዜ በተራራ ላይ አሳልፈዋለሁ

1.5 አንዳንድ ግዜ ወደ ባሕር ዳርቻ እሔዳለሁ

1.6 አብዛኛውን ግዜ ውጭ አገር እሔዳለሁ

1.7 ዘንድሮ የዕረፍት ግዜህን/ ግዜሽን ለማሳለፍ የት ትሔዳለህ/ ትሔጂያለሽ?

1.8 ወደ ፍሎረንስ እሔዳለሁ

1.9 የክረምቱን ዕረፍት የት ያሳልፈዋል/ ታሳልፈውአለች?

1.10 ወደ ፍሎረንስ ይሔዳል/ትሔዳለች

1.11 የክረምት ዕረፍታችሁን የት ታሳልፋትአላችሁ?

1.12 ወደ ፍሎረንስ እንሔዳለን

1.13 የክረምት ዕረፍታቸውን የት ያሳልፋታል?

1.14 ወደ ፍሎረንስ ይሔዳሉ

1.15 እንግሊዝ አገር እቆያለሁ

VACANZE

Come ...
1. dire e chiedere dove si trascorrono generalmente le vacanze e quanto tempo durano
2. dire come si trascorrono le vacanze e con chi

1.1 Dove vai di solito in vacanza?

1.2 Di solito vado in Italia.

1.3 Dove passi di solito le vacanze?

1.4 Di solito vado in montagna.

1.5 Qualche volta vado al mare.

1.6 Spesso vado all'estero.

1.7 Dove andrai quest'anno in vacanza?

1.8 Andrò a Firenze.

1.9 Dove andrà quest'estate in vacanza?

1.10 Andrà a Firenze.

1.11 Dove andrete quest'estate in vacanza?

1.12 Andremo a Firenze.

1.13 Dove andranno quest'estate in vacanza?

1.14 Andranno a Firenze.

1.15 Resterò in Inghilterra.

1.16 How long will you stay on holiday? 1.18 How long will you be on holiday?	1.17 Two weeks. 1.19 About a fortnight.
1.20 Where would you like to go on holiday?	1.21 I'd like to go to Italy. 1.22 I'd like to go to Addis Ababa. 1.23 I'd like to go to Axum.
2.1 What do you usually do on holiday ? 2.3 What do you usually do during your holidays?	2.2 I go for walks. 2.4 I do some sport. 2.5 I go to the discotheque. 2.6 I go skiing. 2.7 I go to the seaside.
2.8 Who are you spending your holidays with? 2.10 Who are you going on holiday with?	2.9 (I'm going) with my friends. 2.11 (I'm going) with my parents.

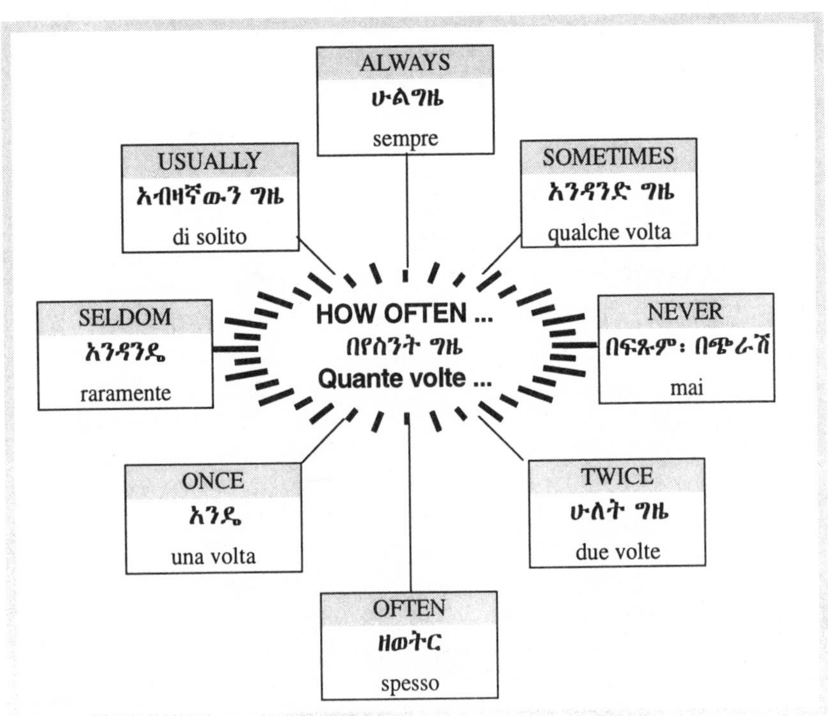

1.16 በዕረፍትህ ግዜ ምን ያህል ትቆያለህ/ ትቆያለሽ?

1.17 ለሁለት ሳምንት

1.18 ምን ያህል በዕረፍት ላይ ትቆያለህ/ ትቆያለሽ?

1.19 ለሁለት ሳምንት ያህል

1.20 ለዕረፍት የት ብትሔድ/ብትሔጂ ትወዳለህ/ ትወጂያለሽ?

1.21 ወደ ጣልያን አገር ብሔድ ደስ ይለኝ ነበር

1.22 አዲስ አበባ ብሔድ ደስ ይለኝ ነበር

1.23 አክሱም ብሔድ ደስ ይለኝ ነበር

2.1 አብዛኛውን ግዜ በዕረፍትህ/ሽ ግዜ ምን ታደርጋለህ/ታደርጊያለሽ?

2.2 እንሸራሸራለሁ

2.3 አብዛኛውን ግዜ በዕረፍት ግዜ ምን ታደርጋለህ/ታደርጊያለሽ?

2.4 ስፖርት እሰራለሁ

2.5 ወደ ዲስኮተክ እሔዳለሁ

2.6 በበረዶ ላይ እንሸራተታለሁ

2.7 ወደ ባሕር ዳር እሔዳለሁ

2.8 የዕረፍት ግዜህን/ግዜሽን ከማን ጋር ታሳልፊዋለህ/ታሳልፊዋለሽ?

2.9 ከጓደኞቼ ጋር እሔዳለሁ

2.10 ለዕረፍት ከማን ጋር ትሔዳለህ/ ትሔጂያለሽ?

2.11 ከቤተሰቦቼ ጋር እሔዳለሁ

1.16 Per quanto tempo resterai in vacanza?

1.17 Due settimane.

1.18 Per quanto tempo stai in vacanza?

1.19 Una quindicina di giorni.

1.20 Dove ti piacerebbe andare in vacanza?

1.21 Mi piacerebbe andare in Italia.

1.22 Mi piacerebbe andare ad Addis Abeba.

1.23 Mi piacerebbe andare ad Axum.

2.1 Che cosa fai di solito in vacanza?

2.2 Faccio delle passeggiate.

2.3 Che cosa fai di solito durante le vacanze?

2.4 Pratico qualche sport.

2.5 Vado in discoteca.

2.6 Vado a sciare.

2.7 Vado al mare.

2.8 Con chi passi le vacanze?

2.9 Con i miei amici.

2.10 Con chi andrai in vacanza?

2.11 Con i miei genitori.

7 TOURIST INFORMATION

HOW TO ...
1. Ask for information about a town and region
2. Ask for details of excursions
3. React (i.e. welcome or reject) to suggestions about activities

1.1 What places of interest are there to see ... ?

1.2 There's a museum.
1.3 There's a sea-front promenade.
1.4 There are a lot of tourist itineraries.
1.5 There are a lot of historical monuments.

1.6 What are the city's main attractions?

2.1 Do they organize any tourist itineraries?
2.2 Do they organize any excursions?
2.3 Could you recommend some excursions?
2.4 Could you recommend a guided tour?

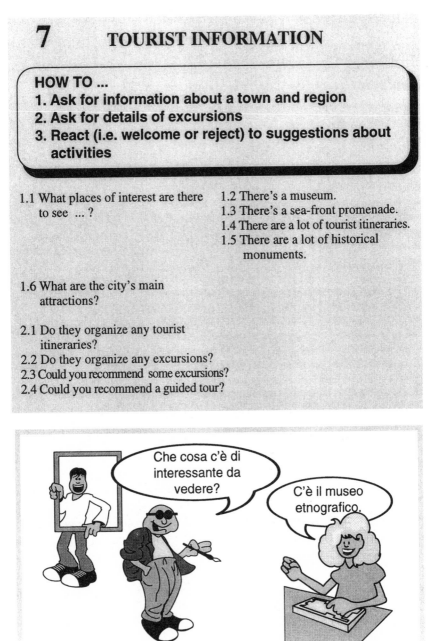

Che cosa c'è di interessante da vedere?
C'è il museo etnografico.

የቱሪስት መረጃ

እንዴት ...
1. ስለ ከተማውና አከባቢው እንደምትጠይቅ
2. ስለ ጉዞ ዝርዝር መረጃ እንደምትጠይቅ
3. ስለ አንዳንድ እንቅስቃሴዎችና ሐሳቦች መቀበልና ውድቅ ማድረግ

1.1 ምን የሚታዩ አስደናቂ ቦታዎች አሉ?

1.2 ቤተመዘክር አለ
1.3 የባሕር ዳርቻ ጎዳና አለው
1.4 ብዙ የጎብኚዎች የሽርሽር ቦታዎች አሉት
1.5 ብዙ የታሪክ ቅርሳ ቅርስ አሉት

1.6 የከተማው ዋና ማራኪ ነገሮች የትኞቹ ናቸው?

2.1 የቱሪስት ጉብኝት ያዘጋጃሉ ወይ?
2.2 ጉብኝት ይዘጋጃል ወይ?
2.3 ስለ ጉብኝት ምን ትመክረኛለህ?
2.4 አስቀድሞ ስለተዘጋጀ ጉብኝት ምን ትመክረኛለህ?

INFORMAZIONI TURISTICHE

Come ...
1. chiedere informazioni su una città o una regione
2. chiedere informazioni su escursioni
3. rispondere (es. accettare o rifiutare) a proposte di attività

1.1 Che cosa c'è di interessante da vedere in questa zona?

1.2 C'è il museo.
1.3 C'è la passeggiata a mare.
1.4 Ci sono molti itinerari turistici.
1.5 Ci sono molti monumenti storici.

1.6 Quali sono le principali attrattive di questa città?

2.1 Organizzano qualche giro turistico?
2.2 Organizzano delle escursioni?
2.3 Può consigliarmi delle escursioni?
2.4 Può consigliarmi delle visite guidate?

3.1 We could go to the museum.
3.3 We could go to the cinema.
3.5 You could go to the theatre.

3.2 Yes, that's a great idea.
3.4 No, I'm tired.
3.6 No, I don't feel like it.
3.7 No, I'm busy.

3.1 ወደ ቤተመዘክር ለመሔድ እንችላለን
3.3 ወደ ሲነማ ለመሔድ እንችላለን
3.5 ወደ ትያትር ለመሔድ ትችላለህ / ትችያለሽ

3.2 መልካም ሐሳብ
3.4 አይቻልም፡ ደክሞኛል
3.6 ደስ አላለኝም
3.7 ሥራ በዝቶብኛል

3.1 Potremmo andare al museo.
3.3 Potremmo andare al cinema.
3.5 Potresti andare a teatro.

3.2 Sì, è un'ottima idea.
3.4 No, sono stanco.
3.6 No, non ne ho voglia.
3.7 No, sono impegnato.

SOME SUGGESTIONS ABOUT THE DIFFERENT PARTS OF THE LETTER

INFORMAL	FORMAL
• Dear ...,	• To • Dear Mr./Mrs., • Dear Sir,
• Sorry I haven't written for ages ... • How are things? • You haven't written for ages ...	• I am/We are ... • The undersigned ... • This is to inform you ... • In answer to your letter of ... • With reference to your letter of ...
• I passed my exam ... • Why don't you come and see us ... • Could you do me a favour?	• I would be grateful if you could send us ... • We would be grateful if you could book ... • Please could you cancel ...
• Bye, bye. • Say hello to everyone from me. • Love and kisses, see you soon. • Lots of love (to everyone). • Love.	• Yours faithfully/sincerely. • Best regards/wishes. • I look forward to hearing from you. Yours faithfully.
• Name	• Name and surname
• Caro/a/i/e ...,	• A/Al/Alla/All' ..., • Caro/a Signor/a ..., • Egregio/Gentile Signore/a ...,
• Scusami se non ti ho scritto prima ... • Come va? • Da molto non mi scrivi ...	• Sono/Siamo ... • Il/La sottoscritto/a ... • Le/Vi comunico ... • In risposta alla Sua lettera del ... • Con riferimento alla Sua del ...
• Sono stato promosso ... • Perché non vieni a trovarci ... • Potresti farmi un favore?	• Le sarei grato se potesse inviarci ... • Vi saremmo grati se poteste prenotare ... • Vi preghiamo di annullare ...
• Ciao. • Saluta tutti da parte mia. Ciao. • Un bacio, a presto. • Tanti cari saluti (a tutti). • Affettuosi saluti.	• Distinti saluti. • Cordiali saluti. • In attesa di Vostre notizie, porgo distinti saluti.
• Nome	• Nome e cognome

8 HOTEL

HOW TO ...
1. Identify yourself
2. Say that you have (not) made a reservation
3. Ask if there are rooms available
4. State when you require a room and for how long
5. Ask the cost per night, per person, per room
6. Ask if meals are included
7. Say you would like to pay

1.1 Good morning. Can I help you?

1.2 Good morning, I'm Mr. Skelton.

2.1 I booked a room.
2.2 I have a room booked.
2.3 I haven't booked.

3.1 Do you have a single room?

3.2 At the moment we're full.

3.3 Do you have a double room?

3.4 For how long?
3.5 For how many nights?

4.1 From ... to ...
4.2 For one night.
4.3 For two weeks.

ሆቴል

እንዴት ...
1. ራስህን እንደምታስተዋውቅ
2. አልጋ አስመዝግበህ እንደምትቆይ
3. ያልተያዙ ክፍሎች ካሉ እንደምትጠይቅ
4. አልጋውን ለመቼና ለስንት ግዜ እንደምትፈልገው እንደምትጠይቅ
5. የአንድ አልጋ ዋጋ ላንድ ሌሊት ላንድ ሰው ስንት መሆኑ እንደምትጠይቅ
6. ዋጋው ምግብን የሚጨምር መሆኑን እንደምትጠይቅ
7. ሒሳብ እንዲቀርብልህ እንደምትጠይቅ

1.1 እንደምን አደሩ፡ ምን ልታዘዝ?

1.2 እንደምን አደሩ (አቶ ስከልቶን)

2.1 አንድ መኝታ ክፍል አስመዝግቤ ነበር
2.2 አንድ የተመዘገበ መኝታ ክፍል አለኝ
2.3 አላስመዘገብኩም

3.1 ላንድ ሰው የሚሆን መኝታ ክፍል አላችሁ ወይ?
3.3 ለሁለት ሰው መኝታ አላችሁ ወይ?

3.2 ለጊዜው ሁሉም ተይዘዋል
3.4 ለስንት ግዜ?
3.5 ለስንት ሌሊት?

4.1 ከ ... እስከ
4.2 ላንድ ሌሊት
4.3 ለሁለት ሳምንት

ALBERGHI

Come ...
1. presentarsi
2. dire se si è prenotato o no
3. chiedere se ci sono camere disponibili
4. dire per quando e per quanto tempo si richiede una camera
5. chiedere il costo per una notte, per persona, per camera
6. chiedere se i pasti sono inclusi
7. chiedere il conto

1.1 Buongiorno, desidera?

1.2 Buongiorno, sono il signor Skelton.

2.1 Ho prenotato una camera.
2.2 Ho una camera prenotata.
2.3 Non ho prenotato.

3.1 Avete una camera singola?
3.3 Avete una camera doppia?

3.2 Per il momento è tutto esaurito.
3.4 Per quanto tempo?
3.5 Per quante notti?

4.1 Dal ... al ...
4.2 Per una notte.
4.3 Per due settimane.

5.1 How much is it for one night ?
5.2 How much is it for one person?
5.3 How much is it for one room?
5.4 How much is it for full board?
5.5 How much is it for half board?

6.1 Is breakfast included?
6.2 Yes, it's all included.
6.3 Are meals included?
6.4 No, they're not included in the price.

7.1 (I would like) the bill, please.
7.2 Here you are, thank you.
7.3 Could you prepare the bill, please?

5.1 ለአንድ ሌሊት ዋጋው ስንት ነው?
5.2 ለአንድ ሰው ዋጋው ስንት ነው?
5.3 ለአንድ መኝታ ክፍል ዋጋው ስንት ነው?
5.4 ለሙሉ መስተንግዶ ዋጋው ስንት ነው?
5.5 ለከፊል(ግማሽ) መስተንግዶ ዋጋው ስንት ነው?

6.1 ክፍያው ቍርስን ይጨምራል ወይ?
6.2 አዎ፡ ሁሉንም ያጠቃልላል
6.3 ክፍያው ምግብን ይጨምራል ወይ?
6.4 አይደለም፡ ሁሉንም አያጠቃልልም

7.1 እባክዎን ሒሳብ ያምጡልኝ
7.2 ይኸውልህ፡ አመሰግናለሁ
7.3 እባክዎን ሒሳብ ይንገሩኝ

5.1 Qual è il prezzo per una notte?
5.2 Qual è il prezzo per una persona?
5.3 Qual è il prezzo per una camera?

5.4 Quant'è la pensione completa?
5.5 Quant'è la mezza pensione?

6.1 E' compresa la prima colazione?
6.2 Sì, è tutto compreso.
6.3 Sono compresi i pasti?
6.4 No, non sono compresi nel prezzo.

7.1 (Vorrei) il conto, per favore.
7.2 Ecco a Lei, grazie.
7.3 Potrebbe prepararmi il conto, per favore?

Common words in hotels
በሆቴሎች የምንጠቀምባቸው ቃላት
Principali parole negli alberghi

drinking water	የሚጠጣ ውኃ	acqua potabile
deposit	ተቀማጭ	caparra
safe	ካዝና	cassaforte
out of order	ከጥቅም ውጪ	fuori servizio
half board	ከፊል መስተንግዶ	mezza pensione
youth hostel	የወጣቶች ሆስቴል	ostello della gioventù
attended car-park	ለመኪናዎች የተያዘ	parcheggio custodito
full board	ሙሉ መስተንግዶ	pensione completa
seaside resort	የመዝናኛ ባህር ዳርቻ	stazione balneare
spa	ዘመናዊ ጠበል	stazione termale
all included	የተሟላ	tutto compreso
emergency exit	የአደጋ ማውጫ	uscita di sicurezza
no camping	ድንኳን አትትከሉ	vietato campeggiare
no admittance	መግባት ክልክል ነው	vietato l'ingresso
no parking	መኪና ማቆም ክልክል ነው	vietato il parcheggio
board and lodging	ምግብና መኝታ	vitto e alloggio
bed and breakfast	አልጋና ቁርስ	alloggio e prima colazione

Reservations are valid only if they are made and confirmed in writing

ቦታ መያዝ ከፈለጉ፣ አስቀድመው በጽሑፍ ያመልክቱ

Le prenotazioni hanno valore solo se effettuate e confermate per iscritto

9 RESTAURANT

HOW TO ...
1. Ask for a table
2. Attract the waiter's attention
3. Order a drink or a snack
4. Order a meal
5. Express an opinion about a meal or dish
6. Ask for the bill

1.1 Hello, is that "Bologna" restaurant?

1.2 Yes, what can I do for you?

1.3 I'd [I would] like (to book) a table for two (people).

1.4 I'd like (to book) a table for five.

1.5 For what time?

1.6 For eight o'clock.

1.7 Fine, what's your name?

ምግብ ቤት

እንዴት...
1. ጠረጴዛ እንደምትይዝ
2. አስተናጋጁን እንደምትስበው
3. መጠጥ ወይም ቍርስ እንደምታዝዝ
4. ምግብ እንደምታዝዝ
5. ስለ ምግብ ሐሳብ እንደምትሰጥ
6. ሒሳብ እንደምትጠይቅ

1.1 ሀሎ፡ ቦሎኛ ምግብ ቤት ነው?

1.2 አዎ፡ ምን ልታዘዝ?

1.3 ለሁለት ሰው ቦታ እፈልግ ነበር

1.4 ለአምስት ሰው ቦታ እፈልግ ነበር

1.5 ለስንት ሰዓት?

1.6 ለስምንት ሰዓት

1.7 በጣም ጥሩ፡ ማን ልበል?

RISTORANTE

Come ...
1. chiedere un tavolo
2. attirare l'attenzione del cameriere
3. ordinare una bevanda o uno spuntino
4. ordinare un pasto
5. esprimere un'opinione sul cibo
6. chiedere il conto

1.1 Pronto, ristorante "Bologna"?

1.2 Sì, dica!

1.3 Vorrei (prenotare) un tavolo per due.

1.4 Vorrei (prenotare) un tavolo per cinque.

1.5 Per che ora?

1.6 Per le otto.

1.7 Va bene, qual è il Suo nome?

2.1 Waiter!
2.2 Waitress!

2.3 Yes, what would you like?

3.1 I'd like a coffee.
3.2 I'd like a cappuccino.
3.3 I'd like a sandwich.
3.4 I'd like a cheese roll.
3.5 I'd like a 'croissant'.
3.6 I'd like an orangeade.
3.7 I'd like a small pizza.
3.8 I'd like to see the menu.

4.1 (As a starter) I'd like ham and melon.
4.2 (As a starter) I'd like Russian salad.

2.1 አሳላፊ (አስተናጋጅ)!
2.2 አሳላፊ (አስተናጋጅ)!

2.3 እሺ፡ ምን ልታዘዝ?

3.1 ቡና አለ?
3.2 ቡና በወተት አለ (ካፑቺኖ አለ)?
3.3 ሳንድዊች አለ?
3.4 የፎርማጆ ሳንድዊች አለ?
3.5 ብርዮሽ አለ?
3.6 አረንቻታ አለ?
3.7 ፒሳ አለ?
3.8 የምግብ ዝርዝር ለማየት እፈልጋለሁ

4.1 በቅድሚያ የአሳማ ስጋና መሎን ብታቀርብልኝ
4.2 በቅድሚያ የሩስያ ሰላጣ ብታቀርብልኝ

2.1 Cameriere!
2.2 Cameriera!

2.3 Prego! Desidera?

3.1 Vorrei un caffè.
3.2 Vorrei un cappuccino.
3.3 Vorrei un tramezzino.
3.4 Vorrei un panino al formaggio.
3.5 Vorrei un cornetto.
3.6 Vorrei un'aranciata.
3.7 Vorrei una pizzetta.
3.8 Vorrei vedere il menù.

4.1 Come antipasto vorrei del prosciutto e melone.
4.2 Come antipasto vorrei dell'insalata russa.

4.3 For first course I'd like (some) lasagna.
4.4 For first course I'd like (some) tagliatelle with tomato sauce.
4.5 For first course I'd like (some) spaghetti.

4.6 And what would you like to drink?

4.7 I'd like an orangeade.
4.8 I'd like a bottle of red/white wine.
4.9 I'd like some fizzy/natural mineral water.

4.10 (For the second course) what do you recommend?

4.11 I recommend the dish of the day.
4.12 I recommend this (dish).
4.13 (I recommend the) fried fish.

4.14 All right, I'll have this with mixed salad.
4.15 Thanks, but I prefer French fries.
4.16 Thanks, but I prefer cooked vegetables.

4.3 መጀመርያ ላዛኛ እፈልጋለሁ
4.4 መጀመርያ ታልያተሊ ከቲማቲም ስጎ ጋር እፈልጋለሁ
4.5 መጀመርያ ስፓገቲ እፈልጋለሁ

4.6 ምን መጠጣት ይፈልጋሉ?

4.7 አረንቻታ እፈልጋለሁ
4.8 ቀይ/ነጭ ወይን ጠጅ እፈልጋለሁ
4.9 ጋዝ ያለው አምቦ ውኃ/ ጋዝ የሌለው አምቦ ውኃ/ እፈልጋለሁ

4.10 ሰኮንዶ ምን ይሻለኛል?

4.11 የቀኑ ምግብ ይሻለዎታል
4.12 ይህ ምግብ ይሻለዎታል
4.13 የተጠበሰ ዓሣ ይሻለዎታል

4.14 እሺ፡ ከሱ ጋር ድብልቅ ሰላጣ አምጣልኝ
4.15 አመሰግናለሁ፡ ሆኖም የተጠበሰ ድንች ይሻለኛል
4.16 አመሰግናለሁ፡ ሆኖም የተጠበሰ አትክልት ይሻለኛል

4.3 Come primo vorrei delle lasagne.
4.4 Come primo vorrei delle tagliatelle al pomodoro.
4.5 Come primo vorrei degli spaghetti.

4.6 E da bere (cosa desidera)?

4.7 Da bere vorrei un'aranciata.
4.8 Da bere vorrei una bottiglia di vino rosso/ bianco.
4.9 Da bere vorrei dell'acqua minerale (naturale/gassata).

4.10 Di secondo che cosa mi consiglia?

4.11 Le consiglio il piatto del giorno.
4.12 Le consiglio questo piatto.
4.13 (Le consiglio) la frittura di pesce.

4.14 Va bene, prendo questo, con contorno di insalata mista.
4.15 Grazie, ma preferisco patatine fritte.
4.16 Grazie, ma preferisco verdure cotte.

4.17 Do you have any sweet/cake?
4.18 I'm sorry, it's finished.
4.19 Do you have (any) ice-cream?
4.20 Do you have (any) cheese?
4.21 Do you have (any) fresh fruit?

5.1 It's all very nice.
5.2 It's very nice.
5.3 The soup is too salty/needs more salt.
5.4 The meat is over-cooked/underdone.
5.5 The pizza is burnt.
5.6 The plate/glass is dirty.

6.1 Can I have the bill, please?

4.17 ኬክ አላችሁ ወይ?
4.18 ይቅርታ፡ አልቋል
4.19 ጀላቲ አላችሁ ወይ?
4.20 ፎርማጆ አላችሁ ወይ?
4.21 አዳዲስ ፍራፍሬዎች አሏችሁ ወይ?

5.1 ሁሉም ጣፋጭ ነው
5.2 በጣም ጣፋጭ ነው
5.3 ይህ መረቅ ጨው በዝቶበታል/ ይህ መረቅ ጨው ያንሰዋል
5.4 ስጋው በጣም በስሏል/ ስጋው ብዙም አልበሰለም
5.5 ፒሳው አሯል
5.6 ሳህኑ ቆሽሿል/ ብርጭቆው ቆሽሿል

6.1 ቢሉን ቢያቀርቡልኝ

4.17 Avete del dolce?
4.18 Ci dispiace, l'abbiamo finito.
4.19 Avete del gelato?
4.20 Avete del formaggio?
4.21 Avete della frutta fresca?
4.22 Ci dispiace, l'abbiamo finita.

5.1 E' tutto molto buono.
5.2 E' buonissimo.
5.3 La minestra è salata/insipida.
5.4 La carne è troppo cotta/cruda.
5.5 La pizza è bruciata.
5.6 Il piatto/bicchiere è sporco.

6.1 Mi porta il conto, per favore?

Common words in recipes
በምግብ አሰራር ዘዴ የሚገኙ ቃላት
Principali parole nelle ricette

1. to toast, to roast	1. መቍላት	1. abbrustolire
2. to slice, to cut	2. መክተፍ	2. affettare
3. to add	3. መጨመር	3. aggiungere
4. herbs	4. ቅመማ ቅመም	4. aromi
5. to boil	5. መቀቀል	5. bollire
6. saucepan	6. መቂያ	6. casseruola
7. to cook	7. ምግብ መስራት	7. cuocere
8. to bake	8. መጋገር	8. cuocere al forno
9. to stew	9. ወጥ መስራት	9. cuocere in umido
10. to steam	10. በእንፋሎት ማብሰል	10. cuocere a vapore
11. to grill	11. መጥበስ	11. cuocere ai ferri
12. to fry	12. መጥበስ	12. friggere
13. to whisk, to whip	13. መውቃት	13. frullare
14. to grate	14. መፈግፈግ	14. grattugiare
15. to knead	15. ማብኳት	15. impastare
16. to flour	16. መፍጨት	16. infarinare
17. to rise	17. ማብኳት	17. lievitare
18. to mix, to stir	18. ማማሰል	18. mescolare
19. ladle	19. ወጥ ማውጣት	19. mestolo
20. to put	20. ማስገባት	20. mettere
21. breadcrumb	21. ፍርፋሪ	21. pane grattugiato
22. to peel	22. መላጥ	22. pelare
23. stuffing	23. መክተት	23. ripieno
24. to brown	24. ማቅላት	24. rosolare
25. to fry lightly	25. ማሞቅ	25. soffriggere
26. to squeeze	26. መጭመቅ	26. spremere
27. to cut	27. መክተፍ	27. tagliare
28. frying pan	28. መጥበሻ	28. tegame
29. tureen, bowl	29. የሸክላ ድስት	29. terrina
30. to mince, to chop	30. አድቅቆ መክተፍ	30. tritare

10 SHOPPING

HOW TO ...

1. **Find out about opening and closing times**
2. **Ask for information about supermarkets, shopping centres, etc.**
3. **Ask where specific departments are**
4. **Express quantity required (including expressions of weight, container; etc.)**
5. **Ask for particular items**
6. **Find out how much things cost**

1.1 At what time do (clothes) shops open?

1.2 They open at eight thirty.

1.3 At what time do (clothes) shops close?

1.4 They close at...

2.1 Is there a supermarket?
2.2 Where's the shopping centre?
2.3 Where's the market?

YES... WE ARE OPEN

SORRY... WE ARE CLOSED

መግዛትና መሸመት

እንዴት ...
1. ስለ ሱቆች መከፈትና መዘጋት መረጃ እንደምትጠይቅ
2. ስለ ሱፐርማርኬቶችና የገበያ አደራሾች መረጃ እንደምትጠይቅ
3. ልዩ የገበያ ክፍል የት እንደሚገኝ እንደምትጠይቅ
4. ስለ ብዛትና ክብደት እንዲሁም ይዞታ እንደምትገልጽ
5. ስለ አንድ ልዩ ዕቃ እንደምትጠይቅ
6. ዋጋ እንደምትጠይቅ

1.1 የልብስ ሱቁ በስንት ሰዓት ይከፈታል?
1.2 በሁለት ሰዓት ተኩል ይከፈታል
1.3 የልብስ ሱቁ በስንት ሰዓት ይዘጋል?
1.4 በ ... ይዘጋል

2.1 እዚህ አካባቢ ሱፐርማርኬት አለ ወይ?
2.2 የገበያ አደራሽ የት ነው?
2.3 ገበያው የት ነው?

COMPERARE

Come ...
1. informarsi sugli orari di apertura e di chiusura
2. chiedere informazioni su supermercati, centri commerciali, ecc.
3. chiedere dove si trova un determinato reparto
4. esprimere la quantità richiesta
5. chiedere un particolare prodotto
6. chiedere il prezzo dei prodotti

1.1 A che ora aprono i negozi (di abbigliamento)?
1.2 Aprono alle otto e mezzo.
1.3 A che ora chiudono i negozi (di abbigliamento)?
1.4 Chiudono alle ...

2.1 C'è un supermercato?
2.2 Dov'è un centro commerciale?
2.3 Dov'è un mercato?

2.4 Where is a greengrocer's?
2.5 Where is a bureau de change/an exchange bureau?
2.6 Where is a chemist's?
2.7 Where is a butcher's?
2.8 Where is a baker's?
2.9 Where is a pastry shop?
2.10 Where is a jeweller's?

3.1 Where's the food department?
3.2 Where's the clothing department?
3.3 Where's the book department?
3.4 Where's the electrical department?

4.1 I'd like a litre of milk.
4.2 I'd like a kilo of bread.
4.3 I'd like a dozen eggs.
4.4 I'd like a plastic bag.
4.5 I'd like a bottle of wine.

2.4 የአትክልትና የፍራፍሬ ገበያ የት ነው?
2.5 ፍራንክ የሚመነዘርበት ቦታ የት ነው?
2.6 መድሓኒት ቤት የት ነው?
2.7 የስጋ መሸጫ ቤት የት ነው?
2.8 ዳቦ ቤት የት ነው?
2.9 ኬክ ቤት የት ነው?
2.10 ወርቅ ሰሪ ቤት የት ነው?

3.1 የመመገብያ ክፍል የት ነው?
3.2 የልብስ መሸጫ ክፍል የት ነው?
3.3 የመጻሕፍት መሸጫ ክፍል የት ነው?
3.4 የኤሌክትሪክ ዕቃዎች መሸጫ ክፍል የት ነው?

4.1 አንድ ሊትር ወተት እፈልጋለሁ
4.2 አንድ ኪሎ ዳቦ እፈልጋለሁ
4.3 አንድ ደርዘን እንቍላል እፈልጋለሁ
4.4 አንድ የፕላስቲክ ሻንጣ እፈልጋለሁ
4.5 አንድ ጠርሙስ የወይን ጠጅ እፈልጋለሁ

2.4 Dov'è un fruttivendolo?
2.5 Dov'è una agenzia di cambio?
2.6 Dov'è una farmacia?
2.7 Dov'è una macelleria?
2.8 Dov'è una panetteria?
2.9 Dov'è una pasticceria?
2.10 Dov'è una gioielleria?

3.1 Dov'è il reparto alimentari?
3.2 Dov'è il reparto vestiti?
3.3 Dov'è il reparto libri?
3.4 Dov'è il reparto elettricità?

4.1 Vorrei un litro di latte.
4.2 Vorrei un chilo di pane.
4.3 Vorrei una dozzina di uova.
4.4 Vorrei un sacchetto di plastica.
4.5 Vorrei una bottiglia di vino.

5.1 I'd like a pullover.
5.2 I'd like a raincoat.
5.3 I'd like an umbrella.
5.4 I'd like a bag.
5.5 I'd like a jacket.
5.6 I'd like a coat.
5.7 I'd like a pair of shoes.

5.8 Made of nylon.
5.9 Made of leather.
5.10 Made of plastic.
5.11 Made of silk.
5.12 Made of cotton.

6.1 How much (is it)?

6.2 Can I pay by cheque?
6.3 Can I pay by credit card?

5.1 አንድ ሹራብ እፈልጋለሁ
5.2 አንድ የዝናም ካፖርት እፈልጋለሁ
5.3 አንድ ጃንጥላ እፈልጋለሁ
5.4 አንድ የእጅ ሻንጣ እፈልጋለሁ
5.5 አንድ ጃኬት እፈልጋለሁ
5.6 አንድ ኮት እፈልጋለሁ
5.7 ጫማ እፈልጋለሁ

5.8 ከናይሎን የተሰራ
5.9 ከቆዳ የተሰራ
5.10 ከፕላስቲክ የተሰራ
5.11 ከሀር የተሰራ
5.12 ከጥጥ የተሰራ

6.1 ይህ፡ ዋጋው ስንት ነው?

6.2 በቼክ መክፈል ይቻላል ወይ?
6.3 በክሬዲት ካርድ መክፈል ይቻላል ወይ?

5.1 Vorrei un pullover.
5.2 Vorrei un impermeabile.
5.3 Vorrei un ombrello.
5.4 Vorrei una borsa.
5.5 Vorrei una giacca.
5.6 Vorrei un cappotto.
5.7 Vorrei un paio di scarpe.

5.8 Di nailon.
5.9 Di pelle.
5.10 Di plastica.
5.11 Di seta.
5.12 Di cotone.

6.1 Quanto costa?

6.2 Posso pagare con un assegno?
6.3 Posso pagare con la carta di credito?

11 SERVICES

POST OFFICE

HOW TO ...
1. **Ask where a post office, a tobacconist or post box is.**
2. **Find out opening and closing times**
3. **Ask how much it costs to send letters, postcards or parcels to a particular country**
4. **Buy stamps of a particular value**
5. **Say whether you would like to send letters, postcards or parcels**

1.1 Excuse me, where is a post office?
1.2 It's there, near the bank.
1.3 Excuse me, where is a tobacconist's?
1.4 It's down there, on the right.
1.5 Excuse me, where is a post box?
1.6 I'm sorry, I don't know.

2.1 At what time does the post office open?
2.2 It opens at eight fifteen.
2.3 At what time does the post office close?
2.4 It closes at 2.00 pm.

ፖስታ ቤት

1. ፖስታ ቤት፡ ሲጋራ የሚሸጥበት ቦታ፡ የፖስታ ሣጥን፡ የት እንደሚገኝ እንደምትጠይቅ
2. የሚከፈትበትና የሚዘጋበት ሰዓት እንደምትጠይቅ
3. ደብዳቤዎች፡ፖስት ካርዶች፡ እንዲሁም ጥቅሎች ወደ ተወሰነ አገር ለመላክ ስንት እንደሚያስከፍል እንደምትጠይቅ
5. የተወሰነ ዋጋ ያላቸውን ቴምብሮች እንደምትገዛ
6. ደብዳቤዎች፡ፖስት ካርዶች፡ጥቅሎች፡ለመላክ እንደምትፈልግ እንደምትገልጽ

1.1 ይቅርታ፡ ፖስታ ቤት የት ነው?
1.2 እዚያው፡ ባንኩ አጠገብ ነው
1.3 ይቅርታ፡ ሲጋራ የሚሸጥበት ሱቅ ቤት የት ነው?
1.4 እታች፡ ወደ ቀኝ ነው
1.5 ይቅርታ፡ የፖስታ ሣጥን የት ነው?
1.6 ይቅርታ፡ አላውቀውም

2.1 ፖስታ ቤቱ በስንት ሰዓት ይከፈታል?
2.2 በሁለት ሰዓት ከሩብ ይከፈታል
2.3 ፖስታ ቤቱ በስንት ሰዓት ይዘጋል?
2.4 በስምንት ሰዓት ከምሽቱ ይዘጋል

UFFICIO POSTALE

Come ...

1. **chiedere dov'è un ufficio postale, una tabaccheria o una buca della lettere**
2. **informarsi sugli orari di apertura e di chiusura**
3. **chiedere quanto costa spedire una lettera, una cartolina o un pacco in un determinato paese**
4. **comprare francobolli di un determinato valore**
5. **dire se si desidera spedire lettere, cartoline o pacchi**

1.1 Scusi, dov'è un ufficio postale?
1.2 Scusi, dov'è una tabaccheria?
1.3 Scusi, dov'è una buca delle lettere?
1.4 E' là, vicino alla banca.
1.5 E' laggiù, sulla destra.
1.6 Non lo so, mi dispiace.

2.1 A che ora apre l'ufficio postale?
2.2 A che ora chiude l'ufficio postale?
2.3 Apre alle otto e quindici.
2.4 Chiude alle quattordici.

3.1 How much is it to send a letter to Germany?
3.2 How much is it to send a card to Belgium?
3.3 How much is it to send a parcel to Ireland?
3.4 How much is it to send a greeting card?

4.1 Would you give me a stamp for Great Britain, please?
4.2 Would you give me a stamp for a letter, please?
4.3 Would you give me a stamp for a card, please?

5.1 I'd like to send this letter by air-mail to Holland.
5.2 I'd like to send this parcel to Denmark.
5.3 I'd like to send a registered letter (with advice of receipt) to Australia.

3.1 ደብዳቤ ወደ ጀርመን አገር ለመላክ ዋጋው ስንት ይደርሳል?
3.2 ፖስት ካርድ ወደ በልጂዩም አገር ለመላክ ዋጋው ስንት ይደርሳል?
3.3 አንድ ጥቅል ወደ አየርላንድ ለመላክ ዋጋው ስንት ይደርሳል?
3.4 የሰላምታ ካርድ ለመላክ ዋጋው ስንት ይደርሳል?

4.1 እባክዎን ለእንግሊዝ አገር ቴምብር ይስጡኝ?
4.2 እባክዎን የደብዳቤ ቴምብር ይስጡኝ?
4.3 እባክዎን የካርድ ቴምብር ይስጡኝ?

5.1 ይችን ደብዳቤ ወደ ሆላንድ በአየር ለመላክ እፈልግ ነበር
5.2 ይችን ካርድ ወደ ዴንማርክ በአየር ለመላክ እፈልግ ነበር
5.3 ያደራ ደብዳቤ ወደ አውስትራልያ ለመላክ እፈልግ ነበር

3.1 Quanto costa spedire una lettera in Germania?
3.2 Quanto costa spedire una cartolina in Belgio?
3.3 Quanto costa spedire un pacco in Irlanda?
3.4 Quanto costa spedire un biglietto d'auguri?

4.1 Mi dia un francobollo per la Gran Bretagna, per favore.
4.2 Mi dia un francobollo per lettera, per favore.
4.3 Mi dia un francobollo per cartolina, per favore.

5.1 Vorrei spedire questa lettera per via aerea in Olanda.
5.2 Vorrei spedire questo pacco in Danimarca.
5.3 Vorrei spedire una raccomandata (con ricevuta di ritorno) in Australia.

TELEPHONE

HOW TO ...
1. Give and seek information about where phone calls can be made
2. Ask if you can make a call
3. Ask for a telephone number
4. Answer a phone call
5. Make a phone call and ask to speak to someone

1.1 Where's the nearest phone-box?
1.2 In Piazza Dante, next to the newspa per kiosk.
1.3 Where's the nearest public phone?
1.4 A hundred metres on your right.

2.1 Can I make a phone call to my parents?
2.2 Yes, of course!
2.3 Could I make a phone call?
2.4 Can I phone Sandra?

3.1 What's your phone number?
3.2 My number is (0184) 357136.
3.3 What is the code for Florence?
3.4 The code for Florence is 055.
3.5 What number do I have to dial for Great Britain?

4.1 Hello!
4.2 This is Mr. Haile.
4.3 Hello! Who's speaking?
4.4 This is Anna.

5.1 Could I speak to Dr. Brandi?
5.2 I can't hear you, please speak louder!
5.3 Is Sonia there?
5.4 Yes, one moment!
5.5 Yes, it's me.
5.6 I'll [I will] call him for you.
5.7 I'll call her for you.
5.8 You've got the wrong number.
5.9 I'm sorry, but he has just gone out.
5.10 Could you phone tonight?
5.11 Could you call back later?
5.12 Could you call back in ten minutes?

ቴሌፎን

እንዴት ...
1. የት እንደሚደወል መረጃ እንደምትሰጥና እንደምትጠይቅ
2. ለመደወል ፈቃድ እንዳለ እንደምትጠይቅ
3. የቴሌፎን ቍጥር እንደምትጠይቅ
4. ቴሌፎን ሲደወል መልስ እንደምትሰጥ
5. ደውለህ ከሌላ ሰው ጋር ለማነጋገር እንደምትፈልግ እንደምትጠይቅ

1.1 የቴሌፎን ሣጥን የት ነው?
1.2 ፒያሳ ዳንተ የጋዜጣ መሸጫ ቤት በስተጀርባ
1.3 የህዝብ ቴሌፎን የት ነው?
1.4 መቶ ሜትር በስተቀኝ

2.1 ለቤተሰቦቼ ልደውል እችላለሁ ወይ?
2.2 አዎ፡ እንዴታ
2.3 መደወል እችላለሁ ወይ?
2.4 ለሳንድራ ልደውልላት?

3.1 ቴሌፎን ቍጥርህ ስንት ነው?
3.2 የተሌፎን ቍጥሬ [0184] 357136 ነው
3.3 የፍሎረንስ ኮድ ስንት ነው?
3.4 የፍሎረንስ ኮድ 055 ነው
3.5 ወደ እንግሊዝ አገር ለመደወል የትኛውን ቍጥር ልጠቀም?

4.1 ሀሎ
4.2 አቶ ኃይለ እባላለሁ
4.3 ሀሎ፡ ማን ልበል?
4.4 አና እባላለሁ

5.1 ዶክተር ብራንዲን ለማነጋገር እችላለሁ ወይ?
5.2 አይሰማም፡ ጮክ ይበሉ
5.3 ሶኒያ እዚያው አለች ወይ?
5.4 አዎ፡ አንዴ
5.5 አዎ፡ እኔ ነኝ
5.6 ልጥራልዎት
5.7 ልጥራልዎት
5.8 ተሳስተዋል
5.9 ይቅርታ፡ አሁኑኑ ወጥትዋል/ ወጥታለች
5.10 ከምሽቱ ሊደውሉ ይችላሉ ወይ?
5.11 ትንሽ ቆይተው ሊደውሉ ይችላሉ ወይ?
5.12 ከአሥር ደቂቃ በኋላ ሊደውሉ ይችላሉ ወይ?

TELEFONO

Come ...
1. **dare e chiedere informazioni su dove si può telefonare**
2. **chiedere se si può telefonare**
3. **chiedere un numero di telefono**
4. **rispondere ad una telefonata**
5. **telefonare e chiedere di parlare con qualcuno**

1.1 Dov'è una cabina telefonica?
1.3 Dov'è un telefono (pubblico)?

1.2 In Piazza Dante, accanto all'edicola.
1.4 A cento metri, sulla destra.

2.1 Posso fare una telefonata ai miei genitori?
2.3 Posso telefonare a Sandra?
2.4 Potrei telefonare?

2.2 Sì, certamente!

3.1 Qual è il Suo numero di telefono?
3.3 Qual è il prefisso di Firenze?
3.3 Che numero devo fare per la Gran Bretagna?

3.2 Il mio numero di telefono è (0184) 357136.
3.4 Il prefisso di Firenze è 055.

4.1 Pronto!
4.3 Pronto! Chi parla?

4.2 Sono il signor Haile.
4.4 Sono Anna.

5.1 Potrei parlare con il dottor Brandi?
5.3 C'è Sonia?

5.2 Non la sento, parli più forte!
5.4 Sì, un attimo!
5.5 Dica! Sono io.
5.6 Glielo chiamo.
5.7 Gliela chiamo.
5.8 Ha sbagliato numero.
5.9 Mi dispiace, ma è appena uscito.
5.10 Potrebbe telefonare stasera?
5.11 Potrebbe richiamare più tardi?
5.12 Potrebbe richiamare tra dieci minuti?

BANK

HOW TO ...
1. Say you would like to change travellers' cheques or money
2. Ask for coins or notes of a particular denomination

1.1 I'd like to change some travellers' cheques.
1.2 I'd like to change dollars.
1.3 I'd like to change lire.
1.4 I'd like to change pounds.

1.5 Have you any means of identification?

1.6 Yes, I have my passport.

1.7 Sign here, please!

1.8 What is the exchange rate for the Australian Dollar?
1.9 What is the exchange rate for the Pound?
1.10 What is the exchange rate for the Yen?

2.1 Could you give me some ten thousand lire notes?
2.2 Could you give me two five thousand lire notes?
2.3 Could you give me some change?

2.4 And the change, how would you like it?

2.5 I would like it in thousand lire notes.
2.6 It doesn't matter!
2.7 As you like!

ባንክ

እንዴት ...
1. የጉዞ ቼክ ወይም ገንዘብ ለመመንዘር የምትፈልግ መሆንህን እንደምትገልጽ
2. የተወሰነ ዋጋ ያለው ዝርዝርና ጥቅል ገንዘብ እንደምትጠይቅ

1.1 ጥቂት የጉዞ ቼክ ለመቀየር እፈልግ ነበር
1.2 ዶላር ለመቀየር እፈልግ ነበር
1.3 ሊረ ለመቀየር እፈልግ ነበር
1.4 ፓውንድ ለመቀየር እፈልግ ነበር

1.5 የመታወቅያ ወረቀት አለዎት ወይ?

1.6 አዎ፡ ፓስፖርት ይዣለሁ

1.7 እባክዎ እዚህ ጋ ይፈርሙ

1.8 የአውስትራልያ ገንዘብ ስንት ይመነዘራል?
1.9 አንድ ፓውንድ ስንት ይመነዘራል?
1.10 አንድ የን ስንት ይመነዘራል?

2.1 የአስር ሺ ሊረ ጥቅሎች ሊሰጡኝ ይችላሉ ወይ?
2.2 ሁለት የአምስት ሺ ሊረ ጥቅሎች ሊሰጡኝ ይችላሉ ወይ?
2.3 ጥቂት ምንዛሪ ሊሰጡኝ ይችላሉ ወይ?

2.4 ምንዛሪውን በምን ዓይነት ነው የሚፈልጉት?

2.5 የአንድ ሺ ጥቅሎች እፈልግ ነበር
2.6 ችግር የለም
2.7 እንደ ፈለጉ

BANCA

Come ...
1. dire se si desidera cambiare travellers' chèque o valuta
2. chiedere monete o banconote di un determinato valore

1.1 Vorrei cambiare dei travellers' chèque.
1.2 Vorrei cambiare dei dollari.
1.3 Vorrei cambiare delle lire.
1.4 Vorrei cambiare delle sterline.

1.5 Ha un documento, per favore?

1.6 Sì, ho il passaporto.

1.7 Firmi qui, per favore.

1.8 Quant'è il cambio del dollaro australiano?
1.9 Quant'è il cambio della sterlina?
1.10 Quant'è il cambio dello yen?

2.1 Potrebbe darmi dei biglietti da diecimila?
2.2 Potrebbe darmi due biglietti da cinquemila?
2.3 Potrebbe darmi della moneta?

2.4 E il resto come lo vuole?

2.5 Vorrei dei biglietti da mille (lire).
2.6 Non importa!
2.7 Come vuole lei!

SIGNS AND KEY WORDS

CHEQUE	Assegno
TRAVELLER'S CHEQUE	Assegno turistico Travellers' cheque
BANK	Banca
BILL, NOTE	Bolletta
STOCK EXCHANGE	Borsa
EXCHANGE	Cambio
CHEQUE CARD	Carta assegni
CREDIT CARD	Carta di credito
CASH DESK	Cassa
NIGHT SAFE	Cassacontinua
SAVING BANK	Cassa di risparmio
SAFE DEPOSIT BOX	Cassetta di sicurezza
TO ENDORSE	Girare
CHEQUE BOOK	Libretto di assegni
FORM	Modulo
COIN	Moneta
LOAN	Mutuo
TO CASH	Riscuotere
TO PAY	Versare
SMALL CHANGE	Spiccioli
COUNTER	Sportello
CASH TILL	Sportello automatico
FOREIGN CURRENCY	Valute estere

12 HEALTH

HOW TO ...

1. **State how you feel**
2. **Refer to parts of the body where you are in pain or discomfort**
3. **Report minor ailments**
4. **Report injuries**
5. **Ask for items in a chemist's**
6. **Call for help**
7. **Warn about danger**

1.1 How are you?
1.2 I am well/I'm fine.
1.3 How is it going?
1.4 I am not well/I don't feel well.
1.5 How do you feel?
1.6 I feel weak.
1.7 I feel better.

2.1 What's wrong with you?
2.2 I've got toothache.
2.3 What's wrong?
2.4 I've got a sore throat.

ጤና

እንዴት ...
1. ምን እንደሚሰማህ እንደምትገልጽ
2. የት እንደሚያምህ እንደምትገልጽ
3. ስለ አነስተኛ በሽታዎች እንደምትገልጽ
4. ህመምህን እንደምትገልጽ
5. መድኃኒት ቤት መድኃኒቶች እንደምትጠይቅ
6. እርዳታ እንደምትጠይቅ
7. ስለ አደጋ ማስጠንቀቅያ እንደምትሰጥ

1.1 እንደ ምን ነህ/ነሽ?
1.2 ደግ፡ መልካም [ደህና ነኝ]
1.3 ሁኔታው እንዴት ነው?
1.4 መጥፎ ይሰማኛል
1.5 ምን ይሰማሃል/ይሰማሻል?
1.6 በጣም ድካም ይሰማኛል
1.7 አሁን ይሻለኛል

2.1 የሚያስቸግርህ/የሚያስቸግርሽ ምንድ ነው?
2.2 ጥርሴን ያመኛል
2.3 ችግሩ ምንድ ነው?
2.4 ጉሮሮየን ያመኛል

SALUTE

Come ...
1. dire come ci si sente
2. dire dove si prova dolore o fastidio
3. riferire ad altri su piccoli malesseri
4. dire ad altri che ci si è fatti male
5. chiedere un determinato prodotto in farmacia
6. chiedere aiuto
7. avvertire di un pericolo

1.1 Come stai?
1.2 (Sto) bene.
1.3 Come va?
1.4 (Sto) male.
1.5 Come ti senti?
1.6 Mi sento debole.
1.7 Mi sento meglio.

2.1 Che cos'hai?
2.2 Ho mal di denti.
2.3 Cos'è che non va?
2.4 Ho mal di gola.

2.5 I've got stomach-ache.
2.6 I've got backache.
2.7 I've got a headache.
2.8 My feet hurt.
2.9 My eyes hurt.

2.10 I'm hot.
2.11 I'm cold.
2.12 I'm hungry.
2.13 I'm thirsty.

3.1 Where does it hurt?

3.2 I have a pain here.

3.3 What symptoms do you have?

3.4 I've got cramps.
3.5 I've got sun-stroke.
3.6 I've got diarrhoea.
3.7 I've vomited.
3.8 I have a temperature.
3.9 I've got flu.
3.10 I've got high/low blood pressure.

2.5 ሆዴን ያመኛል
2.6 ወገቤን ያመኛል
2.7 ራሴን ያመኛል
2.8 እግሬን ያመኛል
2.9 ዐይኔን ያመኛል

2.10 ሙቀት ይሰማኛል
2.11 ብርድ ይሰማኛል
2.12 ርቦኛል
2.13 ጠምቶኛል

3.1 ምንህን/ሽን ያምሃል/ያምሻል?
3.2 እዚህ ላይ ሕመም ይሰማኛል
3.3 ምን ይሰማሃል/ይሰማሻል?
3.4 ቁርጥማት ይሰማኛል
3.5 ፀሐይ መትቶኛል
3.6 ተቅማጥ ይዞኛል
3.7 አስታወከኝ
3.8 ትኩሳት አለብኝ
3.9 ጉንፋን ይዞኛል
3.10 የደም ብዛት/የደም ማነስ አለብኝ

2.5 Ho mal di pancia.
2.6 Ho mal di schiena.
2.7 Ho mal di testa.
2.8 Ho male ai piedi.
2.9 Ho male agli occhi.

2.10 Ho caldo.
2.11 Ho freddo.
2.12 Ho fame.
2.13 Ho sete.

3.1 Dove ha male?
3.2 Ho un dolore qui.
3.3 Che disturbi ha?
3.4 Ho i crampi.
3.5 Ho preso un colpo di sole.
3.6 Ho la diarrea.
3.7 Ho rimesso.
3.8 Ho la febbre.
3.9 Ho l'influenza.
3.10 Ho la pressione alta/bassa.

4.1 I've burnt myself.
4.2 I've hurt myself.
4.3 I've injured myself.
4.4 I've pricked myself.
4.5 I've cut myself.

5.1 I would like some aspirin.
5.2 I would like some bandages.
5.3 I would like some plasters.
5.4 I would like some tablets.
5.5 I would like cotton-wool.
5.6 I would like a cough syrup.
5.7 I would like something for a head-ache.
5.8 I would like something to treat a burn/scald.
5.9 I would like something for an insect bite.

5.10 Take one spoonful of this medicine twice a day.
5.11 Take three drops ... every two hours.
5.12 Take one tablet before each meal.
5.13 Take half a dose ... in the evening.

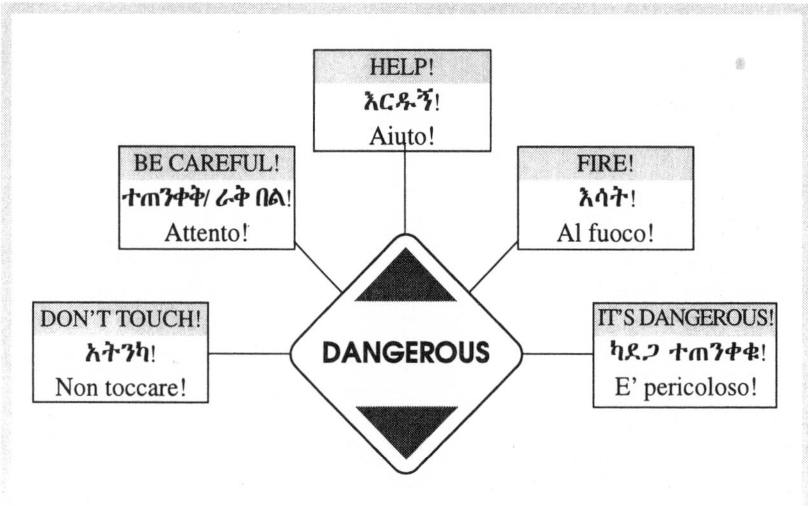

4.1 እሳት ፈጀኝ
4.2 ጉዳት ደርሶብኛል
4.3 ተጐድቻለሁ
4.4 ተወግቻለሁ
4.5 ተቆረጥኩ

5.1 አስፕሪን አላችሁ ወይ?
5.2 ፋሻ አላችሁ ወይ?
5 .3 ፕላስተር አላችሁ ወይ?
5.4 ኪኒን አላችሁ ወይ?
5.5 ጥጥ አላችሁ ወይ?
5.6 የሳል ሽሮፖ አላችሁ ወይ?
5.7 የሆነ የራስ ምታት መድኃኒት አላችሁ ወይ?
5.8 የሆነ የቃጠሎ መድኃኒት አላችሁ ወይ?
5.9 የሆነ የተባዮች መከላከያ መድኃኒት አላችሁ ወይ?

5.10 ከዚሁ መድኃኒት አንድ ማንኪያ በቀን ሁለት ግዜ ይውሰዱ
5.11 ሦስት ጠብታ በየሁለት ሰዓት ይውሰዱ
5.12 ከመመገብዎ በፊት አንድ ኪኒን ይውሰዱ
5.13 ማታ ግማሽ ዶዝ ... ይውሰዱ

4.1 Mi sono bruciato.
4.2 Mi sono fatto male.
4.3 Mi sono ferito.
4.4 Mi sono punto.
4.5 Mi sono tagliato.

5.1 Vorrei delle aspirine.
5.2 Vorrei delle bende.
5.3 Vorrei dei cerotti.
5.4 Vorrei delle compresse.
5.5 Vorrei del cotone.
5.6 Vorrei dello sciroppo per la tosse.
5.7 Vorrei qualcosa per il mal di testa.
5.8 Vorrei qualcosa per le scottature.
5.9 Vorrei qualcosa per le punture d'insetti.

5.10 Prenda un cucchiaino di questa medicina due volte al giorno.
5.11 Prenda tre gocce ... ogni due ore.
5.12 Prenda una compressa prima dei pasti.
5.13 Prenda metà dose ... la sera.

13 FREE TIME

HOW TO ...

1. Say what your hobbies and interests are and inquire about those of others

2. Discuss your evening, weekend and holiday activities

3. Express simple opinions about TV, films, etc.

4. Find out the starting and finishing time (of a film or concert)

1.1 What is your favourite hobby?	1.2 (I like) collecting stamps.
	1.3 (I like) collecting post cards.
1.4 How do you spend your free time?	1.5 (I like) playing draughts.
1.6 What do you do in your free time?	1.7 (I like) playing chess.
	1.8 (I like) playing cards.
	1.9 (I like) playing billiards.

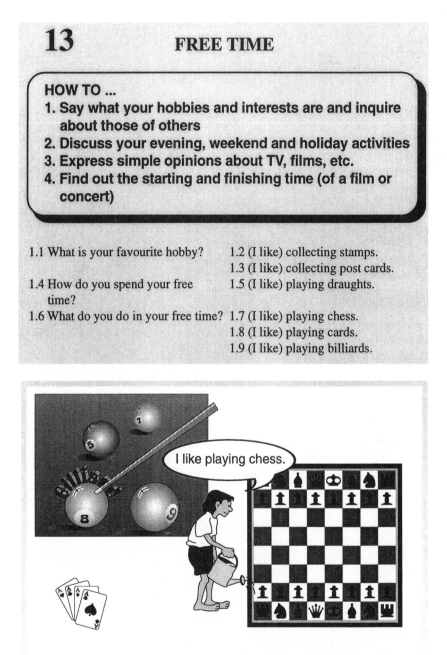

ትርፍ ግዜ

እንዴት...
1. ፍላጎትህና በትርፍ ግዜ የምትሰራውን ስራ እንደምትገልጽና እንዲሁም ሌሎቹንም እንደምትጠይቅ
2. ማታ፣ቅዳሜና እሁድ እንዴት እንደምታሳልፈው እንደምትገልጽ
3. ስለ ተለቪዥንና ፊልም ያለህን አስተያየት እንደምትገልጽ
4. ስለ ፊልም ወይም ኮንሰርት የሚጀመርበትና የሚጨረስበት ሰዓቶች እንደምትጠይቅ

1.1 በጣም የሚማርክህ የግዜ ማሳለፍያ የትኛው ነው?
1.4 ትርፍ ግዜህን እንዴት ታሳልፈዋለህ?
1.6 በትርፍ ግዜህ ምን ታደርጋለህ?

1.2 ቴምብር መሰብሰብ ደስ ይለኛል
1.3 ፖስትካርዶች መሰብሰብ ደስ ይለኛል
1.5 ዳማ መጫወት ደስ ይለኛል
1.7 ቸስ መጫወት ደስ ይለኛል
1.8 ካርታ መጫወት ደስ ይለኛል
1.9 ከረንቡላ መጫወት ደስ ይለኛል

TEMPO LIBERO

Come ...
1. dire quali sono i propri passatempi e interessi e chiederlo ad altri
2. discutere di quello che si fa la sera, il fine settimana e durante le vacanze
3. esprimere opinioni sulla TV, sui film, ecc.
4. informarsi sull'orario di inizio e di fine di un film o di un concerto

1.1 Qual è il tuo passatempo preferito?
1.4 Come passi il tuo tempo libero?
1.6 Che cosa fai nel tempo libero?

1.2 Mi piace collezionare francobolli.
1.3 Mi piace collezionare cartoline.
1.5 Mi piace giocare a dama.
1.7 Mi piace giocare a scacchi.
1.8 Mi piace giocare a carte.
1.9 Mi piace giocare a biliardo.

	1.10 (I like) photography. 1.11 (I like) model making. 1.12 (I like) computers. 1.13 (I like) football. 1.14 (I like) music. 1.15 (I like) playing the guitar. 1.16 (I like) ballet. 1.17 (I like) walking.
1.18 Do you do any sport?	1.19 Yes, I go cross-country running. 1.20 Yes, I do high-jumps. 1.21 Yes, I go swimming. 1.22 Yes, I go cycling. 1.23 Yes, I play football. 1.24 Yes, I play tennis. 1.25 Yes, I play basketball. 1.26 Yes, I play handball. 1.27 Yes, I play rugby.

1.10 ፎቶግራፍ ማንሳት ደስ ይለኛል
1.11 ስነ-ጥበብ ደስ ይለኛል
1.12 ኮምፒዩተር ደስ ይለኛል
1.13 የግር ኳስ ደስ ይለኛል
1.14 ሙዚቃ ደስ ይለኛል
1.15 ጊታር መጫወት ደስ ይለኛል
1.16 ክላሲካል ዳንስ ደስ ይለኛል
1.17 በእግር መጓዝ ደስ ይለኛል

1.18 ስፖርት ትሰራለህ ወይ?

1.19 አዎ፡ አገር አቋራጭ ሩጫ እሮጣለሁ
1.20 አዎ፡ እዘላለሁ
1.21 አዎ፡ እዋኛለሁ
1.22 አዎ፡ በቢሲክለት ውድድር እሳተፋለሁ
1.23 አዎ፡ የግር ኳስ እጫወታለሁ
1.24 አዎ፡ ቴንስ እጫወታለሁ
1.25 አዎ፡ የመረብ ኳስ እጫወታለሁ
1.26 አዎ፡ የእጅ ኳስ እጫወታለሁ
1.27 አዎ፡ ራግቢ እጫወታለሁ

1.10 Mi piace la fotografia.
1.11 Mi piace il modellismo.
1.12 Mi piace il computer.
1.13 Mi piace il calcio.
1.14 Mi piace la musica.
1.15 Mi piace suonare la chitarra.
1.16 Mi piace la danza classica.
1.17 Mi piace passeggiare.

1.18 Pratichi qualche sport?
Fai qualche sport?

1.19 Sì, faccio corsa campestre.
1.20 Sì, faccio salto in alto.
1.21 Sì, faccio nuoto.
1.22 Sì, faccio ciclismo.
1.23 Sì, gioco a calcio.
1.24 Sì, gioco a tennis.
1.25 Sì, gioco a pallacanestro.
1.26 Sì, gioco a pallamano.
1.27 Sì, gioco a rugby.

2.1 What do you usually do in the evening?	2.2 I watch television.
	2.3 I listen to music.
2.4 How do you spend your evenings?	2.5 I go out with my friends.
	2.6 I read a book.
	2.7 I play cards.
	2.8 Nothing in particular.
2.9 What do you like to read?	2.10 I like adventure books.
	2.11 I like science fiction books
	2.12 I like sports papers.
	2.13 I like comics.
	2.14 I like fashion magazines.
	2.15 I like music magazines.
2.16 What kind of music do you prefer?	2.17 (I prefer) pop music.
	2.18 (I prefer) classical music.
	2.19 (I prefer) jazz.
	2.20 (I prefer) folk music.

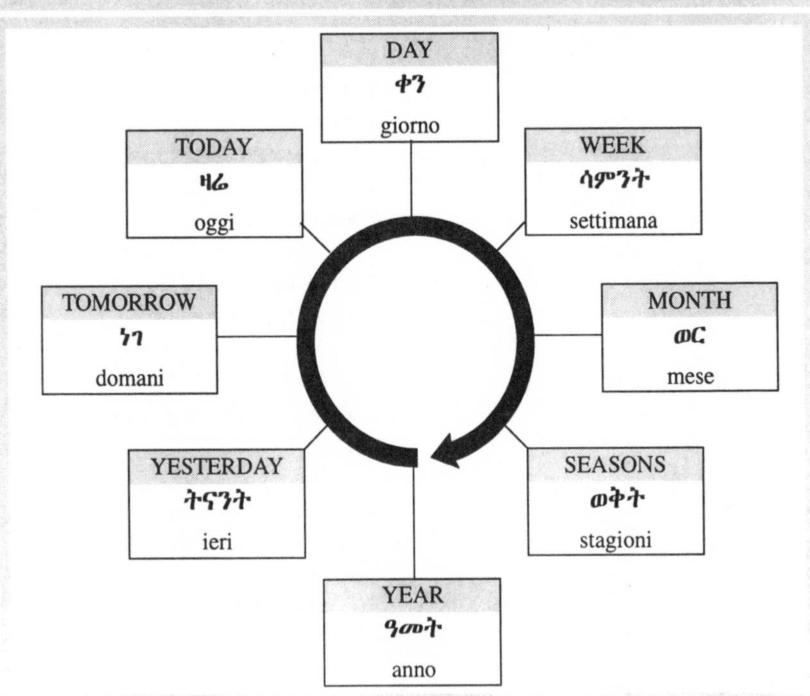

2.1 አብዛኛውን ግዜ ማታ ምን ትሰራለህ?

2.2 ቴለቪዥን አያለሁ
2.3 ሙዚቃ አዳምጣለሁ

2.4 ማታ እንዴት ታሳልፈዋለህ?

2.5 ከጓደኞቼ ጋር እወጣለሁ
2.6 መጽሐፍ አነባለሁ
2.7 ካርታ እጫወታለሁ
2.8 ምንም ልዩ ነገር አልሰራም

2.9 ምን ማንበብ ደስ ይለሃል?

2.10 የአድቬንቸር መጻሕፍት ደስ ይሉኛል
2.11 የሳይንስ ልቦለዶች ደስ ይሉኛል
2.12 የስፖርት ጋዜጦች ደስ ይሉኛል
2.13 ካርቱን ማንበብ ደስ ይሉኛል
2.14 የፋሽን መጽሔቶች ደስ ይሉኛል
2.15 የሙዚቃ መጽሔቶች ደስ ይሉኛል

2.16 ምን ዓይነት ሙዚቃ ትመርጣለህ?

2.17 ፖፕ ሙዚቃ እመርጣለሁ
2.18 ክላሲካል ሙዚቃ እመርጣለሁ
2.19 ጃዝ ሙዚቃ እመርጣለሁ
2.20 የባህል ሙዚቃ እመርጣለሁ

2.1 Che cosa fai di solito la sera?

2.2 Guardo la televisione.
2.3 Ascolto musica.

2.4 Come passi le serate?

2.5 Esco con gli amici.
2.6 Leggo qualche libro.
2.7 Gioco a carte.
2.8 Non faccio niente di particolare.

2.9 Che cosa ti piace leggere?

2.10 Mi piacciono i libri di avventura.
2.11 Mi piacciono i libri di fantascienza.
2.12 Mi piacciono i giornali sportivi.
2.13 Mi piacciono i fumetti.
2.14 Mi piacciono le riviste di moda.
2.15 Mi piacciono le riviste di musica.

2.16 Che tipo di musica preferisci?

2.17 (Preferisco) la musica pop.
2.18 (Preferisco) la musica classica.
2.19 (Preferisco) la musica jazz.
2.20 (Preferisco) la musica folk.

2.21 What do you do at weekends ?	2.22 I sometimes go horse-riding.
2.23 What do you do during the holidays?	2.24 I often go to play ...
	2.25 I usually go dancing.
	2.26 I usually go fishing.
	2.27 I usually go to the theatre.
	2.28 I usually go to see friends.
	2.29 I usually go to the cinema.
	2.30 I usually go to the sports club.
	2.31 I usually go to concerts.
	2.32 I usually go to discos.
3.1 Which television programmes do you prefer?	3.2 I like cartoons.
3.2 Which are your favourite programmes?	3.4 (I like) musical programmes.
	3.5 I like plays.
	3.6 I like documentaries on nature.
	3.7 I like sports programmes.
	3.8 I like current affairs programmes.
	3.9 I like serials.

Che cosa fai
durante le vacanze?

2.21 ቅዳሜና እሁድ ምን ታደርጋለህ?

2.22 አንዳንዴ በፈረስ እንሸራሸራለሁ

2.23 በዕረፍት ግዜህ ምን ታደርጋለህ?

2.24 አብዛኛውን ግዜ ለመጫወት ... እሔዳለሁ
2.25 አብዛኛውን ግዜ ለዳንስ እወጣለሁ
2.26 አብዛኛውን ግዜ ዓሣ ለማጥመድ እሔዳለሁ
2.27 አብዛኛውን ግዜ ትያትር እሔዳለሁ
2.28 አብዛኛውን ግዜ ጓደኞቼን ለማግኘት እወጣለሁ
2.29 አብዛኛውን ግዜ ሲነማ ቤት እሔዳለሁ
2.30 አብዛኛውን ግዜ ስፖርት ክለብ እሔዳለሁ
2.31 አብዛኛውን ግዜ ኮንሰርት እሔዳለሁ
2.32 አብዛኛውን ግዜ ዲስኮ ቤት እሔዳለሁ

3.1 የትኛውን የቴለቪዥን ፕሮግራም ትመርጣለህ?

3.2 ካርቱን ፊልም ደስ ይለኛል

3.3 የትኛውን የቴለቪዥን ፕሮግራም ነው ደስ የሚልህ?

3.4 የሙዚቃ ፕሮግራም ደስ ይለኛል
3.5 ድራማ ደስ ይለኛል
3.6 ደኩሜንታሪ ፊልም ደስ ይለኛል
3.7 የስፖርት ፕሮግራም ደስ ይለኛል
3.8 የዜና ፕሮግራም ደስ ይለኛል
3.9 የፍቅር ፊልም ደስ ይለኛል

2.21 Che cosa fai durante il fine settimana?

2.22 Qualche volta vado a cavallo.

2.23 Che cosa fai durante le vacanze?

2.24 Spesso vado a giocare a ...
2.25 Di solito vado a ballare.
2.26 Di solito vado a pescare.
2.27 Di solito vado a teatro.
2.28 Di solito vado a trovare gli amici.
2.29 Di solito vado al cinema.
2.30 Di solito vado al circolo sportivo.
2.31 Di solito vado ai concerti.
2.32 Di solito vado in discoteca.

3.1 Quali sono i programmi televisivi che preferisci?

3.2 Mi piacciono i cartoni animati.

3.3 Quali sono i tuoi programmi preferiti?

3.4 Mi piacciono i programmi musicali.
3.5 Mi piacciono le commedie.
3.6 Mi piacciono i documentari sulla natura.
3.7 Mi piacciono i programmi sportivi.
3.8 Mi piacciono i programmi di attualità.
3.9 Mi piacciono i teleromanzi.

3.10 Which kind of films do you like?	3.11 I like comedies.
3.12 What kind of films do you like?	3.13 I like westerns.
	3.14 I like dramas.
	3.15 I like adventure films.
	3.16 I like romantic films.
	3.17 I like historical films.
	3.18 I like horror films.
3.19 Why?	3.20 Because they make me laugh.
	3.21 Because they amuse me.
3.22 Did you like Fellini's film?	3.23 I did/didn't like it.
3.24 Did he like Goldoni's play?	3.25 He did/didn't like it.
3.26 Did she like the cartoons?	3.27 She did/didn't like them.
3.28 Did you like the songs ...?	3.29 We did/didn't like them.
4.1 (At) what time does the next show start?	4.2 It starts at eight.
4.3 (At) what time does the next show finish?	4.4 It finishes at half past nine.

3.10 ምን ዓይነት ፊልም ደስ ይልሃል?
3.12 ምን ዓይነት ፊልም ደስ ይልሻል?

3.11 አስቂኝ ፊልም ደስ ይለኛል
3.13 የቴክሳስ ፊልም ደስ ይለኛል
3.14 ድራማ ደስ ይለኛል
3.15 የአድቬንቸር ፊልም ደስ ይለኛል
3.16 የፍቅር ፊልም ደስ ይለኛል
3.17 የታሪክ ፊልም ደስ ይለኛል
3.18 የሚያስፈራ ፊልም ደስ ይለኛል

3.19 ለምን?

3.20 ስለሚያስቀኝ
3.21 ስለሚያዝናናኝ

3.22 የፊሊኒን ፊልም ወደድከው ወይ?
3.23 ወደድኩት/አልወደድኩትም
3.24 የጎልዶኒን ፊልም ወደደው ወይ?
3.25 ወደደው/አልወደደውም
3.26 የካርቱኑን ፊልም ወደደችው ወይ?
3.27 ወደደችው/አልወደደችውም
3.28 ... ዘፈኖቹን ወደዳችኋቸው ወይ?
3.29 ወደድነው/አልወደድነውም

4.1 የሚቀጥለው ትርኢት በስንት ሰዓት ይጀምራል?
4.2 በሁለት ሰዓት ይጀምራል
4.3 የሚቀጥለው ትርኢት በስንት ሰዓት ያልቃል?
4.4 በሦስት ሰዓት ተኩል ያልቃል

3.10 Che tipo di film ti piace?
3.12 Quali film ti piacciono?

3.11 Mi piacciono i film comici.
3.13 Mi piacciono i film western.
3.14 Mi piacciono i film drammatici.
3.15 Mi piacciono i film avventurosi.
3.16 Mi piacciono i film romantici.
3.17 Mi piacciono i film storici.
3.18 Mi piacciono i film dell'orrore.

3.19 Perché?

3.20 Perché mi fanno ridere.
3.21 Perché mi divertono.

3.22 Ti è piaciuto il film di Fellini?
3.23 (Non) mi è piaciuto.
3.24 Gli è piaciuta la commedia di Goldoni?
3.25 (Non) gli è piaciuta.
3.26 Le sono piaciuti i cartoni animati?
3.27 (Non) le sono piaciuti.
3.28 Vi sono piaciute le canzoni ...?
3.29 (Non) ci sono piaciute.

4.1 A che ora inizia il prossimo spettacolo?
4.2 Comincia alle otto.
4.3 A che ora finisce il prossimo spettacolo?
4.4 Termina alle nove e mezzo.

14 EDUCATION AND FUTURE CAREER

HOW TO ...
1. Exchange information about your present school
2. Exchange information about when lessons begin and end
3. Exchange information about how many lessons there are and how long they last
4. Exchange information about homework
5. Exchange information about subjects studied
6. Exchange information about your plans for the future

1.1 What school do you attend?	1.2 I attend the ...
1.3 What year are you in?	1.4 The first (year). 1.5 The second (year).
1.6 What class are you in?	1.7 The third. 1.8 The fourth.

ትምህርትና የወደፊት የሥራ ዕድል

እንዴት ..
1. ስለምትማርበት ትምህርት ቤት መረጃ እንደምትለዋወጥ
2. ስለ ትምህርት ሰዓቶችና የትምህርት ክፍለ ጊዜ መረጃ እንደምትለዋወጥ
3. ስንት የትምህርት ዓይነቶች እንዳሉና ምን ያህል ጊዜ እንደሚወስዱ መረጃ እንደምትለዋወጥ
4. ስለ የቤት ሥራ መረጃ እንደምትለዋወጥ
5. ስለምትማራቸው የትምህርት ዓይነቶች ሐሳብ እንደምትለዋወጥ
6. ስለ የወደፊት ዕቅድህ መረጃ እንደምትለዋወጥ

1.1 የት ትማራለህ?

1.2 ... እማራለሁ

1.3 የስንተኛ ዓመት ተማሪ ነህ?

1.4 አንደኛ (ዓመት)
1.5 ሁለተኛ (ዓመት)

1.6 ስንተኛ ክፍል ትማራለህ?

1.7 ሦስተኛ
1.8 አራተኛ

ISTRUZIONE E CARRIERA

Come ...
1. **scambiarsi informazioni sulla scuola che si frequenta**
2. **scambiarsi informazioni sull'inizio e la fine delle lezioni**
3. **scambiarsi informazioni sulle ore di lezione e sulla loro durata**
4. **scambiarsi informazioni sui compiti**
5. **scambiarsi informazioni sulle materie studiate**
6. **scambiarsi informazioni sui propri programmi per il futuro**

1.1 Che scuola frequenti?

1.2 Frequento ...

1.3 Che anno frequenti?

1.4 Il primo (anno).
1.5 Il secondo (anno).

1.6 Che classe fai?

1.7 La terza
1.8 La quarta

1.9 Where is your school?	1.10 It's in Rome Square. 1.11 It's in the centre.
1.12 Is your school big? 1.14 Is your school small?	1.13 It's quite large.
1.15 Are the classes large?	1.16 No, there are usually about twenty of us.
1.17 Is it a good school?	1.18 Yes, the teachers are very good. 1.19 No, it is lacking in facilities.
1.20 Are there many sports facilities?	1.21 There's a gymnasium. 1.22 There's a swimming pool. 1.23 There's a tennis court. 1.24 There's a volleyball court. 1.25 There's a basketball court.
2.1 At what time do the lessons start? 2.3 At what time do the lessons finish?	2.2 (They start) at eight. 2.4 (They finish) at one.

1.9 ትምህርት ቤትህ የት ነው?

1.10 በሮም አደባባይ
1.11 ማሐል ከተማ

1.12 ትምህርት ቤትህ ትልቅ ነው ወይ?
1.14 ትምህርት ቤትህ ትንሽ ነው ወይ?

1.13 በመጠኑ ትልቅ ነው

1.15 ብዙ ተማሪዎች አሉት ወይ?

1.16 የሉትም፣ አብዛኛውን ግዜ ወደ ሀያ ገደማ ነን

1.17 ጥሩ ትምህርት ቤት ነው ወይ?

1.18 አዎ፣ አስተማሪዎቹ በጣም ጐበዞች ናቸው
1.19 አይደለም፣ የመሳሪያዎች እጥረት አለው

1.20 ብዙ የስፖርት መሳሪያዎች አሉት ወይ?

1.21 አንድ የስፖርት ክፍል አለው
1.22 አንድ መዋኛ አለው
1.23 አንድ የተኒስ ሜዳ አለው
1.24 አንድ የመረብ ኳስ መጫወቻ አለው
1.25 አንድ የቅርጫት ኳስ መጫወቻ አለው

2.1 ትምህርቱ በስንት ሰዓት ይጀምራል?

2.2 በሁለት ሰዓት ይጀመራል

2.3 ትምህርቱ በስንት ሰዓት ያልቃል?

2.4 በአንድ ሰዓት ያልቃል

1.9 Dove si trova la tua scuola?

1.10 E' in Piazza Roma.
1.11 E' in centro.

1.12 E' una scuola grande?
1.14 E' una scuola piccola?

1.13 E' una scuola piccola.

1.15 Le classi sono numerose?

1.16 No, siamo in genere una ventina.

1.17 E' una buona scuola?

1.18 Sì, gli insegnanti sono molto bravi.
1.19 No, è carente di molte strutture.

1.20 Ci sono molte attrezzature sportive?

1.21 C'è una palestra.
1.22 C'è una piscina.
1.23 C'è un campo da tennis.
1.24 C'è un campo da pallavolo.
1.25 C'è un campo da pallacanestro.

2.1 A che ora iniziano le lezioni?

2.2 (Iniziano) alle otto.

2.3 A che ora finiscono le lezioni?

2.4 (Finiscono) alle tredici.

3.1 How many hours (of lessons) do you have?	3.2 (Usually) five hours.
3.3 How long does a lesson last?	3.4 One hour. 3.5 Fifty minutes.
4.1 Are you given much class-work? 4.3 Are you given much homework?	4.2 Too much! 4.4 Quite a lot! 4.5 Yes, mostly Mathematics, ...
5.1 What subjects do you study?	5.2 (I study) Italian and French. 5.3 (I study) English and Amharic. 5.4 (I study) German and Arabic. 5.5 (I study) Maths. 5.6 (I study) Science. 5.7 (I study) History. 5.8 (I study) Geography. 5.9 (I study) Art. 5.10 (I study) P.E. 5.11 (I study) Music.

3.1 ምን ያህል የትምህርት ሰዓቶች አሉዋችሁ?	3.2 አብዛኛውን ግዜ አምስት ሰዓቶች
3.3 አንድ ክፍለ ግዜ ምን ያህል ደቂቃ ነው?	3.4 አንድ ሰዓት 3.5 አምሣ ደቂቃ
4.1 ብዙ የክፍል ሥራ ይሰጡሃል ወይ? 4.3 ብዙ የቤት ሥራ ይሰጡሃል ወይ?	4.2 በጣም ብዙ 4.4 በመጠኑ 4.5 አዎ፡ በተለይ ሂሳብን በሚመለከት
5.1 ምን ዓይነት ትምህርት ትማራለህ?	5.2 ጣልያንኛና ፈረንሳይኛ (እማራለሁ) 5.3 እንግሊዝኛና አማርኛ (እማራለሁ) 5.4 ጀርመንኛና ዓረብኛ (እማራለሁ) 5.5 ሂሳብ(እማራለሁ) 5.6 ሳይንስ (እማራለሁ) 5.7 ታሪክ (እማራለሁ) 5.8 ጂአግራፊ (እማራለሁ) 5.9 ስዕል (እማራለሁ) 5.10 ስፖርት (እማራለሁ) 5.11 ሙዚቃ (እማራለሁ)

3.1 Quante ore di lezione avete?	3.2 (Di solito) cinque ore.
3.3 Quanto dura una lezione?	3.4 Un'ora. 3.5 Cinquanta minuti.
4.1 Ti danno molti compiti in classe? 4.3 Ti danno molti compiti a casa?	4.2 Troppi! 4.4 Abbastanza! 4.5 Sì, soprattutto di matematica.
5.1 Che materie studi?	5.2 (Studio) italiano e francese. 5.3 (Studio) inglese e amarico. 5.4 (Studio) tedesco e arabo 5.5 (Studio) matematica. 5.6 (Studio) scienze. 5.7 (Studio) storia. 5.8 (Studio) geografia. 5.9 (Studio) educazione artistica. 5.10 (Studio) educazione fisica. 5.11 (Studio) educazione musicale.

5.12 What's your favourite subject?

5.13 Which are your favourite subjects?

5.14 Do you like Mathematics?

5.15 Yes, I do/I like it.

5.16 Do you like Literature?

5.17 No, I don't (like it).

6.1 What are your plans for the future?

6.2 I am going to university.

6.3 I am going to work.

6.4 What will you do when you have finished school?

6.5 I will look for a job.

6.6 I am going to France for a year.

6.7 (I don't know) we'll see ...

6.8 What kind of work would you like to do?

6.9 I would like to be an architect.

6.10 I would like to be a journalist.

6.11 I would like to be a hairdresser.

6.12 I would like to be a mechanic.

6.13 I would like to be a teacher.

5.12 የትኛው የትምህርት ዓይነት ደስ ይልሃል?
5.13 የትኞቹ የትምህርት ዓይነቶች ደስ ይሉሃል?

5.14 ሂሳብ ትወዳለህ ወይ?
5.16 ስነጽሑፍ ትወዳለህ ወይ?

5.15 አዎ፡ ደስ ይለኛል
5.17 አልወድም፡ ደስ አይለኝም

6.1 የወደፊት እቅዶችህ ምንድ ናቸው?

6.2 ዩኒቨርሲቲ ለመማር ነው
6.3 ሥራ ለመጀመር ነው

6.4 ትምህርት ከጨረስክ በኋላ ምን ታደርጋለህ?

6.5 ሥራ ልፈልግ ነው
6.6 ለአንድ ዓመት ፈረንሳይ አገር ልሔድ ነው
6.7 (አላወቅኩም) እናየዋለን

6.8 ምን ዓይነት ሥራ መስራት ደስ ይልሃል?

6.9 አናጢ መሆን ደስ ይለኝ ነበር
6.10 ጋዜጠኛ መሆን ደስ ይለኝ ነበር
6.11 ጠጉር አስተካካይ መሆን ደስ ይለኝ ነበር
6.12 መካኒክ መሆን ደስ ይለኝ ነበር
6.13 አስተማሪ መሆን ደስ ይለኝ ነበር

5.12 Qual è la tua materia preferita?
5.13 Quali sono le tue materie preferite?

5.14 Ti piace la matematica?
5.16 Ti piace la letteratura?

5.15 Sì, mi piace.
5.17 No, non mi piace ...

6.1 Quali sono i tuoi progetti per il futuro?

6.2 Andrò all'università.
6.3 Andrò a lavorare.

6.4 Che cosa farai, quando avrai finito la scuola?

6.5 Cercherò un impiego.
6.6 Andrò un anno in Francia.
6.7 (Non lo so) vedremo ...

6.8 Che lavoro ti piacerebbe fare?

6.9 Mi piacerebbe fare l'architetto.
6.10 Mi piacerebbe fare il giornalista.
6.11 Mi piacerebbe fare il parrucchiere.
6.12 Mi piacerebbe fare il meccanico.
6.13 Mi piacerebbe fare l'insegnante.

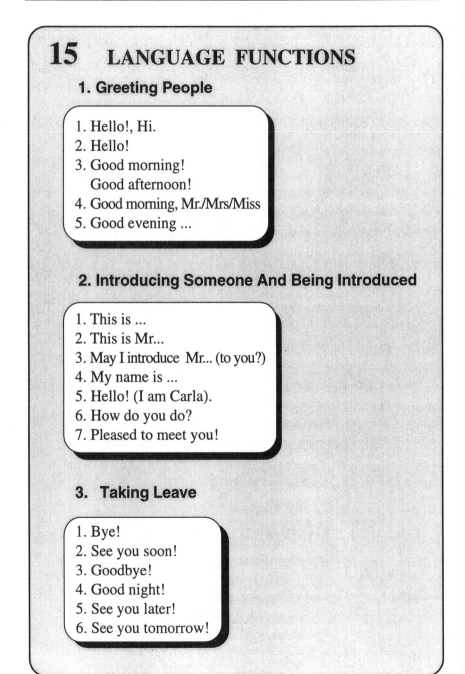

15 LANGUAGE FUNCTIONS

1. Greeting People

1. Hello!, Hi.
2. Hello!
3. Good morning!
   Good afternoon!
4. Good morning, Mr./Mrs/Miss
5. Good evening ...

2. Introducing Someone And Being Introduced

1. This is ...
2. This is Mr...
3. May I introduce Mr... (to you?)
4. My name is ...
5. Hello! (I am Carla).
6. How do you do?
7. Pleased to meet you!

3. Taking Leave

1. Bye!
2. See you soon!
3. Goodbye!
4. Good night!
5. See you later!
6. See you tomorrow!

1. ሰላምታ መለዋወጥ

1. ሰላም
2. ጤና'ስጥልኝ
3. እንደምን አደሩ
   እንደምን ዋሉ
4. እንደምን አደሩ
   አቶ/ወይዘሮ/ወይዘሪት
5. እንደምን አመሹ

1. Salutare

1. Ciao!
2. Salve!
3. Buongiorno!
4. Buongiorno,
   signor/signora/signorina ...
5. Buonasera ...

2. ሰውን ማስተዋወቅና ራስህን ማስተዋወቅ

1. ይህ ... (m)
   ይቺ ... (f)
2. አቶ ... ይባላሉ
3. ከአቶ ... ላስተዋውቅህ
4. ስሜ ... ይባላል
5. ጤና'ስጥልኝ (ካርላ እባላለሁ)
6. እንደምን ነህ? (m)
   እንደምን ነሽ? (f)
7. መልካም ትውውቅ
   ያድርግልን

2. Presentare qualcuno e presentarsi

1. Questo è...
   Questa è ...
2. Le presento il signor ...*
3. Posso presentarle il signor ... *
4. Mi chiamo ...
5. Ciao, (io sono Carla).
6. Piacere!
7. Molto lieto!

3. መነሳት

1. ደህና ሁን/ሁኚ (m/f)
2. በደህና ያገናኘን
3. ደህና ሁን/ሁኚ (m/f)
4. ደህና እደር/እደሪ (m/f)
5. እንገናኛለን
6. ነገ እንገናኛለን

3. Congedarsi

1. Ciao!
2. (Ciao), a presto!
3. Arrivederci!
3.1. ArrivederLa! *
4. Buonanotte!
5. A più tardi!
6. A domani!

* FORMALE

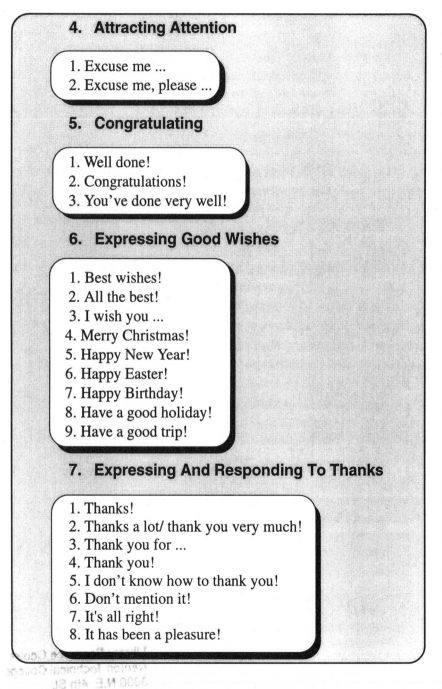

4. Attracting Attention

1. Excuse me ...
2. Excuse me, please ...

5. Congratulating

1. Well done!
2. Congratulations!
3. You've done very well!

6. Expressing Good Wishes

1. Best wishes!
2. All the best!
3. I wish you ...
4. Merry Christmas!
5. Happy New Year!
6. Happy Easter!
7. Happy Birthday!
8. Have a good holiday!
9. Have a good trip!

7. Expressing And Responding To Thanks

1. Thanks!
2. Thanks a lot/ thank you very much!
3. Thank you for ...
4. Thank you!
5. I don't know how to thank you!
6. Don't mention it!
7. It's all right!
8. It has been a pleasure!

4. ሰውን መሳብ

1. ይቅርታ
2. ይቅርታ አድርግልኝ

4. Richiamare l'attenzione

1. Scusa ...
   (Mi) scusi ... *
2. Senta, per favore ... *

5. እንኳን ደስ አለህ ማለት

1. ጎሽ
2. እንኳን ደስ አለህ
3. አስደሰትከን/አስደሰትሽን

5. Congratularsi

1. Bravo!
2. Congratulazioni!
3. Sei stato bravissimo!

6. መልካም ምኞት መግለጽ

1. መልካም ምኞት
2. መልካም ዕድል
3. ... እመኝልሀለሁ
4. መልካም የገና በዓል
5. መልካም አዲስ ዓመት
6. መልካም ፋሲካ
7. መልካም የልደት በዓል
8. መልካም ዕረፍት
9. መልካም ጉዞ

6. Augurare

1. Auguri!
2. I migliori auguri!
3. Ti auguro ...
   Le auguro ...*
4. Buon Natale!
5. Buon Anno!
6. Buona Pasqua!
7. Buon compleanno!
8. Buone vacanze!
9. Buon viaggio!

7. ለምስጋና መልስ መስጠት

1. እግዚሄር ይስጥልኝ
2. በጣም አመሰግናለሁ
3. ለ ... አመሰግናለሁ
4. አመሰግናለሁ
5. እንዴት እንደማመሰግንህ/ሽ አላውቅም
6. ምንም አይደለም
7. ምንም አይደለም
8. በጣም ደስ ብሎኛል

7. Ringraziare e rispondere ai ringraziamenti

1. Grazie!
2. Grazie mille!
3. Grazie per ...
4. Ti ringrazio!/La ringrazio!*
5. Non so come ringraziarti!
   Non so come ringraziarLa! *
6. Prego!
7. Di niente!
8. E' stato un piacere!

8. Expressing Lack Of Understanding

1. Pardon?
2. (I beg your) pardon?
3./4. I don't understand.
5. I haven't understood.
6. Would you repeat it, please?
7. What does it mean?
8. Can you repeat it, please?
9. It is not clear.

9. Expressing Agreement And Disagreement

1. I agree.
2. You're right!
3. Of course!
4. Right!
5. I don't agree!
6. You are wrong!
7. It's not true!
8. Not at all!

10. Expressing Surprise

1. What a surprise!
2. What a nice surprise!
3. This is a real surprise!
4. No kidding?
5. I can't believe it!
6. No!

8. አለመግባባት

1. ይቅርታ
2. ምን አሉ፡ ይቅርታ

3. ይቅርታ፡አልገባኝም
4. አልገባኝም
5. አልተረዳኝም

6. እባክዎን እንደገና ይድገሙልኝ
7. ምን ማለት ነው
8. ልትደግመው ትችላለህ ወይ?
9. ግልፅ አይደለም

8. Esprimere mancanza di comprensione e chiedere chiarimenti

1. Come, (scusa)?
2. Scusi, come ha detto? *

3. Prego? (Non ho capito!)
4. Non capisco.
5. Non ho capito.

6. Vuole ripetere, prego? *
7. Che cosa vuol dire?
8. Puoi ripetere, per favore?
9. Non è chiaro.

9. መስማማትና አለመስማማት

1. እስማማለሁ
2. ልክ ነህ/ነሽ
3. ግልፅ ነው
4. ትክክል

5. አልስማማም
6. ተሳስተሃል/ሻል (m/f)
7. ውሸት
8. በፍጹም

9. Esprimere accordo e disaccordo

1. Sono d'accordo.
2. Hai (proprio) ragione!
3. Naturalmente!
4. Giusto!

5. Non sono d'accordo!
6. Sbagli!
7. Non è vero!
8. Per niente!

10. መደነቅ

1. ይገርማል
2. የምስራች
3. በጣም የሚገርም ነው
4. ምን ትቀልዳለህ
5. አላምንም
6. አይሆንም

10. Esprimere sorpresa

1. Che sorpresa!
2. Che bella sorpresa!
3. Questa sì che è una sorpresa!
4. Davvero!
5. Non ci credo!
6. No!

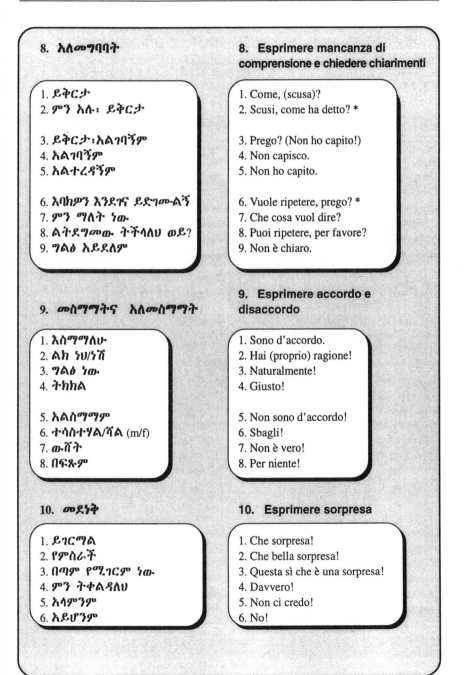

11. Expressing Hope

1. Let's hope so!
2. I hope so!
3. If only!
4. I hope you'll be better.

12. Expressing Satisfaction

1. Wonderful!
2. How lovely!
3. I'm very happy/satisfied ...
4. It's just what I wanted.
5. It's lovely!

13. Expressing Gratitude

1. I am very grateful to you ...
2. You've been very kind ...
3. Thank you!
4. Thanks for everything!

14. Apologizing

1. Sorry!
2. I am so sorry!
3. I apologize for ...
4. I am sorry!

11. ተስፋ መስጠት

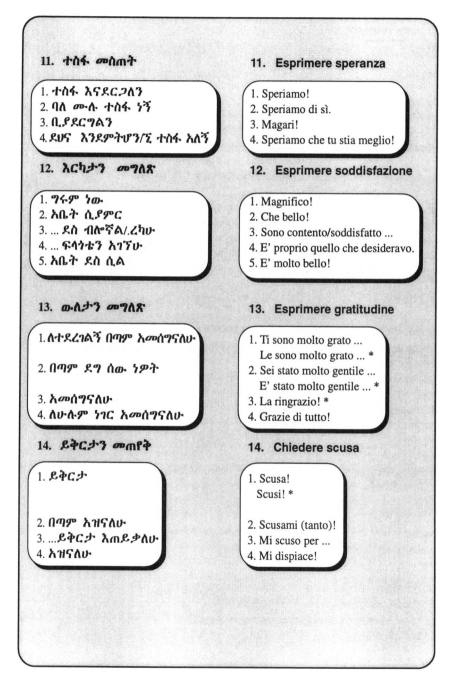

1. ተስፋ እናደርጋለን
2. ባለ ሙሉ ተስፋ ነኝ
3. ቢያደርግልን
4. ደህና እንደምትሆን/ኚ ተስፋ አለኝ

11. Esprimere speranza

1. Speriamo!
2. Speriamo di sì.
3. Magari!
4. Speriamo che tu stia meglio!

12. እርካታን መግለጽ

1. ግሩም ነው
2. አቤት ሲያምር
3. ... ደስ ብሎኛል/.ረካሁ
4. ... ፍላጎቴን አገኘሁ
5. አቤት ደስ ሲል

12. Esprimere soddisfazione

1. Magnifico!
2. Che bello!
3. Sono contento/soddisfatto ...
4. E' proprio quello che desideravo.
5. E' molto bello!

13. ውለታን መግለጽ

1. ለተደረገልኝ በጣም አመሰግናለሁ
2. በጣም ደግ ሰው ነዎት
3. አመሰግናለሁ
4. ለሁሉም ነገር አመሰግናለሁ

13. Esprimere gratitudine

1. Ti sono molto grato ...
   Le sono molto grato ... *
2. Sei stato molto gentile ...
   E' stato molto gentile ... *
3. La ringrazio! *
4. Grazie di tutto!

14. ይቅርታን መጠየቅ

1. ይቅርታ
2. በጣም አዝናለሁ
3. ...ይቅርታ እጠይቃለሁ
4. አዝናለሁ

14. Chiedere scusa

1. Scusa!
   Scusi! *
2. Scusami (tanto)!
3. Mi scuso per ...
4. Mi dispiace!

15. Expressing Indifference

1. I don't care!
2. It's all the same to me.
3. Do as you like!

16. Suggesting A Course Of Action (Including The Speaker)

1. Shall we go ...?
2. We could ...
3. Will you come with us ...?
4. Would you like to ...?

17. Requesting Others To Do Something

1. Could you ...?
2. Would you mind ...?
3. I would be very grateful if you could ...

18. Asking For Advice

1. What do you think of ...?
2. Any ideas?
3. What would you do
(in my situation?)
4. What do you suggest?
5. What would you suggest?

15. ግድ አለማድረግ

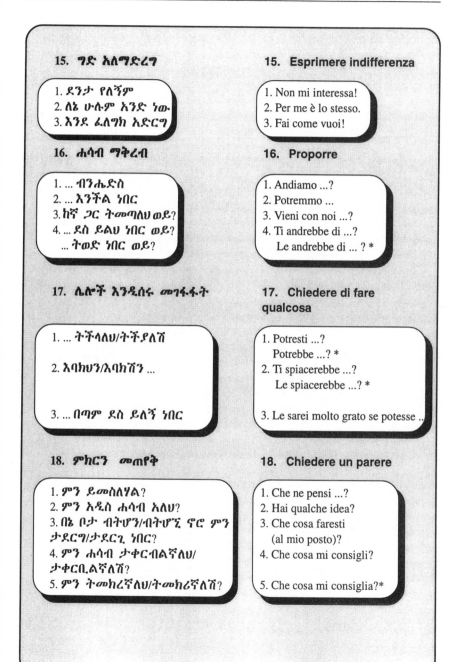

1. ደንታ የለኝም
2. ለኔ ሁሉም አንድ ነው
3. እንደ ፈለግክ አድርግ

15. Esprimere indifferenza

1. Non mi interessa!
2. Per me è lo stesso.
3. Fai come vuoi!

16. ሐሳብ ማቅረብ

1. ... ብንሔድስ
2. ... እንችል ነበር
3. ከኛ ጋር ትመጣለህ ወይ?
4. ... ደስ ይልህ ነበር ወይ?
   ... ትወድ ነበር ወይ?

16. Proporre

1. Andiamo ...?
2. Potremmo ...
3. Vieni con noi ...?
4. Ti andrebbe di ...?
   Le andrebbe di ... ? *

17. ሌሎች እንዲሰሩ መገፋፋት

1. ... ትችላለህ/ትችያለሽ
2. እባክህን/እባክሽን ...
3. ... በጣም ደስ ይለኝ ነበር

17. Chiedere di fare qualcosa

1. Potresti ...?
   Potrebbe ...? *
2. Ti spiacerebbe ...?
   Le spiacerebbe ...? *
3. Le sarei molto grato se potesse ...

18. ምክርን መጠየቅ

1. ምን ይመስለሃል?
2. ምን አዲስ ሐሳብ አለህ?
3. በኔ ቦታ ብትሆን/ብትሆኚ ኖሮ ምን ታደርግ/ታደርጊ ነበር?
4. ምን ሐሳብ ታቀርብልኛለህ/ታቀርቢልኛለሽ?
5. ምን ትመክረኛለህ/ትመክሪኛለሽ?

18. Chiedere un parere

1. Che ne pensi ...?
2. Hai qualche idea?
3. Che cosa faresti (al mio posto)?
4. Che cosa mi consigli?
5. Che cosa mi consiglia?*

GRAMMAR REVIEW

UNIT 1 PERSONAL IDENTIFICATION

What's What is	your name?

(My name is) I'm	Mary. Charles.

Are	you you they	from	Ethiopia? England? Italy?
Is	he she		

Yes,	I am. we are. they are. he is. she is.

No,	I'm not. we aren't. they aren't. he isn't. she isn't.

Are	you you they	Ethiopian? English? Italian?
Is	he she	

No,	I'm we're they're he's she's	French. Australian. American.

Do	you you they	like	Italian? this book? this pen?
Does	he she		

Yes,	I we they	like	it.
	he she	likes	

UNITÀ 1 IDENTIFICAZIONE PERSONALE

Come	ti chiami?

(Mi chiamo)	Maria. Carlo.

Vieni (tu) Venite (voi) Vengono (loro) Viene (lui/lei)	dall'	Etiopia? Inghilterra? Italia?

Sì, No,	(io) vengo (noi) veniamo (loro) vengono (lui/lei) viene	dall'	Etiopia.

Sei (tu)	etiope?
Siete (voi)	inglesi?
Sono (loro)	italiani?
E' (lui)	italiano?
E' (lei)	italiana?

No,		
	(io) sono	francese.
	(noi) siamo	australiani.
	(loro) sono	americani.
	(lui) è	americano.
	(lei) è	americana.

Ti Vi Gli Gli Le	piace	l'italiano? questo libro? questa penna?

Sì,	mi ci gli gli le	piace.

UNIT 2 FAMILY

What's	your	father grandfather brother uncle cousin son husband mother grandmother sister aunt cousin daughter wife	called?
	his/her name?		

He's She's	called ...
His/Her name's ...	

What job	does	your	father mother	do?
	do	you		

He's She's I'm	an architect. a teacher. unemployed.

Do	you you they	have	any pets at home?
Does	he/she		

Yes,	I we they	have	a	cat. dog.
	he/she	has		

UNITÀ 2 FAMIGLIA

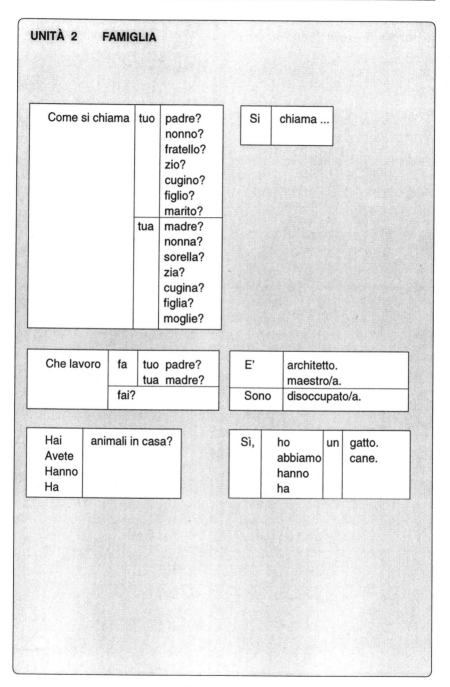

Come si chiama	tuo	padre? nonno? fratello? zio? cugino? figlio? marito?
	tua	madre? nonna? sorella? zia? cugina? figlia? moglie?

Si	chiama ...

Che lavoro	fa	tuo padre? tua madre?
	fai?	

E'	architetto. maestro/a.
Sono	disoccupato/a.

Hai Avete Hanno Ha	animali in casa?

Sì,	ho abbiamo hanno ha	un	gatto. cane.

UNIT 3 HOUSE AND HOME

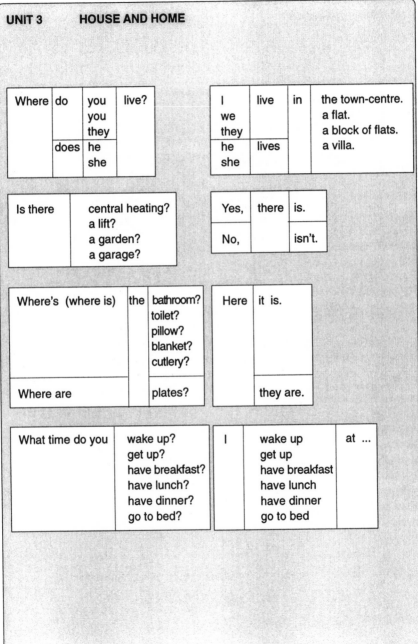

Where	do	you you they	live?
	does	he she	

I we they	live	in	the town-centre. a flat. a block of flats. a villa.
he she	lives		

Is there	central heating? a lift? a garden? a garage?

Yes,	there	is.
No,		isn't.

Where's (where is)	the	bathroom? toilet? pillow? blanket? cutlery?
Where are		plates?

Here	it is.
	they are.

What time do you	wake up? get up? have breakfast? have lunch? have dinner? go to bed?

I	wake up get up have breakfast have lunch have dinner go to bed	at ...

UNITÀ 3 CASA

Dove	abiti? abitate? abitano? abita (lui)? abita (lei)?

Abito Abitiamo Abitano Abita Abita	in	centro. un appartamento. un palazzo. una villa.

C'è	il riscaldamento centrale? l'ascensore? il giardino? il garage?

Sì,	c'è.
No, non	

Dove	è	il bagno? il gabinetto? il cuscino? la coperta?
	sono	le posate? i piatti?

Eccolo.
Eccola.
Eccole. Eccoli.

A che ora	ti	svegli? alzi?
	fai colazione? pranzi? ceni? vai a letto?	

Mi	sveglio alzo	alle ...
Faccio colazione Pranzo Ceno Vado a letto		

UNIT 4a GEOGRAPHICAL SURROUNDINGS

Where do you live?

I live	in	Ethiopia. Italy. England. Rome. London. Chicago.

Where are you from?

I'm	from	Gondar. Addis Ababa.

Where is it?

It's	in	northern central southern the north of the south of	Ethiopia.

Which is	the nearest	city?

It's	near	Gondar. London.

What's the countryside like?

It's	hilly. enchanting. monotonous. picturesque. wonderful.

Is	there	an	airport?
		a	sports centre?
Are		many	monuments?
			industries?

Yes,	there	is ...
No,		isn't ...
Yes,		are ...
No,		aren't ...

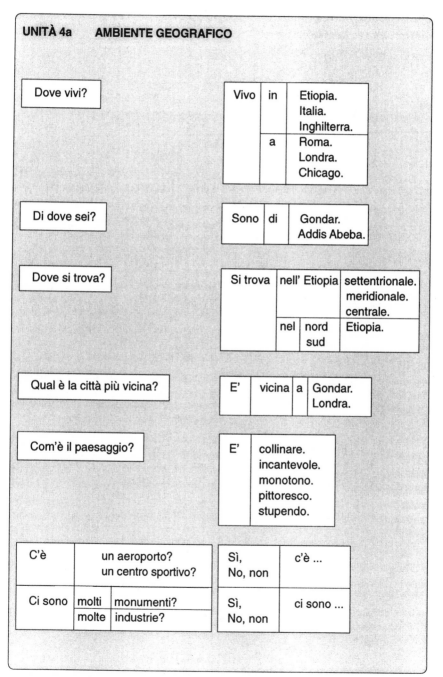

UNITÀ 4a AMBIENTE GEOGRAFICO

Dove vivi?		
Vivo	in	Etiopia. Italia. Inghilterra.
	a	Roma. Londra. Chicago.

Di dove sei?		
Sono	di	Gondar. Addis Abeba.

Dove si trova?			
Si trova	nell' Etiopia		settentrionale. meridionale. centrale.
	nel	nord sud	Etiopia.

Qual è la città più vicina?			
E'	vicina	a	Gondar. Londra.

Com'è il paesaggio?	
E'	collinare. incantevole. monotono. pittoresco. stupendo.

C'è	un aeroporto? un centro sportivo?		Sì, No, non	c'è ...
Ci sono	molti	monumenti?	Sì, No, non	ci sono ...
	molte	industrie?		

UNIT 4b WEATHER

What's the weather like?	It's	fine. bad. hot. cold. cool. raining. snowing. hailing. thundering. sunny. frosty. stormy. windy. foggy. misty.		
		a	fine bad	day.
	It is/The sky is	cloudy. overcast. dark. clear.		

What's the sea like today?	It's	calm. choppy. rough. very rough.

What's the climate like in	Germany? Italy? Spain? Ethiopia?	It's a	continental mediterranean mild splendid	climate.

MONTHS	January, February, March, April, May, June, July, August, September, October, November, December.
SEASONS	Spring, Summer, Autumn, Winter.

UNITÀ 4b TEMPO ATMOSFERICO

Che tempo fa?		
Fa	bel tempo. brutto tempo. caldo. freddo. fresco.	
Piove. Nevica. Grandina. Tuona.		
C'è	il sole. (il) ghiaccio. (il) temporale. vento. nebbia. foschia.	
E' una	bella brutta	giornata.
(Il cielo) è	nuvoloso. coperto. scuro. sereno.	

Com'è il mare oggi?	
E'	calmo. poco mosso. molto mosso. agitato.

Com'è il clima in	Germania? Italia? Spagna? Etiopia?
E' un clima	continentale. mediterraneo. mite. magnifico.

MESI	gennaio, febbraio, marzo, aprile, maggio, giugno, luglio, agosto, settembre, ottobre, novembre, dicembre.
STAGIONI	primavera, estate, autunno, inverno.

UNIT 5 TRAVEL AND TRANSPORT

Where's the	bus stop? station? information centre?

Take the	first second	on the	left. right.
Turn			
It's there, on your			
(Go) straight on.			
Go as far as the	traffic lights. cross-road.		
Cross the road.			

Is there	a	coach bus train	for	Florence?

Yes, there's one	in half an hour. at ten past seven.

What time does	it	leave get to	London? Oxford?

It	leaves gets in	at 3.00 p.m.

I'd like	a	single return	ticket	to	Rome.

At what time	are	you you they	leaving?
	is	he she	

I'm We're They're He's She'	leaving	at	six. seven. eight. nine. ten.

Can you check the	oil, water, tyres,	please?

UNITÀ 5 TRASPORTI

Dov'è	la fermata dell'autobus? la stazione? l'ufficio informazioni?

Prenda la	prima seconda	a	sinistra. destra.
Volti/giri			
E' lì sulla			
Continui Vada	sempre dritto. fino al semaforo. fino all'incrocio.		
Cross the road.			

C'è	una corriera un'autobus un treno	per	Firenze?

Sì, ce n'è uno	tra mezz'ora. alle sette e dieci.

A che ora	parte da arriva a	Londra? Oxford?

Parte Arriva	alle	15.00.

Vorrei	un	biglietto	di	andata andata e ritorno	per Roma.

A che ora	partirai (tu)? partirete (voi)? partiranno (loro)? partirà (lui)? partirà (lei)?

(Io) partirò (Noi) partiremo (Loro) partiranno (Lui) partirà (Lei) partirà	alle	sei. sette. otto. nove. dieci.

Mi controlli	l'olio, l'acqua, le gomme,	per favore?

UNIT 6-7 HOLIDAYS

Where do you	usually	go on holiday? spend your holidays?

Usually Often Sometimes	I go to	Ethiopia. the mountains. the seaside.

Where	are	you you they	going on holiday?
	is	he she	

I'm We're They're	going to staying in	Florence.
He's She's		

Where would you like to go on holiday?

I'd like I would like	to go	to	Italy. America. Venice. Paris.

What do you usually do on holiday?

I go	skiing. to the seaside. for walks.
I do some sport.	

You We	could go to	the museum. the cinema. the theatre

Yes, that's a great idea.	
No,	I'm tired ... I'm busy ...

UNITÀ 6-7 VACANZE

Dove	vai	di solito	in vacanza?
	passi		le vacanze?

Di solito Spesso Qualche volta	vado	in Etiopia. in montagna. al mare.

Dove	andrai andrete andranno	in vacanza?
	andrà andrà	

Andrò Andremo Andranno	a Firenze. in Inghilterra.
Andrà Andrà	
Resterò	

Dove ti piacerebbe andare in vacanza?

Mi piacerebbe andare	in	Italia. America.
	a	Venezia. Parigi.

Che cosa fai di solito in vacanza?

Vado	a sciare. al mare.
Faccio delle passeggiate.	
Pratico qualche sport.	

Potresti Potremmo	andare	al museo. al cinema. a teatro.

Sì, è un'ottima idea.	
No,	sono stanco.... sono impegnato ...

UNIT 8 HOTEL

I have a room I haven't	booked.

Do you have	a	single double	room?

For	one night. two weeks. three days.

With Without	(a) bathroom. (a) shower.

How much is it	for one	night? person? room?

Could I see a room	on the first floor? with a view of the sea? at the front? at the back?

At what time is	breakfast lunch dinner	served?

UNITÀ 8 ALBERGHI

Ho una camera prenotata. Non ho prenotato.

Avete una camera	singola? doppia?

Per	una notte. due settimane. tre giorni.

Con Senza	bagno. doccia.

Qual è il prezzo	per una	notte? persona? camera?

Potrei vedere una camera	al primo piano? con vista sul mare? sul davanti? sul retro?

A che ora servite	la prima colazione? il pranzo? la cena?

UNIT 9 FOOD AND DRINK

I'd like	a	coffee. cappuccino. sandwich. cheese roll.
	an	orangeade.

Do you have	(any)	ice-cream? cheese? fresh fruit?

Do you like	Italian Greek French Chinese Indian	cooking?

At what time do you have	breakfast? lunch? supper?

Could you please	bring me	some bread? the salt? the pepper? the tooth-picks?

UNITÀ 9 CIBI E BEVANDE

Vorrei	un	caffè. cappuccino. tramezzino. panino al formaggio.
	un'aranciata.	

Avete	del dolce? del formaggio? della frutta fresca?

Ti piace	la cucina	italiana? greca? francese? cinese? indiana?

A che ora fai	colazione? pranzi? ceni?

Mi porta	un po' di pane il sale il pepe gli stuzzicadenti	per favore?

UNIT 10 SHOPPING

Is there	a	supermarket? shopping centre? market? chemist's? butcher's? baker's?

Where's	the	food stationery clothing	department?

I'd like a	litre	of milk.
	kilo	of bread.
	dozen	eggs.
	box	of matches.
	plastic	bag.
	bottle	of wine.
	can	of orangeade.
	100 grams	of cheese.

I'd like	a pullover. a raincoat. an umbrella. a bag. a jacket.

Made of	nylon. leather. plastic. china. silk. metal. cotton.

UNITÀ 10 COMPERARE

C'è	un	supermercato? centro commerciale? mercato?
	una	farmacia? macelleria? panetteria?

Dov'è	il reparto	alimentari? cancelleria? vestiti/abbigliamento?

Vorrei	un litro	di latte.
	un chilo	di pane.
	una dozzina	di uova.
	una scatola	di fiammiferi.
	un sacchetto	di plastica.
	una bottiglia	di vino.
	una lattina	di aranciata.
	un etto	di formaggio.

Vorrei	un pullover. un impermeabile. un ombrello. una borsa. una giacca.

Di	nylon. pelle. plastica. porcellana. seta. metallo. cotone.

UNIT 11 SERVICES

How much is it to send	a	letter card parcel	to	Germany? America? Italy?

What stamp do I have to put	for	France? Great Britain? Australia?

I'd like to change	some travellers' cheques. Francs. Lire. Dollars.

What is the exchange rate for the	Pound? Deutsche Mark? French Franc? Dutch Guilder? Swiss Franc? U.S. Dollar? Australian Dollar? Canadian Dollar? Yen? Birr? Nakfa?

I've had	my	car camera	stolen ...

I have lost	my	bag. wallet.

UNITÀ 11 SERVIZI

Quanto costa spedire	una lettera una cartolina un pacco	in	Germania? America? Italia?

Che fracobollo devo mettere	per	la Francia? la Gran Bretagna? l'Australia?

Vorrei cambiare	dei travellers' cheque. dei franchi. delle lire. dei dollari.

Quant'è il cambio Qual è la quotazione	della sterlina? del marco tedesco? del franco francese? del fiorino olandese? del franco svizzero? del dollaro USA? del dollaro australiano? del dollaro canadese? dello yen? del birr? del nakfa?

Mi hanno rubato	la macchina/l'automobile. la macchina fotografica.

Ho perso	la borsa. il portafoglio.

UNIT 12 HEALTH

What's	wrong with you? wrong?
What How	do you feel?

I feel	weak. tired.
I've got	tooth ache. a sore throat. stomach-ache. back-ache. a head-ache. cramp. sun-stroke. diarrhoea. hay-fever. flu. high/low blood pressure.

I've	burnt hurt injured cut	myself.

I need I would like	to lie down. to go to bed. to see a doctor.

I would like	some	aspirin. plasters. tablets for ...

UNITÀ 12 SALUTE

Che cos'hai? Cos'è che non va? Che disturbo sente?* Come ti senti?

Mi sento		debole. stanco/a.
Ho	mal di	denti. gola. pancia. schiena. testa.
	i crampi. preso un colpo di sole. la diarrea. il raffreddore da fieno. l'influenza. la pressione alta/bassa.	

Mi sono	bruciato/a. fatto/a male. ferito/a. tagliato/a.

Ho bisogno di Vorrei	distendermi. coricarmi. un dottore/medico.

Vorrei	delle aspirine. dei cerotti. delle compresse di ...

UNIT 13 FREE TIME

What's your (favourite)	hobby?
What do you do in your	free time?

(I like)	collecting	stamps. post cards. stickers.
	playing	draughts. chess. cards. billiards.
		photography. electronics. model making. computers. football. music.

What do you do	at weekends? during the holidays?

I	usually sometimes often	go	dancing. horse-riding. to play ... fishing. to the theatre. to the cinema. to discos.

I	go	swimming. cycling. ice-skating.
	play	football. tennis. basket-ball.

UNITÀ 13 TEMPO LIBERO

Qual è il tuo hobby preferito? Che cosa fai nel tempo libero?

Mi piace	collezionare	francobolli. cartoline. adesivi.
	giocare a	dama. scacchi. carte. biliardo.
	la fotografia. l'elettronica. il modellismo. il computer. il calcio. la musica.	

Che cosa fai durante	il fine settimana? le vacanze?

Di solito Qualche volta Spesso	vado	a	ballare. cavallo. a giocare. pescare. teatro.
		al in	cinema. discoteca.

Faccio	nuoto. ciclismo. pattinaggio su ghiaccio.
Gioco a	calcio. tennis. pallacanestro.

UNIT 14 EDUCATION

What year are you in?

The	first second third fourth fifth	(year).

What subjects do you study?

(I study)	Arabic. French. German. English. Amharic. Italian. Maths. Science. History. Geography. Religion. Art. P.E. Music.

Do you like	Mathematics? Geography? Literature?

Yes, I like it. No, I don't like it. I prefer ...

What kind of work would you like to do?

I would like to be	an architect. a journalist. a hairdresser. a mechanic. a teacher.

UNITÀ 14 ISTRUZIONE

Che anno frequenti?

Il	primo secondo terzo quarto quinto	(anno).

Che materie studi?

(Studio)	arabo. francese. tedesco. inglese. amarico. italiano. matematica. scienze. storia. geografia. religione. educazione artistica. educazione fisica. musica.

Ti piace la	matematica? geografia? letteratura?

Si, mi piace. No, non mi piace. Preferisco ...

Che lavoro ti piacerebbe fare?

Mi piacerebbe fare	l'architetto. il giornalista. il parrucchiere. il meccanico. l'insegnante.

IRREGULAR VERBS

Infinitive	Past Tense	Past Participle		
to be	was	been	essere	መኖር
to beat	beat	beaten	battere	መደብደብ
to become	became	become	diventare	መሆን
to begin	began	begun	iniziare	መጀመር
to bend	bent	bent	piegare	ማጠፍ
to bite	bit	bitten	mordere	መንከስ
to bleed	bled	bled	sanguinare	መድማት
to break	broke	broken	rompere	መስበር
to bring	brought	brought	portare	ማምጣት
to build	built	built	costruire	ማነጽ
to burn	burnt	burnt	bruciare	መቃጠል
to buy	bought	bought	comperare	መግዛት
to catch	caught	caught	prendere	መያዝ
to choose	chose	chosen	scegliere	መምረጥ
to come	came	come	venire	መምጣት
to cost	cost	cost	costare	ዋጋ ማውጣት
to cut	cut	cut	tagliare	መቍረጥ
to do	did	done	fare	ማድረግ
to draw	drew	drawn	disegnare	መሳል
to drink	drank	drunk	bere	መጠጣት
to drive	drove	driven	guidare	መንዳት
to eat	ate	eaten	mangiare	መብላት
to fall	fell	fallen	cadere	መውደቅ
to feel	felt	felt	sentire	መሰማት
to find	found	found	trovare	ማግኘት
to forget	forgot	forgotten	dimenticare	መርሳት
to forgive	forgave	forgiven	perdonare	ይቅርታ ማድረግ
to get	got	got	ottenere	ማግኘት
to give	gave	given	dare	መስጠት
to go	went	gone	andare	መሔድ
to grow	grew	grown	crescere	ማደግ
to have	had	had	avere	መኖር
to hear	heard	heard	ascoltare	መስማት
to hide	hid	hidden	nascondere	መደበቅ
to hit	hit	hit	colpire	መምታት
to hold	held	held	tenere	መያዝ

IRREGULAR VERBS

to hurt	hurt	hurt	farsi male	መጐዳት
to keep	kept	kept	tenere	መያዝ
to know	knew	known	sapere	ማወቅ
to learn	learnt	learnt	imparare	መማር
to leave	left	left	partire	መነሳት
to lend	lent	lent	imprestare	ማበደር
to lose	lost	lost	perdere	ማጥፋት
to make	made	made	fare	መስራት
to mean	meant	meant	significare	ማለት
to meet	met	met	incontrare	መገናኘት
to pay	paid	paid	pagare	መክፈል
to put	put	put	mettere	ማስቀመጥ
to read	read	read	leggere	ማንበብ
to run	ran	run	correre	መሮጥ
to say	said	said	dire	ማለት
to see	saw	seen	vedere	ማየት
to sell	sold	sold	vendere	መሸጥ
to send	sent	sent	spedire	መላክ
to shake	shook	shaken	scuotere	መነቃነቅ
to shoot	shot	shot	sparare	መተኰስ
to show	showed	shown	mostrare	ማሳየት
to shut	shut	shut	chiedere	መዝጋት
to sing	sang	sung	cantare	መዝፈን
to sit	sat	sat	sedersi	መቀመጥ
to sleep	slept	slept	dormire	መተኛት
to speak	spoke	spoken	parlare	መናገር
to spend	spent	spent	spendere	ማጥፋት
to steal	stole	stolen	rubare	መስረቅ
to swim	swam	swum	nuotare	መዋኘት
to take	took	taken	prendere	መውሰድ
to teach	taught	taught	insegnare	ማስተማር
to tell	told	told	dire	መንገር
to think	thought	thought	pensare	ማሰብ
to understand	understood	understood	capire	መረዳት
to wear	wore	worn	indossare	መልበስ
to win	won	won	vincere	ማሸነፍ
to write	wrote	written	scrivere	መጻፍ

PRINCIPALI VERBI IRREGOLARI

PI= presente indicativo (present indicative)
FI = futuro indicativo (future)
PR = passato remoto (past historic)
PP = participio passato (past participle)

accendere	acceso	accesi	(to turn on; ማብራት)
aprire	aperto	aprii	(to open; መክፈት)
cadere	caduto	caddi	(to fall; መውደቅ)
chiedere	chiesto	chiesi	(to ask; መጠየቅ)
chiudere	chiuso	chiusi	(to close; መዝጋት)
conoscere	conosciuto	conobbi	(to know; ማወቅ)
correre	corso	corsi	(to run; መሮጥ)
correggere	corretto	corressi	(to correct; ማረም)
decidere	deciso	decisi	(to decide; መወሰን)
descrivere	descritto	descrissi	(to describe; መግለጽ)
leggere	letto	lessi	(to read; ማንበብ)
mettere	messo	misi	(to put; ማስቀመጥ)
nascere	nato	nacqui	(to be born; መወለድ)
nascondere	nascosto	nascosi	(to hide; መደበቅ)
offrire	offerto	offrii	(to offer; ማበርከት)
perdere	perso	persi	(to lose; መጥፋት)
prendere	preso	presi	(to take; መውሰድ)
promettere	promesso	promisi	(to promise; ተስፋ መስጠት)
ridere	riso	risi	(to laugh; መሳቅ)
rimanere	rimasto	rimasi	(to remain; መቅረት)
rompere	rotto	ruppi	(to break; መስበር)
rispondere	risposto	risposi	(to answer; መልስ መስጠት)
scegliere	scelto	scelsi	(to choose; መምረጥ)
spegnere	spento	spensi	(to put out, to switch off; ማጥፋት)
scrivere	scritto	scrissi	(to write; መጻፍ)
spendere	speso	spesi	(to spend; ማጥፋት)
vedere	visto	vidi	(to see; ማየት)
vincere	vinto	vinsi	(to win; ማሸነፍ)
vivere	vissuto	vissi	(to live; መኖር)

andare (to go; መሄድ)
PI vado, vai, va, andiamo, andate, vanno
FI andrò, andrai, andrà, andremo, andrete, andranno
PP andato; PR andai
avere (to have; መኖር)
PI ho, hai, ha, abbiamo, avete, hanno
FI avrò, avrai, avrà, avremo, avrete, avranno
PP avuto; PR ebbi
bere (to drink; መጠጣት)
PI bevo, bevi, beve, beviamo, bevete, bevono
FI berrò, berrai, berrà, berremo, berrete, berranno
PP bevuto, PR bevvi
dare (to give; መስጠት)
PI do, dai, dà, diamo, date, danno
FI darò, darai, darà, daremo, darete, daranno
PP dato; PR diedi/detti
dire (to say; ማለት)
PI dico, dici, dice, diciamo, dite, dicono
FI dirò, dirai, dirà; diremo, direte, diranno
PP detto; PR dissi
dovere (must; መገባት)
PI devo, devi, deve, dobbiamo, dovete, devono
FI dovrò, dovrai, dovrà, dovremo, dovrete, dovranno
PP dovuto; PR dovetti
essere (to be; መኖር)
PI sono, sei, è, siamo, siete, sono
FI sarò, sarai, sarà, saremo, sarete, saranno
PP stato; PR fui
fare (to do, to make; ማድረግ)
PI faccio, fai, fa, facciamo, fate, fanno
FI farò, farai, farà, faremo, farete, faranno
PP fatto; PR feci
potere (to be able; መቻል)
PI posso, puoi, può, possono, possiamo, potete
FI potrò, potrai, potrà, potremo, potrete, potranno
PP potuto; PR potei
sapere (to know; ማወቅ)
PI so, sai, sa, sappiamo, sapete, sanno
FI saprò, saprai, saprà, sapremo, saprete, sapranno
PP saputo; PR seppi

stare (to stay;መቆየት)
PI sto, stai, sta, stiamo, state, stanno
FI starò, starai, starà, staremo, starete, staranno
PP stato; PR stetti
tradurre (to translate; መተርጎም)
PI traduco, traduci, traduce, traduciamo, traduciete, traducono;
FI tradurrò, tradurrai, tradurrà, tradurremo, tradurrete, tradurranno
PP tradotto; PR tradussi
uscire (to go out; መውጣት)
PI esco, esci, esce, usciamo, uscite, escono
FI uscirò, uscirai, uscirà, usciremo, uscirete, usciranno
PP uscito; PR uscii
venire (to come; መምጣት)
PI vengo, vieni, viene, veniamo, venite, vengono
FI verrò, verrai, verrà, verremo, verrete, verranno
PP venuto; PR venni
volere (to want; መፈለግ)
PI voglio, vuoi, vuole, vogliamo, volete, vogliono
F vorrò, vorrai, vorrà, vorremo, vorrete, vorranno
PP voluto, PR volli

VOCABULARY LISTS BY TOPICS

ENGLISH

አማርኛ

ITALIANO

VOCABULARY LISTS BY TOPIC

PERSONAL IDENTIFICATION

Nationality

America	America	አሜሪካ
americano	American	አሜሪካዊ/ት
Africa	Africa	አፍሪካ
Africano	African	አፍሪካዊ/ት
Australia	Australia	አውስትራሊያ
australiano	Australian	አውስትራሊያዊ/ት
bandiera	flag	ሰንደቅ ዓላማ
belga	Belgian	በልጂማዊ/ት
Belgio	Belgium	በልጂዩም
britannico	British	እንግሊዛዊ/ት
carta di identità	identity card	መታወቅያ ወረቀት
danese	Danish	ዴንማርካዊ/ት
Danimarca	Denmark	ዴንማርክ
Eritrea	Eritrea	ኤርትራ
eritreo	Eritrean	ኤርትራዊ/ት
Etiopia	Ethiopia	ኢትዮጵያ
etiope	Ethiopian	ኢትዮጵያዊ/ት
Europa	Europe	አውሮጳ
europeo	European	አውሮጳዊ/ት
francese	French	ፈረንሳዊ/ት
Francia	France	ፈረንሳይ አገር
Galles	Wales	ዌልስ
gallese	Welsh	ዌልሳዊ/ት
Germania	Germany	ጀርመን
Gran Bretagna	Great Britain	ታላቋ ብሪታንያ
Grecia	Greece	ግሪክ
greco	Greek	ግሪካዊ/ት
Irlanda	Ireland	አየርላንድ
irlandese	Irish	አየርላንዳዊ/ት
Italia	Italy	ጣልያን
italiano	Italian	ኢጣልያዊ/ት
lussemburghese	Luxemburger	ሉክሰምቡርጋዊ/ት
Lussemburgo	Luxemburg	ሉክሰምቡርግ

Olanda	Holland	ሆላንድ
olandese	Dutch	ሆላንዳዊ/ት
passaporto	passport	ፓስፖርት
Portogallo	Portugal	ፖርቱጋል
portoghese	Portuguese	ፖርቱጋላዊ/ት
Russia	Russia	ሩስያ
russo	Russian	ሩስያዊ/ት
Scozia	Scotland	ስኮትላንድ
scozzese	Scottish	ስኮትላንዳዊ/ት
Spagna	Spain	ስፔን
spagnolo	Spanish	ስፓኛዊ/ት
straniero	foreigner	የውጭ አገር ዜጋ
tedesco	German	ጀርመናዊ/ት

Occupations

assistente di volo (m/f)	steward, stewardess	አስተናጋጅ ሆስተስ
autista (m/f)	driver	ሹፌር
avvocato	lawyer	ጠበቃ
cameriere (m)	waiter	አስተናጋጅ/አሳላፊ
casalinga	housewife	የቤት እመቤት
commerciante (m/f)	trader	ነጋዴ
commercio	trade	ንግድ
commesso	shop-assistant	የሱቅ ቤት ሰራተኛ
dentista (m/f)	dentist	የጥርስ ሐኪም
direttore (m)	manager	ሥራ አስኪያጅ
disoccupato	unemployed	ሥራ አጥ
ditta	firm, company	ድርጅት
dottore (m)	doctor	ሐኪም
essere	to be	መሆን
fabbrica	factory	ፋብሪካ
farmacista (m/f)	chemist, pharmacist	ኬሚስት፡ ፋርማሲስት፡ ቀማሚ
fattoria	farm	እርሻ
guadagnare	to earn	ደሞዝ ማግኘት
impiegato	employee	ሰራተኛ
infermiere (m)	male nurse	አስታማሚ
infermiera	nurse	አስታማሚ
insegnante (m/f)	teacher	አስተማሪ
interessante	interesting	አስደሳች
lavorare	to work	መስራት

lavoro	job, work	ሥራ
macellaio	butcher	ሥጋ ሸያጭ
maestro	teacher (primary)	አስተማሪ
magazzino	store, warehouse	ግምጃ ቤት
meccanico	mechanic	መካኒክ
medico	doctor	ሐኪም
negozio	shop	ሱቅ
operaio	workman	ሰራተኛ
padrone (m)	owner	ባለቤት
paga	pay, salary	ደሞዝ
parrucchiere (m)	hairdresser	ጠጕር ሰሪ
pizzeria	'pizzeria'	ፒሳ የሚሸጥበት
poliziotto	policeman	ፖሊስ
posizione (f)	position	ቦታ
professione (f)	profession	ሞያ
professore (m)	teacher, professor	አስተማሪ፡ ፕሮፌሰር
proprietario	owner	ባለቤት፡ ባለንብረት
salario	wage	ደሞዝ፡ ክፍያ
segretario	secretary	ጸሓፊ
stipendio	salary	ደሞዝ፡ ክፍያ
studente (m)	student	ተማሪ
tassista (m/f)	taxi-driver	ባለ ታክሲ
trovare un impiego	to find a job	ሥራ ማግኘት
ufficio	office	ቢሮ፡ ጽሕፈት ቤት

General descriptions

bambino	child	ልጅ
donna	woman	ሴት
femmina	female	ሴት አንስታይ
figlio	son	ወንድ
maschio	male	ወንድ፡ ተባዕታይ
ragazza	girl	ሴት፡ ልጃገረድ
ragazzo	boy	ልጅ
signorina	young lady	ወይዘሪት
uomo	man	ወንድ
celibe (m)	single	ወንድ ላጤ
congratularsi con	to congratulate	እንኳን ደስ አለህ ማለት
coniugato	married	ያገባ
divorziato	divorced	የተፋታ
fidanzarsi	to become engaged	መታጨት

Physical Appearance

a mio parere	in my opinion	በኔ አስተያየት
alto	tall	ረጅም
anziano	old, elderly	ታላቅ/ሽማግሌ
azzurro	light blue	ውሃ ሰማያዊ
baffi (m, pl.)	moustache	የአፍንጫ ጢም
barba	beard	ሪዝ
basso	short	አጭር
bellezza	beauty	ቊንጅና
bello	beautiful, handsome	ቆንጆ፡ መልከ መልካም
bianco	white	ነጭ
biondo	fair, blonde	ቢጫ
bocca	mouth	አፍ
brutto	ugly	መጥፎ፡ አስቀያሚ
capelli (m, pl.)	hair	ጠጕር
carino	pretty	ደስ የሚል
carnagione (f)	complexion	የቆዳ ቀለም
castano	brown, hazel	ቡና
chiaro	fair	የቀላ
corto	short	አጭር
denti	teeth	ጥርስ
elegante	elegant; smart	ዘናጭ
giovane	young	ወጣት
grasso	fat	ወፍራም
grazioso	pretty	ውብ፡ መልከ መልካም
grosso	big	ትልቅ
lisci (capelli ...)	straight hair	ሉጫ ጠጕር
lungo	long	ረጂም
magro	thin	ቀጭን
naso	nose	አፍንጫ
nero	black, dark	ጥቁር፡ ጨለማ
occhi	eyes	አይኖች
occhiali	glasses, spectacles	መነጽር
ondulato	wavy	ዚግዛግ
orecchino	earring	ጕትቻ
orecchio	ear	ጆሮ
ricci (capelli ...)	curly hair	የተጠቀለለ ጠጕር
robusto	strong, robust	ጠንካራ
snello	slim	ሸንቅጥ፡ ምልምል
somiglianza	likeness	ተመሳሳይ

sorriso	smile	ፈገግታ
statura media	medium height	መካከለኛ ቁመት
vecchio	old	ሽማግሌ (m) አሮጊት (f)
verde	green	አረንጓዴ

Character

abbastanza	rather, enough	በቂ፡ ብቃት ያለው
allegro	cheerful, merry	ደስተኛ
antipatico	unpleasant	ደስ የማይል፡ የማይስማማ
beneducato	well mannered	ሽጋ ጸባይ ያለው/ያላት
bravo	good, clever	ጉበዝ
buffo	funny	አስቂኝ፡ ኮሚክ
calmo	calm	ጸጥ ያለ
comprensivo	understanding	የሚገባባ
contento	happy, pleased	ደስተኛ
cortese	polite	ሰው አክባሪ፡ስነ ስርዓት ያለው
divertente	amusing	አዝናኝ
felice	happy	ደስተኛ
geloso	jealous	ምቀኛ
gentile	kind	ደግ ብሩክ
intelligente	intelligent	ብልህ
maleducato	bad-mannered	ያልተቀጣ፡ ስድ አደግ
meraviglioso	wonderful	ግሩም፡ አስደናቂ
molto	much, very	ብዙ፡ እጅግ በጣም
nervoso	irritable, nervous	ቁጡ፡ ቶሎ የሚቆጣ
noioso	boring	አሰልቺ፡ ደባሪ
onesto	honest	ታማኝ፡ቅኑ
orgoglioso	proud	ኩሩ
pazzo	crazy	እብድ
pigro	lazy	ሰነፍ
piuttosto	rather	ያህል፡ የሚዳረግ
serio	serious	ኮስታራ
severo	severe, strict	ጽኑ ጥብቅ
simpatico	nice	ተወዳጅ
studioso	studious	ተመራማሪ
superbo	proud, haughty	ትዕቢተኛ፡ ኩራተኛ
timido	shy, timid	አይነ አፋር፡ ፈሪ
triste	sad	ሐዘንተኛ፡ የሚያሳዝን
vivace	lively	ንቁ፡ ቀልጣፋ

FAMILY

amico	friend	ጓደኛ
babbo	dad	አባት
bambino	child	ልጅ
cognato	brother-in-law	የእህት ባለቤት
cugino	cousin	ያክስት/ ያጎት ልጅ
famiglia	family	ቤተሰብ
figlio	son	ወንድ ልጅ
figlio unico	only son	ብቸኛ ልጅ
fratello	brother	ወንድም
gemelli	twins	መንትያ
genitore (m)	parent	ወላጆች
giovane	young	ወጣት
grande	big, grown-up	አዋቂ
madre (f)	mother	እናት
maggiore	older	ታላቅ
mamma	mummy	እማማ
marito	husband	ባለቤት፡ ባል
matrimonio	marriage, wedding	ጋብቻ
minore	younger	ታናሽ
moglie (f)	wife	ሚስት፡ ባለቤት
nipote (m/f)	nephew, niece, grand-son, grand-daughter	የአክስት/ የአጎት ልጅ፡ የልጅ ልጅ
nonno	grand-father	የወንድ አያት
nozze (f, pl.)	wedding	ሰርግ
numeroso	numerous; large	ብዙ፡ ሰፊ
padre (m)	father	አባት
papà	daddy	አብየ
parente (m/f)	relative	ዘመድ አዝማድ
piccolo	small	ትንሽ
rassomigliare a	to look like	መምሰል
sorella	sister	እህት
suocero	father-in-law	የወንድ አማች
unire	to unite	መተባበር
zio	uncle	አጎት

HOUSE AND HOME

Accommodation and Services

accendere	to switch on	ማብራት
acqua	water	ውኃ
(al piano) di sopra	upstairs	ላይኛው ፎቅ
(al piano) di sotto	downstairs	ታችኛው ፎቅ
al piano superiore	on the upper floor	እላይኛው ፎቅ
al pianterreno	on the ground floor	እታችኛው ፎቅ
al primo piano	on the first floor	ባንደኛው ፎቅ
aprire	to open	መክፈት
automobile (f)	car	መኪና
balcone (m)	balcony	በረንዳ
bottone/pulsante (m)	button	ቍልፍ
caldo	hot	ሙቅ
camera (da letto)	bedroom	መኝታ ክፍል
cantina	cellar	መሬት ስር የሚገኝ ግምጃ ቤት
chiudere	to shut	መዝጋት
confortevole	comfortable	ምቹ፡ ድሎት ያለው
cucina	kitchen	ማድ ቤት
dormire	to sleep	መተኛት
elettricità	electricity	የኤለክትሪክ ኃይል
elettrico	electric	ኤለክትሪክ
entrata	entrance	መግቢያ
fiammifero	match	ክብሪት
finestra	window	መስኮት
fornello	cooker	ወጥ ማብሰያ
freddo	cold	ብርድ፡ ቀዝቃዛ
gabinetto	toilet	መጸዳጃ
garage (m)	garage	ጋራዥ፡ የመኪና ማቆምያ
ingresso	entrance, hallway	መግቢያ፡ ደጃፍ
lavandino	wash basin, sink	የፊት፡ የዕቃ መታጠቢያ
macchina	car, machine	መኪና
non funziona	out of order	ከሥራ ውጭ
porta	door	በር
premere	to press	መጫን
rubinetto	tap	ቧንቧ
sala da pranzo	dining room	መመገቢያ ክፍል
salotto	sitting-room	የእንግዶች መቀበያ
scale (f, pl.)	stairs	ደረጃ

soggiorno	living-room	ሳሎን
spegnere	to switch off	ማጥፋት
stanza	room	ክፍል
(stanza da) bagno	bathroom	መጸዳጃ (ገላ መታጠብያ)
studio	study	የጥናት ቤት

Furniture, household equipment and appliances

apparecchiare	to lay the table	ምግብ ማቅረብ
armadio	wardrobe	ቁም ሣጥን
arredare	to furnish	የቤት ዕቃዎች መደርደር
asciugamano	hand towel	የእጅ ፎጣ
aspirapolvere (m)	vacuum-cleaner	ቤት የማጽጃ መኪና
bicchiere (m)	glass	ብርጭቆ
bottiglia	bottle	ጠርሙስ
caffettiera	coffee pot	ጀበና
casseruola	saucepan	ባለእጀታ ድስት
cassetto	drawer	መሳብያ
coltello	knife	ቢላዋ
congelatore (m)	freezer	ማቀዝቀዣ
coperta	cover, blanket	ብርድ ልብስ
cosa	thing	ዕቃ፡ነገር
credenza	sideboard	ኮመዲኖ
cucchiaino	teaspoon	የሻይ ማንኪያ
cucchiaio	spoon	ማንኪያ
cucina	kitchen	ማድ ቤት
cuscino	cushion, pillow	ትራስ
dentifricio	toothpaste	የጥርስ ሳሙና
disco	record	ሸክላ
divano	settee	ሶፋ
doccia	shower	ሻወር
elettricità	electricity	የኤለክትሪክ ኃይል
elettrico	electric	ኤለክትሪክ
elettrodomestici	electric household appliances	የቤት ውስጥ የኤለክትሪክ መገልገያዋች
federa	pillow-case	የትራስ ሽፋን
forchetta	fork	ሹካ

forno	oven	ምጣድ
frigorifero	refrigerator	ማቀዝቀዣ
lampada	lamp	መብራት ፋና
lampadina	light bulb	የእጅ መብራት
lavastoviglie (f)	dish-washer	የሰሀን፡ድስት፡ብርጭቆ ወዘተ ማጠብያ
lavatrice (f)	washing machine	የልብስ ማጠብያ
lenzuolo	sheet	አንሶላ
letto	bed	አልጋ
libreria	bookcase	የመጻሕፍት መደርደርያ
lucidatrice (f)	floor-polisher	ሸራ፡የወለል መወልወያ
mobile (m)	piece of furniture	የቤት ዕቃ
orologio	clock	የጠረጴዛ ሰዓት
padella	pan	መጥበሻ
parecchi	many, several	ብዙ፡ በብዛት
pattumiera	dustbin	የቆሻሻ ማጠራቀምያ
pentola	pot; pan	ድስት
pianoforte (m)	piano	ፒያኖ
piattino	saucer	የስኒ ማስቀመጫ
piatto	plate, dish	ሰሀን
poltrona	arm-chair	ሶፋ
portacenere (m)	ash-tray	የሲጋራ መተርኰሻ
quadro	picture	ስዕል
radio (f)	radio	ረዲዮ
registratore (m)	tape-recorder	ቴፕ
sapone (m)	soap	ሳሙና
scaffale (m)	shelf	መደርደርያ
sedia	chair	ወንበር
sparecchiare	to clear the table	ምግቡን ማንሳት
spazzolino da denti	toothbrush	የጥርስ ብሩሽ
sveglia	alarm clock	የሚቀሰቅስ ሰዓት
tappeto	carpet	ምንጣፍ
tazza	cup	ስኒ
tazzina	coffee-cup	የቡና ስኒ
tegame	saucepan	መቁያ
teiera	tea-pot	የሻይ ጀበና
televisione (f)	television	ቴለቪዥን
tende	curtains	መጋረጃ
tovaglia	table cloth	የጠረጴዛ ልብስ
tovagliolo	napkin, serviette	የአፍ ማበሻ (ናፕኪን)
video registratore	video recorder	ቪደዮ ቀጂ

GEOGRAPHICAL SURROUNDINGS AND WEATHER

Location

abitante (m)	inhabitant	ተቀማጭ
c'è, ci sono	there is, there are	አለ፡ አሉ
camminare	to walk	መሔድ
campagna (in ...)	country (in the ...)	ገጠር ውስጥ
capitale (f)	capital	ዋና ከተማ
centro	centre	መሃል
chilometro	kilometre	ኪሎሜትር
cielo	sky	ሰማይ
città (in ...)	city, town (in the ...)	ከተማ ውስጥ ...
dove, dov'è	where, where is	የት፡ የት ነው
est (m)	east	ምሥራቅ
giro	tour	ዙረት
gita	excursion, trip	ሽርሽር
località	locality, place	ቦታ፡ ሰፈር
lontano da	far from	ከ ... ሩቅ የሆነ
mare; (al ...)	sea; (at the seaside)	ባሕር፡ በባሕር ዳር
mondo	world	ዓለም
montagna (in ...)	mountain (in the ...s)	ኰረብታ፡ በኰረብታ ላይ
nord (m)	north	ሰሜን
ovest (m)	west	ምዕራብ
passeggiare	to stroll, to walk	መሸራሸር
passeggiata	stroll, walk	ሽርሽር
periferia (in ...)	suburb (in the ...)	አከባቢ በ ...
regione (f)	region	ወረዳ አውራጃ
sud (m)	south	ደቡብ
vedere	to see	ማየት
visitare	to visit	መድረስ
vista	view	ትዕይንት/ትርኢት

Amenities/features of interest

aeroporto	airport	የአውሮፕላን ማረፍያ
albergo	hotel	ማረፍያ ቤት
altro	other	ሌላ
antico	ancient	ጥንታዊ
architettura	architecture	ስነ-ቅየሳ
abbazia	abbey	ደብር
bello	beautiful	መልካም፡ ውብ

bosco	wood	ጫካ
brutto	ugly	መጥፎ፣ አስቀያሚ
campeggio	camping site	ማረፍያ ቦታ
carta geografica	map	የዓለም ካርታ
castello	castle	የነገስታት ግንብ
cattedrale (f)	cathedral	ትልቅ ቤተክርስትያን
chiesa	church	ቤተክርስትያን
cinema (m)	cinema	ሲኒማ
collina	hill	ኰረብታ
discoteca	discotheque	ዲስኮተክ
edificio	building	ፎቅ ህንፃ
epoca	age, epoch	ዘመን
fabbrica	factory	ፋብሪካ
fattoria	farm	እርሻ
fiume (m)	river	ወንዝ፣ ጐርፍ
fontana	fountain	የውኃ ምንጭ
foresta	forest	ጫካ
interessante	interesting	ማራኪ፣ አስፈላጊ
isola	island	ደሴት
lago	lake	ሀይቅ
moderno	modern	ዘመናዊ
monumento	monument	ሐወልት
moschea	mosque	መስጊድ
municipio	town-hall	ማዘጋጃ ቤት
museo	museum	ቤተ መዘክር
paesaggio	landscape, scenery	መልክዐ ምድር
panorama (m)	view, panorama	ግሩም የመሬት ትርኢት
parco	park	መናፈሻ፣ የአትክልት ቦታ
piscina	swimming pool	መዋኛ
ponte (m)	bridge	ድልድይ
settentrionale	northern	ሰሜናዊ
spiaggia	beach	ባሕር ዳር
stadio	stadium	ስታድዩም
stazione (f)	station	ጣብያ
storico	historic	ታሪካዊ
teatro	theatre	ትያትር
villaggio	village	አገር ቤት

Weather

asciutto	dry	ደረቅ
autunno	autumn	በልግ
brezza	breeze	ቀዝቃዛ ነፋስ
caldo	hot	ሙቀት
che tempo fa?	what's the weather like?	የአየር ሁኔታው ምን ይመስላል
cielo	sky	ሰማይ
clima (m)	climate	የአየር ሁኔታ
coperto	cloudy, overcast	ደመና
estate (f)	summer	በጋ
far bel tempo/bello	to be good weather	መልካም የአየር ሁኔታ
brutto tempo	to be bad weather	መጥፎ የአየር ሁኔታ
caldo	to be hot	ይሞቃል
freddo	to be cold	ይበርዳል
fulmine (m)	lightning	መብረቅ
ghiaccio	ice	በረዶ
grandine (f)	hail	በረዶ ያለው ዝናም
inverno	winter	ክረምት
lampo	flash of lightning	መብረቅ
mite	mild	ደህና
nebbia	fog	ጉም
neve (f)	snow	በረዶ ውርጭ
nevicare	to snow	በረዶ መዝነም
nuvola	cloud	ደመና
pioggia	rain	ዝናም
piovere	to rain	መዝነም
piovigginare	to drizzle	ያካፋል
primavera	spring	በልግ
secco	dry	ደረቅ
sereno	clear, cloudless	ደመና የሌለው
sole (m)	sun	ፀሐይ
soleggiato	sunny	ፀሐያማ
stagione (f)	season	ወራት
temperatura	temperature	የሙቀት መጠን
tempesta	storm	ማዕበል፡ አውሎነፋስ፡ኃይለኛ ዝናም
temporale (m)	thunder storm	ነጐድጓድ የተቀላቀለበት ኃይለኛ ዝናም
umidità	humidity	እርጥበት ያዘለ አየር
vento	wind	ነፋስ

TRAVEL AND TRANSPORT

Public Transport

bagaglio	luggage	ሻንጣ
biglietteria	ticket office	ቲኬት መሸጫ
biglietto	ticket	ቲኬት
binario	platform	መድረክ
conducente (m/f)	driver	ሹፌር
controllore (m)	inspector	ተቆጣጣሪ
corriera	coach	አውቶቡስ
cuccetta	couchette	መኝታ [ባቡር ውስጥ]
fermata	(bus) stop	ፌርማታ
ferrovia	railway	ሐዲድ
finestrino	window	መስኮት
nave (f)	ship	መርከብ
orario	timetable	የግዜ መደብ
partire	to leave	መሔድ
passeggero	passenger	መንገደኛ ተሳፋሪ
prenotare	to book	መመዝገብ
pullman (m)	coach	አሰልጣኝ
sala d'aspetto	waiting room	እንግዳ መቀበያ
stazione (f)	station	የባቡር ጣብያ
tassì	taxi	ታክሲ
treno	train	ባቡር
ufficio informazioni	information office	የመረጃ ጽሕፈት ቤት
valigia	suitcase	ሻንጣ
viaggiatore (m)	traveller	መንገደኛ

Travel by Air/Sea

aereo	aeroplane	አውሮፕላን
assistente di volo (m/f)	steward, stewardess	ሆስተስ አስተናጋጅ
atterrare	to land	መድረስ፡ መውረድ
carta d'imbarco	boarding pass	የመሳፈርያ ወረቀት
cintura di sicurezza	safety belt	የአደጋ መከላከያ ቀበቶ
controllo	check	ቊጥጥር
crociera	cruise	ጉዞ
decollare	to take off	መነሳት
dogana	customs	ጉምሩክ
frontiera	frontier	ኬላ

'hostess'	air hostess	ሆስተስ
hovercraft (m)	hovercraft	ሆቨርክራፍት
imbarcare	to embark, board	መሳፈር
nave (f)	ship	መርከብ
passaporto	passport	ፓስፖርት
pilota	pilot	ፓይሎት
porto	port, harbour	ወደብ
sbarcare	to disembark	መውረድ
traghetto (nave ...)	ferry (boat)	መሸጋገርያ መርከብ
traversata	crossing	መተላለፍያ
uscita	exit, gate	መውጫ
volare	to fly	መብረር
volo	flight	በረራ

Private Transport

agente di polizia	policeman	ፖሊስ
assicurazione	insurance	መድህን
autista (m/f)	driver	ሹፌር
autostrada	motorway	የመኪና መንገድ
batteria	battery	ባትሪ
benzina	petrol	ነዳጅ
bicicletta	bicycle	ብሲክሌት
cambio	gear stick	ማርሽ
camion (m)	lorry	የጭነት መኪና
candela	spark plug	ካንዴላ
casco	helmet	ሀልመት
cintura di sicurezza	seat belt	የአደጋ መከላከያ ቀበቶ
copertone (m)	tyre	የመኪና ጐማ
dare la precedenza	to give way	ማሳለፍ
distributore (di ben.)	petrol pump	የነዳጅ ማደያ
forare	to have a puncture	ጐማው ፈነዳ
frenare	to brake	ፍሬን መያዝ
freno	brake	ፍሬን
frizione	clutch	ፍርስዮን
furgone (m)	van	የጭነት መኪና፡ ካሚዮን
gomma	tyre	የመኪና ጐማ
gonfiare	to inflate	መንፋት
guidare	to drive	መንዳት
incidente (m)	accident	አደጋ

incrocio	crossroads	መስቀለኛ መንገድ
ingorgo	traffic jam	የትራፊክ መጨናነቅ
lavaggio	washing; car wash	የመኪና ማጠብያ
lavori in corso	work in progress	በመሰራት ላይ ያለና ያላለቀ
limite di velocità	speed limit	የፍጥነት ገደብ
macchina	car	መኪና
moto (cicletta) (f)	motorcycle	ሞቶር ብሲክሊት
motore (m)	engine	ሞተር
multa	fine	መቀጮ
nafta	diesel	ዲዘል፡ ናፍታ
noleggiare	to hire	መከራየት
olio	oil	ዘይት
ore di punta	rush hours	የሩጫ ሰዓቶች
panne (in ...)	breakdown	መሰበር
parcheggiare	to park	ማቆም
patente (f)	driving licence	የመንጃ ፈቃድ
pezzi di ricambio	spare parts	የመኪና መለዋወጫ
pieno; (fare il ...)	full; (to fill it up)	ሙሉ (መሙላት)
pneumatico	tyre	ጐማ
pompa (di benzina)	petrol pump	ፓምፕ
posteggio	parking space	የመኪና ማቆምያ
pressione (f)	pressure	የአየር ግፊት
rallentare	to slow down	በዝግታ መንዳት
ruota	wheel	ቸርኪዮ
scontro	bump, collision	ግጭት
semaforo	traffic lights	የትራፊክ መብራት
senso (a ... unico)	one way	መግቢያ ብቻ
senza piombo (benzina)	unleaded (petrol)	ሊድ የሌለበት በንዚን
sorpassare	to overtake	ደርሶ ማለፍ
sosta	parking	የመኪና ማቆምያ
targa	number plate	የሰሌዳ ቁጥር
traffico	traffic	ትራፊክ
velocità	speed	ፍጥነት
volante (m)	steering wheel	መሪ

HOLIDAYS

abbronzarsi	to get a tan	ቆዳን በፀሐይ ማጥቆር
abbronzato	sun-tanned	በፀሐይ የጠቆረ
affittare	to rent, to hire	መከራየት
agenzia di viaggi	travel agency	የጉዞ ወኪል
bagnino	lifeguard	ነፍስ አዳኝ
barca	boat	ጀልባ
benvenuto	welcome	እንኳን በደህና መጡ
costume da bagno	bathing costume	የመዋኛ ልብስ
crema solare	suntan lotion	ፀሐይ መከላከያ ሎሽን
diapositiva	slide, transparency	ስላይድ
estero (all'...)	abroad	ውጭ አገር
ferie	holidays	በዓላት
foto (f)	photograph	ስዕል
giro	trip	ጉዞ
gita	excursion; school trip	የመዝናኛ ቦታ
guida	guide	መንገድ የሚያሳይ
in macchina	by car	በመኪና
lago	lake	ሀይቅ
macchina fotografica	camera	ካሜራ
mare (m)	sea	ባሕር
montagna	mountain	ተራራ
monumento	monument	ሐውልት
occhiali da sole	sun-glasses	የፀሐይ መነጽር
ombrellone (m)	beach umbrella	የባሕር ዳር ጃንጥላ
ospitalità	hospitality	እንግዳ ተቀባይነት
rullino/rollino	film (for camera)	ፊልም
sabbia	sand	አሸዋ
sciare	to ski	በረዶ ላይ መንሸራተት
sedia a sdraio	deck-chair	ወንበር
sole (m)	sun	ፀሐይ
spiaggia	beach	ባሕር ዳር
turismo	tourism	ቱሪዝም
turista (m/f)	tourist	ቱሪስት
vacanza	holiday	በዓል
visitare	to visit	መድረስ፡ መጎብኘት

TOURIST INFORMATION

(see also Hotel and Free Time)

albergo	hotel	ሆቴል
cartina geografica	(small) map	ትንሽ የዓለም ካርታ
cercare	to look for	መፈለግ
cinema (m)	cinema	ሲነማ ቤት
città	town, city	ከተማ
concerto	concert	ኮንሰርት
dépliant (m)	leaflet, brochure	ፓምፍሌት
giocare (a tennis ...)	to play (tennis...)	መጫወት (ቴንስ ...)
informare	to inform	ማሳወቅ
museo	museum	ቤተመዘክር
musica	music	ሙዚቃ
negozio	shop	ሱቅ ቤት
opera	opera	ኦፔራ
opuscolo	booklet,brochure	የኪስ መጽሐፍ
parco	park	መናፈሻ
pianta (della città)	map (of the town)	የከተማ ፕላን
regione (f)	region, area	ዞን
ristorante (m)	restaurant	ምግብ ቤት
spettacolo	show, performance	ምርኢት
sport (m)	sport	ስፖርት
teatro	theatre	ትያትር
ufficio informazioni	information office	የማስታወቅያ ጽሕፈት ቤት

HOTEL

albergo	hotel	ፔንስዮን
ascensore (m)	lift	ሊፍት
bagagli (m, pl.)	luggage	ሻንጣዎች
camera	room	የቤት ክፍል
... per una persona	single ...	ሲንግል
... matrimoniale	double ...	ለጥንድ
... a due letti	... with twin beds	ባለ ሁለት አልጋ
... a un letto	... with a single bed	ባለ አንድ አልጋ
... con (il) bagno	... with a bath	ከገላ መታጠብያ ጋር
... con (la) doccia	... with a shower	ከሻወር ጋር
chiave (f)	key	ቍልፍ
completo	full	በሙሉ
compreso, incluso	inclusive	የሚያጠቃልል
conto	bill, amount	ሂሳብ፡ ቢል፡ ብዛት
direttore (m)	manager	ሥራ አስኪያጅ
direzione (la ...)	management	አሰተዳደር
padrone (m)	owner	ባለቤት
pagare	to pay	መክፈል
passaporto	passport	ፓስፖርት
piano	floor, storey	ፎቅ
pianterreno	ground floor	ታችኛው ፎቅ
portare	to carry, to bring, to take	መሸከም፡ ማምጣት፡ መውሰድ
prenotare	to book	መመዝገብ፡ ክፍል መያዝ
ricevuta	receipt	ፋክቱር
riservare	to reserve	አስቀድሞ መያዝ
ristorante (m)	restaurant	ምግብ ቤት
scale	stairs	ደረጃ
telefono	telephone	ቴሌፎን
televisore (m)	television set	ቴለቪዥን
uscita di sicurezza	emergency exit	የአደጋ መውጭያ
valigia	suitcase	ሻንጣ
vista	view	ትርኢት
visto	visa	ቪዛ

FOOD AND DRINK

General

aceto	vinegar	ቆምጣጤ
acqua minerale	mineral water	አምቦ ውኃ
aranciata	orangeade	አረንቻታ
arrosto	roast	የተጠበሰ፡የተቆላ፡ጥብስ
bere	to drink	መጠጣት
bevanda	drink	መጠጥ
birra	beer	ቢራ
biscotto	biscuit	ብስኩት
brindare	to toast	ለጤናችን
buon appetito	enjoy your meal	መልካም ምግብ
burro	butter	ቅቤ
caffettiera	coffee pot/maker	ጀበና
caffè (m)	coffee	ቡና
caldo	hot	ትኩስ
cappuccino	cappuccino	ቡና በወተት (ካፑቺኖ)
caramelle	sweets	ከረሜላ
cena	dinner; supper	እራት
cibo	food	ምግብ
cincin!	cheers!	ለጤናችን
cioccolata	chocolate	ቸኮላታ
colazione (prima ...)	breakfast	ቍርስ
dolce, dessert (m)	sweet, dessert	ጣፋጭ፡ ፍራፍሬ
formaggio	cheese	ፎርማጆ
frittata	omelet	የተጠበሰ እንቍላል
gelato	ice cream	ጀላቲ
lasagne (f, pl.)	lasagna	ላዛኛ
latte (m)	milk	ወተት
limonata	lemonade	የሎሚ ጭማቂ
macedonia	fruit salad	ማቸዶንያ
minestra	soup	የአትክልት ሾርባ
mozzarella	'mozzarella'	ሞዛሬላ
olio di semi	vegetable oil	የአትክልት ዘይት
pane (m)	bread	ዳቦ
patate fritte	chips, French fries	ፍሬንች ፍራይስ
patatine	crisps, chips	የተጠበሰ ድንች
piccante	spicy, hot	ቅመም የበዛበት፡ የሚያቃጥል
pizza	pizza	ፒሳ

ravioli	ravioli	ራቪዮሊ
ricetta	recipe	የምግብ አሰራር ዘዴ
riso	rice	ሩዝ
sale (m)	salt	ጨው
salute (alla ...!)	cheers!	ለጤናችን
spremuta	fresh fruit juice	አዲስ የፍራፍሬ ጭማቂ
succo di frutta	fruit juice	የፍራፍሬ ጭማቂ
tè (m)	tea	ሻይ
torta	cake	ኬክ
uovo	egg	እንቁላል
vino (bianco, rosso)	wine (white, red)	የወይን ጠጅ፡ነጭ/ ቀይ
zucchero	sugar	ስኳር

Café, Restaurant and other Public Places

acqua	water	ውኃ
bar (m)	bar, café	ቡናቤት
bicchiere (m)	glass	ብርጭቆ
birra	beer	ቢራ
cameriere (m)	waiter	አስተናጋጅ፡አሳላፊ
conto	bill	ቢል
contorno	vegetables, side dish	ተጨማሪ አትክልት
espresso	espresso (coffee)	ኤስፕሬሶ
fiasco	flask	ብርለ
ghiaccio	ice	በረዶ
litro	litre	ሊትር
panino; (... imbottito)	roll (filled roll, sandwich)	ሳንድዊች
piatto (del giorno)	dish (of the day)	የቀኑ ምግብ
pizzeria	'pizzeria'	ፒሳ የሚሸጥበት
primo (piatto)	first (course)	ፕሪሞ
ristorante (m)	restaurant	ምግብ ቤት
secondo (piatto)	second (course)	ሴኮንዶ
spumante (m)	'sparkling wine'	ጋዝ ያለው ወይን ጠጅ
tovagliolo	napkin	ናፕኪን

Fruit and vegetables

aglio	garlic	ነጭ ሽንኩርት
albicocca	apricot	አፕሪኮት
ananas (m)	pineapple	አናናስ
anguria	water melon	ወተር ሜሎን
arancia	orange	ብርትኳን
banana	banana	ሙዝ
carciofo	artichoke	ካርችዮፊ
carota	carrot	ካሮት
cavolfiore (m)	cauliflower	የአበባ ጐመን
cavolo	cabbage	ጥቅል ጐመን
zucchino	courgette	ዝኩኒ
ciliegia	cherry	አዳም
cipolla	onion	ቀይ ሽንኩርት
fagioli	beans	ባቄላ
fagiolini	French beans	የፈረንሳይ ባቄላ
fragola	strawberry	እንጆሪ
frutta	fruit	ፍራፍሬ
fungo	mushroom	የጅብ ጥላ
insalata	salad, lettuce	ሰላጣ
lampone (m)	raspberry	ዓጋም
limone (m)	lemon	ሎሚ
mango	mango	ማንጎ
mela	apple	ፖም
melanzana	aubergine	መለንዛኒ
oliva	olive	ወይራ
papaia	papaw	ፓፓያ
patata	potato	ድንች
pepe (m)	pepper	ቃርያ
peperone	pepper (red ...)	የፈረንጅ ቃርያ
pera	pear	ፐረ
pesca	peach	ኮክ
piselli	peas	ዓተር
pomodoro	tomato	ቲማቲም
pompelmo	grapefruit	ኮምጣጤ
porro	leek	ሊክ
sedano	celery	ሰደኖ
uva (f, sing.)	grapes	ወይን/ፍሬወይን
verdura (f, sing.)	vegetables, greens	አትክልት

Meat and Fish

agnello	lamb	ጠቦት
aragosta	lobster	ሎብስተር
baccalà (m)	dried salted cod	የዓሳ ቋንጣ
bistecca, (...ai ferri)	steak, (grilled ...)	ቢስቴክ
bollito	boiled meat	የበሰለ ስጋ (በውኃ)
capretto	kid	ግልገል (ካፕሬቶ)
coniglio	rabbit	ጥንቸል
cozze	mussels	የባሕር ቀንድ አውጣ
frittura di pesce	mixed fried fish	ዓሣ በያይነቱ
frutti di mare	seafood	ከባሕር የሚገኝ ምግብ
gamberetti	shrimps/prawns	ሽሪምፕ
granchio	crab	ክራብ
maiale (m)	pork	ያሳማ ስጋ
manzo	beef	የከብት ስጋ
merluzzo	cod	ኮድ
montone (m)	mutton	የበግ ስጋ
mortadella	mortadella	ሞርታዴላ
ostrica	oyster	ኦይስተር
pesce (m)	fish	ዓሣ
pollo	chicken	ዶሮ
prosciutto	ham	ሀም
salame (m)	salami	ሳላመ
salmone (m)	salmon	ሳልሞን
sardina	sardine	ሰርዲን
scampi	scampi	ስካምፕ
sogliola	sole	ሶል
tacchino	turkey	ደንድ
tonno	tuna	ቱና
trota	trout	ትሮት
vitello	veal	የጥጃ ስጋ
vongola	clam	ክላም

SHOPPING

Shops

abbigliamento (n. di ...)	clothes shop	የልብስ ሱቅ
alimentari (negozio di ...)	grocer's (shop)	ግሮሰሪ
cartoleria	stationery (shop)	የጽሕፈት መሳሪያ ሱቅ
edicola	newspaper kiosk	የጋዜጣ መሸጫ ኪዮስክ
farmacia	pharmacy; chemist's	መድኃኒት ቤት
fioraio	florist	የአበባ ሱቅ
fruttivendolo	greengrocer's	አትክልትና ፍራፍሬ ሻጭ
gelateria	ice-cream (shop)	አይስ ክሬም ቤት
gioielleria	jeweller's (shop)	ብርና ወርቅ ሰሪ
giornalaio	newsagent	ጋዜጣ ሻጭ
grande magazzino	department store	ግምጃ ቤት
lavanderia	laundry	ላውንድሪ
libreria	bookshop	ቤተ መጻሕፍት
macelleria	butcher's (shop)	ልኳንዳ
mercato	market	ገበያ፡ ሱቅ
panetteria/fornaio	baker's (shop)	ዳቦ ቤት
parrucchiere (m)	hairdresser	የቍንጅና ሳሎን
pasticceria	confectioner's (shop)	ኬክ ቤት
pescheria	fishmonger's (shop)	የዓሣ ገበያ
profumeria	perfumer's shop	ሽቶ ቤት
salumeria	delicatessen (shop)	ግሮሰሪ
supermercato	supermarket	የገበያ አዳራሽ
tabaccheria	tobacconist's (shop)	ሲጋራ የሚሸጥበት ሱቅ

Clothes

calze	socks, stockings	የግር ሹራብ
camicia	shirt	ሸሚዝ
cappello	hat	ቆብ
cappotto	(over) coat	ካፖርት
cintura	belt	ቀበቶ
costume da bagno	bathing costume	የመዋኛ ልብስ
cravatta	tie	ክራቫታ
fazzoletto	handkerchief	መሐረብ
giacca	jacket	ጃኬት
gonna	skirt	ጉርድ ቀሚስ
impermeabile (m)	raincoat	የዝናም ልብስ
maglia	jersey	ሹራብ

pantaloni, (paio di)	trousers, (pair of)	ሱሪ
pigiama (m)	pyjamas	ፒጃማ
scarpa	shoe	ጫማ
stivale (m)	boot	ቦት
vestiti/abiti	clothes	ልብስ
vestito	suit, dress	ልብስ፡ቀሚስ

Materials

argento	silver	ብር
carta	paper	ወረቀት
cotone (m)	cotton	ጥጥ
ferro	iron	ብረት
lana	wool	ሱፍ
legno	wood	እንጨት
metallo	metal	ብረት፡ሜታል
nailon	nylon	ናይሎን
oro	gold	ወርቅ
pelle	leather	ቆዳ
plastica	plastic	ፕላስቲክ
seta	silk	ሀር
stoffa	cloth, material	ጨርቅ
velluto	velvet	ቨሉቶ፡ቬልቪት
vetro	glass	ጠርሙስ

Colours

arancione	orange	ብርቱኳን
bianco	white	ነጭ
celeste	light blue	ቀላ ያለ ሰማያዊ
chiaro	light	ቀላ ያለ
colore	colour	ቀለም
giallo	yellow	ቢጫ
grigio	grey	ግራጫ
marrone	brown	ቡና
nero	black	ጥቁር
rosa	pink	ሮዝ
rosso	red	ቀይ
verde	green	አረንጓዴ
viola	violet	ሃምራዊ

SERVICES

Post Office & Telephone

all'estero	abroad	ውጭ ሀገር
ascoltare	to listen	ማዳመጥ፡ መስማት
attimo	moment	ግዜ
bolletta	bill	ደረሰኝ
buca delle lettere	letter box, post box	የፖስታ ሣጥን
busta	envelope	ፖስታ
cabina (telefonica)	telephone box	ቴሌፎን መደወያ
cartolina (postale)	postcard	ፖስትካርድ
centralino	telephone exchange	የስልክ መለዋወጫ
centralinista (m/f)	operator	ኦፐሬተር
chi parla?	who is speaking?	ማን ልበል
destinatario	addressee	ተቀባይ
elenco telefonico	telephone directory	የቴሌፎን ማውጫ
fare il numero	to dial the number	መደወል
francobollo	stamp	ቴምብር
impostare/imbucare	to post	መላክ
indirizzo	address	አድራሻ
interno	extension	ኤክስተንሽን
lettera	letter	ደብዳቤ
libero	free	ነጻ
mittente (m/f)	sender	ላኪ
numero	number	ቍጥር
occupato	engaged	ተይዟል
pacchetto (postale)	(small) parcel	ጥቅል
Pagine Gialle	Yellow Pages	ማስታወቅያ
posta	mail	ደብዳቤዎች
postino/portalettere	postman	ፖስተኛ
prefisso	area code (telephone)	የዞን ኮድ
pronto!	hallo!	ሀሎ
richiamare	to call back	እንደገና መደወል
segreteria telefonica	answerphone	መልስ ሰጪ ቴሌፎን
spedire	to send	መላክ
suonare	to ring	መደወል
telefonare	to telephone	መደወል
telefono	telephone	ቴሌፎን
ufficio postale	post office	ፖስታ ቤት

Bank or Exchange Office

agenzia di cambio	exchange bureau	የውጭ ምንዛሪ ጽሕፈት ቤት
assegno (bancario)	cheque	ቼክ
banca	bank	ባንክ
banconota	banknote	የባንክ ኖት
Birr	Birr	ብር
cambiare	to change	መመንዘር፡ መቀየር
cambio	exchange	ምንዛሪ
carta assegni	cheque card	ቼክ ካርድ
carta di credito	credit card	የብድር ቼክ
cassa	cash desk, till	ገንዘብ የሚከፈልበት
commissione (f)	commission	ኮሚሽን
conto corrente	current account	ተንቀሳቃሽ ሒሳብ
denaro	money	ገንዘብ
firmare	to sign	መፈረም
interesse (m)	interest	ወለድ
istituto di credito	bank	ባንክ
libretto di assegni	cheque book	የቼክ ሊብሬቶ
Lira	Lira	ሊረ
Nakfa	Nakfa	ብር
modulo	form	ቅርጽ
moneta	coin	ሳንቲም
passaporto	passport	ፓስፖርት
per cento	per cent	መቶኛ
prestito	loan	ብድር
ritirare	to withdraw	ገንዘብ ማውጣት
saldo	balance	ሚዛን
soldi (m, pl.)	money	ገንዘብ
spiccioli (m, pl.)	small change	ዝርዝር
Sterlina	Pound (sterling)	ፓውንድ
travellers' cheque	travellers' cheque	የመንገደኛ ቼክ
ufficio di cambio	bureau de change	የምንዛሪ ጽሕፈት ቤት
valore	value	ዋጋ
valuta	currency	ገንዘብ

HEALTH

General

aiuto	help	እርዳታ
aver mal di denti	to have a tooth ache	የጥርስ ሕመም
... gola	... sore throat	የጉረሮ ሕመም
... schiena	... back ache	የወገብ ሕመም
... stomaco	... stomach ache	የሆድ ሕመም
... testa	... head ache	የራስ ምታት
ammalarsi	to fall ill	የታመመ
ammalato	ill	የታመመ
bocca	mouth	አፍ
braccio	arm	ክንድ
caldo	hot, warm	ትኩስ፡ሙቅ
caviglia	ankle	ቍርጭምጭሚት
cuore (m)	heart	ልብ
dito	finger	ጣት
fegato	liver	ጉበት
freddo	cold	ቀዝቃዛ
gamba	leg	እግር
ginocchio	knee	ጉልበት
lingua	tongue	ምላስ
malato	ill	የታመመ
mano (f)	hand	እጅ
occhio	eye	ዓይን
orecchio	ear	ጆሮ
osso	bone	አጥንት
pelle (f)	skin	ቆርበት፡ ቆዳ
pericoloso	dangerous	አደገኛ
piede (m)	foot	እግር
salute (f)	health	ጤና
sangue (m)	blood	ደም
spalla	shoulder	ትከሻ
stare meglio	to feel/be better	መሻል
va bene	it is all right, fine	ችግር የለም

Illness and injury

annegare	to drown	መስመጥ
aspirina	aspirin	አስፐሪን
attacco	fit, stroke, attack	ሽባ የሚያደርግ በሽታ
benda	bandage	ፋሻ
bruciarsi la mano	to burn one's hand	እጅን ማቃጠል
cancro	cancer	ነቀርሳ
cerotto (adesivo)	(sticking) plaster	ፕላስተር
colpo di sole	sunstroke	የፀሐይ ምች
cotone idrofilo	cotton-wool	የጥጥ ሱፍ
dentista (m/f)	dentist	የጥርስ ሐኪም
diarrea	diarrhoea	ተቅማጥ
dolore (m)	pain	ሕመም፡ስቃይ
farmacia	chemist's (shop)	መድኃኒት ቤት
febbre (f)	fever, high temp.	ትኩሳት
febbre da fieno	hay fever	ጉንፋን
ferito	wounded	ቍስለኛ
guarire	to recover	መዳን
indigestione (f)	indigestion	የአለመፈጨት ችግር
influenza	infuenza	ኢንፍሉወንዛ
ingessare	to put in plaster	ፕላስተር ማድረግ
malattia	illness	በሽታ
mal di mare	sea-sickness	የጉዞ በሽታ (የሚያቅለሸልሽ)
medico	doctor	ሐኪም
medicina	medicine	መድኃኒት
mordere	to bite	መንከስ
ospedale (m)	hospital	ሆስፒታል
otturazione (f)	filling	መሙላት
pastiglia	tablet	ኪኒን
pomata	ointment, cream	መድኃኒትነት ያለው ቅባት
pronto soccorso	first aid	የመጀመርያ እርዳታ
puntura	injection	መርፌ መውጋት
raffreddato (essere...)	to have a cold	ጉንፋን መያዝ
ricetta	prescription	የሐኪም ትእዛዝ፡የመድኃኒት ማዘዣ
salute (f)	health	ጤና
sanguinare	to bleed	መድማት
sciroppo	syrup, mixture	ሲሩፕ፡ ሽሮፖ
tagliarsi	to cut	መቍረጥ
tosse (f)	cough	ሳል
vomitare	to vomit	ማስመለስ፡ ማስታወክ

Accident

(moto) ciclista	(motor) cyclist	ባለ ቢሲክለት
aiutare	to help	መርዳት
all'improvviso	suddenly	ድንገት
ambulanza	ambulance	አምቡላንስ
attenzione!	Look out!, Caution!	ልብ አድርግ፡ ተጠንቀቅ
attraversare	to cross	መሻገር
autobus (m)	bus	አውቶቡስ
autocarro	lorry	የጭነት መኪና
bruciare	to burn	መቃጠል
cadere	to fall	መውደቅ
collisione (f)	collision	ግጭት
colpa	fault	ስህተት
consolato	consulate	ቆንስል
correre	to run, to speed	መሮጥ፡ በፍጥነት
corriera	coach	አውቶቡስ
danno	damage	ጉዳት
fare attenzione	to be careful	መጠንቀቅ
ferito	wounded	የተጐዳ ፡ቊስለኛ
fuoco, (al ...!)	fire, (fire!)	እሳት
grave	serious	ኰስታራ፡ጥብቅ፡ አሳሳቢ
improvvisamente	suddenly	ድንገት
incidente (m)	accident	አደጋ
investire	to collide with, to run over	መጋጨት፡መዳጥ
macchina	car	መኪና
marciapiede (m)	pavement	የእግረኛ መንገድ
morto	dead	የሞተ
passante (m/f)	passer-by	መንገደኛ
pedone (m)	pedestrian	እግረኛ
pericolo	danger	አደጋ
polizia	police	ፖሊስ
presto!	quick!	ቶሎ
scontro	collision, crash	የመኪና ግጭት
senso unico	one way	መግቢያ ብቻ
sorpassare	to overtake	ማለፍ
targa	number plate	የሰሌዳ ቊጥር
testimone (m/f)	witness	ምስክር
urto	collision, impact	ግጭት
vigili del fuoco	firemen	የእሳት አደጋ ሰራተኞች

FREE TIME AND ENTERTAINMENT

andare a cavallo	to ride	መጋለብ
... in bicicletta	to cycle	በቢሲክሌት መንሸራሸር
... al mare	to go to the seaside	ወደ ባሕሩ ዳር መሔድ
... in campagna	... the countryside	ወደ ገጠር መሔድ
... in montagna	... the mountains	ተራራ ላይ መውጣት
atletica	athletics	አትሌቲክስ
attore (m)	actor	ተዋናይ
ballare	to dance	መደነስ፡ መጨፈር
biblioteca	library	ቤተመጻሕፍት
calcio	football	እግር ኳስ
camminare	to walk	በእግር መንሸራሸር
cantare	to sing	መዝፈን
chitarra	guitar	ጊታር
ciclismo	cycling	ቢሲክለት መንዳት
cinema (m)	cinema	ሲነማ
collezionare	to collect	ገንዘብ መሰብሰብ፡ ማጠራቀም
computer (m)	computer	ኮምፕዩተር
concerto	concert	ኮንሰርት
dama	draughts	ዳማ
discoteca	discotheque	ዲስኮተክ
fotografia	photography	ስዕል
giocare a pallone	to play football	እግር ኳስ መጫወት
leggere	to read	ማንበብ
museo	museum	ቤተ መዘክር
musica classica	classical music	ክላሲካል ሙዚቃ
nuotare	to swim	መዋኘት
opera	opera	ኦፐራ
pallanuoto	water-polo	የውኃ ኳስ
pallacanestro	basket-ball	የቅርጫት ኳስ
pescare	to fish	ዓሣ ማጥመድ
pianoforte (m)	piano	ፒያኖ
piscina	swimming pool	መዋኛ
rivista	magazine	መጽሔት
scacchi	chess	ቸስ
sciare	to ski	በበረዶ ላይ መንሸራተት
teatro	theatre	ትያትር
televisione (f)	television	ቴለቪዥን
tennis (m)	tennis	ቴኒስ

EDUCATION

General

alunno	pupil	ተማሪ
aula	classroom	ክፍል
banco	desk	ጠረጴዛ
biblioteca	library	ቤተመጻሕፍት
bocciare	to fail	መውደቅ፡ መቅረት
borsa di studio	grant, scholarship	ማኅደረ ትምህርት
cattedra	teacher's desk	መንበረ መምህር
certificato	certificate	የምስክር ወረቀት
classe (f)	class	ክፍል
compito	homework	የቤት ሥራ
correggere	to correct, to mark	ማረም
esame (m)	exam	ፈተና
frequentare	to attend	መሳተፍ፡ መከታተል
gesso	chalk	ጠመኔ
gomma	rubber	ላጲስ
imparare	to learn	መማር
insegnare	to teach	ማስተማር
intervallo	break	ዕረፍት
iscrizione (f)	enrolment	ምዝገባ
laurea	degree	ዲግሪ
lavagna	blackboard	ጥቁር ሰሌዳ
lezione (f)	lesson	ትምህርት
libro	book	መጽሐፍ
maestro	(primary) teacher	አስተማሪ
orario	timetable	የግዜ ሰሌዳ
preside (m/f)	headmaster/mistress	ርእሰ መምህር
professore (m)	teacher, professor	አስተማሪ
professoressa	teacher, professor	አስተማሪ
promuovere	to pass	ማለፍ
quaderno	exercise book	ደብተር
sbaglio	mistake	ስህተት
scrivere	to write	መጻፍ
studente (m)	student	ተማሪ
studentessa (f)	student	ተማሪ
studiare	to study	ማጥናት
uniforme	uniform	ዩኒፎርም
università	university	ዩኒቨርሲቲ

Subjects

amarico	Amharic	አማርኛ
arabo	Arabic	ዓረብኛ
biologia	biology	ባዮሎጂ
ceramica	pottery	የሸክላ ሥራ
chimica	chemistry	ኬሚስትሪ
dattilografia	typing	የመኪና ጽሕፈት
economia	economics	ኤኮኖሚ
educazione artistica	art	ስነ ጥበብ
educazione fisica	physical education	የሰውነት ማጎልመሻ
educazione musicale	music	ሙዚቃ
elettronica	electronics	ኤሌክትሮኒክስ
fisica	physics	ፊዚክስ
francese (m)	French	ፈረንሳይኛ
geografia	geography	ሕብረት-ትምህርት
greco	Greek	የግሪክ ቋንቋ
informatica	computer science	ኮምፕዩተር
inglese (m)	English	እንግሊዝኛ
italiano	Italian	ጣልያንኛ
latino	Latin	ላቲን
letteratura	literature	ስነ ጽሑፍ
lingue moderne	modern languages	ዘመናዊ ቋንቋ
matematica	maths	ሂሳብ
morale (f)	ethics	ሞራል/ግብረ ገብ
musica	music	ሙዚቃ
ragioneria	accounting	የሒሳብ አያያዝ
religione (f)	religious education	የሀይማኖት ትምህርት
scienze (f, pl.)	science	ሳይንስ
scienze naturali	natural sciences	የተፈጥሮ ሳይንስ
scienze umane	human sciences	የሰው ልጅ ሳይንስ
sociologia	sociology	የኅብረተሰብ ጥናት
spagnolo	Spanish	የስፓኝ ቋንቋ
stenografia	shorthand	ሾርት ሀንድ
storia dell'arte	history of art	የስነ ጥበብ ታሪክ
storia	history	ታሪክ
teatro	drama	ድራማ
tedesco	German	ጀርመን
tigrino	Tigrinya	ትግርኛ

How To Say It

IN
AMHARIC

PHONETIC TRANSCRIPTION

CONTENTS

Key to Phonetic Symbols

Vowels:

e	as in pet
é	It has a closed pronunciation, approximately like that of the "vowel" **a** in d**a**y (similar to the French **é** in **été**)
u	as in p**u**t
i	as in p**i**t
a	as in c**a**t
ï	as in French p**eu** (but very short, **almost silent**)
o	as in p**o**t

Consonants:

ch	as in **ch**air
ch (underlined)	as **c** explosive
g	as in **g**ame
h	as in **h**ave
j	as in vi**s**ion or French **j**oli
dj	as **in j**ob
ñ	as in o**ni**on
k	as in **c**at
q	as **k** explosive
r	slightly rolled (like the Scottish r)
s	as in **s**un
sh	as in **sh**ip
t (underlined)	**t** explosive (not to be confused with double t)
w	as in **w**et
y	as in **y**es
z	as in **z**ero
ts	as in pi**ts** (z explosive)
'	glottal stop (not to be confused with the apostrophe)

• When a double consonant is used, the pronunciation must be reinforced.

AMHARIC ALPHABET

1° Gï‘ïz	2° Ka‘ïb	3° Salïs	4° Rabï‘	5° Hamïs	6° Sadïs	7° Sabï‘
ሀ ha	ሁ hu	ሂ hi	ሃ ha	ሄ hé	ህ h(ï)	ሆ ho
ለ le	ሉ lu	ሊ li	ላ la	ሌ lé	ል l(ï)	ሎ lo
ሐ ha	ሑ hu	ሒ hi	ሓ ha	ሔ hé	ሕ h(ï)	ሖ ho
መ me	ሙ mu	ሚ mi	ማ ma	ሜ mé	ም m(ï)	ሞ mo
ሠ se	ሡ su	ሢ si	ሣ sa	ሤ sé	ሥ s(ï)	ሦ so
ረ re	ሩ ru	ሪ ri	ራ ra	ሬ ré	ር r(ï)	ሮ ro
ሰ se	ሱ su	ሲ si	ሳ sa	ሴ sé	ስ s(ï)	ሶ so
ሸ she	ሹ shu	ሺ shi	ሻ sha	ሼ shé	ሽ sh(ï)	ሾ sho
ቀ qe	ቁ qu	ቂ qi	ቃ qa	ቄ qé	ቅ q(ï)	ቆ qo
በ be	ቡ bu	ቢ bi	ባ ba	ቤ bé	ብ b(ï)	ቦ bo
ተ te	ቱ tu	ቲ ti	ታ ta	ቴ té	ት t(ï)	ቶ to
ቸ che	ቹ chu	ቺ chi	ቻ cha	ቼ ché	ች ch(ï)	ቾ cho
ኀ ha	ኁ hu	ኂ hi	ኃ ha	ኄ hé	ኅ h(ï)	ኆ ho
ነ ne	ኑ nu	ኒ ni	ና na	ኔ né	ን n(ï)	ኖ no
ኘ ñe	ኙ ñu	ኚ ñi	ኛ ña	ኜ ñé	ኝ ñ(ï)	ኞ ño
አ (‘)a	ኡ (‘)u	ኢ (‘)i	ኣ (‘)a	ኤ (‘)é	እ (‘)(ï)	ኦ (‘)o
ከ ke	ኩ ku	ኪ ki	ካ ka	ኬ ké	ክ k(ï)	ኮ ko
ኸ he	ኹ hu	ኺ hi	ኻ ha	ኼ hé	ኽ h(ï)	ኾ ho
ወ we	ዉ wu	ዊ wi	ዋ wa	ዌ wé	ው w(ï)	ዎ wo
ዐ ‘a	ዑ ‘u	ዒ ‘i	ዓ ‘a	ዔ ‘é	ዕ (‘)(ï)	ዖ ‘o
ዘ ze	ዙ zu	ዚ zi	ዛ za	ዜ zé	ዝ z(ï)	ዞ zo
ዠ je	ዡ ju	ዢ ji	ዣ ja	ዤ jé	ዥ j(ï)	ዦ jo
የ ye	ዩ yu	ዪ yi	ያ ya	ዬ yé	ይ y(ï)	ዮ yo
ደ de	ዱ du	ዲ di	ዳ da	ዴ dé	ድ d(ï)	ዶ do
ጀ dje	ጁ dju	ጂ dji	ጃ dja	ጄ djé	ጅ dj(ï)	ጆ djo
ገ ge	ጉ gu	ጊ gi	ጋ ga	ጌ gé	ግ g(ï)	ጎ go
ጠ <u>t</u>e	ጡ <u>t</u>u	ጢ <u>t</u>i	ጣ <u>t</u>a	ጤ <u>t</u>é	ጥ <u>t</u>(ï)	ጦ <u>t</u>o
ጨ <u>ch</u>e	ጩ <u>ch</u>u	ጪ <u>ch</u>i	ጫ <u>ch</u>a	ጬ <u>ch</u>é	ጭ <u>ch</u>(ï)	ጮ <u>ch</u>o
ጰ <u>p</u>e	ጱ <u>p</u>u	ጲ <u>p</u>i	ጳ <u>p</u>a	ጴ <u>p</u>é	ጵ <u>p</u>(ï)	ጶ <u>p</u>o
ጸ tse	ጹ tsu	ጺ tsi	ጻ tsa	ጼ tsé	ጽ ts(ï)	ጾ tso
ፀ tse	ፁ tsu	ፂ tsi	ፃ tsa	ፄ tsé	ፅ ts(ï)	ፆ tso
ፈ fe	ፉ fu	ፊ fi	ፋ fa	ፌ fé	ፍ f(ï)	ፎ fo
ፐ pe	ፑ pu	ፒ pi	ፓ pa	ፔ pé	ፕ p(ï)	ፖ po
ቨ ve	ቩ vu	ቪ vi	ቫ va	ቬ vé	ቭ v(ï)	ቮ vo
ኈ hwe		ኊ hwi	ኋ hwa	ኌ hwé	ኍ hw(ï)	
ኰ kwe		ኲ kwi	ኳ kwa	ኴ kwé	ኵ kw(ï)	
ቈ qwe		ቊ qwi	ቋ qwa	ቌ qwé	ቍ qw(ï)	
ጐ gwe		ጒ gwi	ጓ gwa	ጔ gwé	ጕ gw(ï)	

- Letters and symbols in parenthesis are used only if necessary.
- Nowadays, the letter ጰ (ጱ:ጲ:ጳ:ጴ:ጵ:ጶ) is often replaced by: ፀ (ፁ:ፂ:ፃ:ፄ:ፅ:ፆ).

Personal Identification

Name

What's [What is] your name?	• **Sïmïh man new?**	ስምህ ማን ነው? (m)
(My name is) Charles.	• **Sïmé Charles new.**	ስሜ ቻርለስ ነው
What's your name?	• **Sïmïsh man new?**	ስምሽ ማን ነው? (f)
(My name is) Mary.	• **Sïmé Mïryam new.**	ስሜ ሚርያም ነው

Address

What's your address?	• **Adrashah yet new?**	አድራሻህ የት ነው? (m)
	• **Adrashash yet new?**	አድራሻሽ የት ነው? (f)
(My address is) 5, Market Street.	• **Gebeya godena qwïtr ammïst new.**	ገበያ ጎደና ቍ. 5 ነው

Telephone number

What's your telephone number?	• **Yesïlk qwïtrïh sïnt new?**	የስልክ ቍጥርህ ስንት ነው? (m)
	• **Yesïlk qwïtrïsh sïnt new?**	የስልክ ቍጥርሽ ስንት ነው? (f)
(My telephone number is) 340 1256.	• **Yesïlk qwïtré 340 1256 new.**	የስልክ ቍጥሬ 340 1256 ነው

Age

How old are you?	• **Ïdméh sïnt new?**	ዕድሜህ ስንት ነው? (m)
	• **Ïdmésh sïnt new?**	ዕድሜሽ ስንት ነው? (f)
I'm fourteen.	• **Ïdméyé asr'arat new.**	ዕድሜዬ 14 ነው
I'm fifteen.	• **Ïdméyé asr'ammïst new.**	ዕድሜዬ 15 ነው
I'm sixteen.	• **Ïdméyé asra sïddïst new.**	ዕድሜዬ 16 ነው
When were you born?	• **Meché teweledkï?**	መቼ ተወለድክ? (m)
	• **Meché teweledsh?**	መቼ ተወለድሽ? (f)
(I was born) on the 2nd of January 1974.	• **Tïr 2, 1974.**	ጥር 2/1974
When is your birthday?	• **Yeteweledkïbet ïlet meché new?**	የተወለድክበት ዕለት መቼ ነው? (m)
	• **Yeteweledshïbet ïlet meché new?**	የተወለድሽበት ዕለት መቼ ነው? (f)
The 3rd of February.	• **Yekatit sost.**	የካቲት 3
The 4th of March.	• **Megabit arat.**	መጋቢት 4

Nationality

What nationality are you?	• **Zégïnetïh mïnd new?**	ዜግነትህ ምንድ ነው? (m)
	• **Zégïnetïsh mïnd new?**	ዜግነትሽ ምንድ ነው? (f)
I'm English.	• **Ïnglizawi/t neñ.**	እንግሊዛዊ/ት ነኝ
I'm Italian.	• **Italyawi/t neñ.**	ኢጣልያዊ/ት ነኝ
I'm American.	• **Amerikawi/t neñ.**	አመሪካዊ/ት ነኝ
I'm Ethiopian.	• **Ityopyawi/t neñ.**	ኢትዮጵያዊ/ት ነኝ
Are you Italian?	• **Italyawi neh?**	ኢጣልያዊ ነህ? (m)
	• **Italyawit nesh?**	ኢጣልያዊት ነሽ? (f)

• **Abbreviations used:** m. masculine; f. feminine; s. singular; p. plural.
• In colloquial Amharic ወይ (wey) is sometimes ometted.

Is he/she English?	• Ïnglizawi new?	እንግሊዛዊ ነው? (m)
	• Ïnglizawit nat?	እንግሊዛዊት ናት? (f)
Are you Italian?	• Italyawyan nachuh?	ኢጣልያውያን ናችሁ?
Are they English?	• Ïnglizawyan nachew?	እንግሊዛውያን ናቸው?
No, I'm Spanish.	• Aydelehum, Ïspañawi/t neñ.	አይደለሁም፡ እስፓኛዊ/ት ነኝ
No, he/she is American.	• Aydellem/aydelechm, Amerikawi/t new/nat.	አይደለም/አይደለችም፡ አመሪካዊ/ት ነው/ናት
No, we are Spanish.	• Aydellenm, Ïspañawyan neñ.	አይደለንም፡ እስፓኛውያን ነን
No, they are American.	• Aydellum, Amerikawyan nachew.	አይደሉም፡ አመሪካውያን ናቸው
Where were you born?	• Yet new yeteweledkew?	የት ነው የተወለድከው? (m)
	• Yet new yeteweledshïw?	የት ነው የተወለድሽው? (f)
(I was born) in Gondar.	• Gonder new yeteweledkut.	ጎንደር ነው የተወለድኩት
(I was born) in Addis Ababa.	• Addis Abeba new yeteweledkut.	አዲስ አበባ ነው የተወለድኩት
(I was born) in Italy.	• Talyan ager new yeteweledkut.	ጣልያን አገር ነው የተወለድኩት
(I was born) in England.	• Ïngliz ager new yeteweledkut.	እንግሊዝ አገር ነው የተወለድኩት
Where are you from?	• Keyet new yemetahaw?	ከየት ነው የመጣሃው? (m)
	• Keyet new yemetashïw?	ከየት ነው የመጣሽው? (f)
I'm from England.	• Ke Ïngliz ager.	ከእንግሊዝ አገር
I'm from Italy.	• Ke Talyan ager.	ከጣልያን አገር
I'm from the United States.	• Ke Tebaberut ye Amerika Mengïstat.	ከተባበሩት የአመሪካ መንግስታት
I'm from Ethiopia.	• Ke Ityopya.	ከኢትዮጵያ

Likes and dislikes

Do you like Italian?	• Talyaniña tïweddalleh wey?	ጣልያንኛ ትወዳለህ ወይ? (m)
	• Talyaniña tïwedjïyallesh wey?	ጣልያንኛ ትወጂያለሽ ወይ? (f)
Do you like this book?	• Yïchi mezhaf des tlïhallech wey?	ይቺ መጽሓፍ ደስ ትልሃለች ወይ? (m)
	• Yïchi mezhaf des tlïshallech wey?	ይቺ መጽሓፍ ደስ ትልሻለች ወይ? (f)
Do you like this pen?	• Yïchi ïskripto des tlïhallech wey?	ይቺ እስክሪፕቶ ደስ ትልሃለች ወይ? (m)
	• Yïchi ïskripto des tlïshallech wey?	ይቺ እስክሪፕቶ ደስ ትልሻለች ወይ? (f)
Do you like these books?	• Ïneñih mezahïft des yluhal wey?	እነኚህ መጻሕፍት ደስ ይሉሃል ወይ? (m)
	• Ïneñih mezahïft des ylushal wey?	እነኚህ መጻሕፍት ደስ ይሉሻል ወይ? (f)
Do you like these pens?	• Ïneñih ïskriptowoch des yluhal wey?	እነኚህ እስክሪፕቶዎች ደስ ይሉሃል ወይ? (m)
	• Ïneñih ïskriptowoch des ylushal wey?	እነኚህ እስክሪፕቶዎች ደስ ይሉሻል ወይ? (f)
Yes, I do [I like it].	• Awo, ïweddallehuñ/des tleñallech.	አዎ፡ እወዳለሁኝ/ደስ ትለኛለች
Yes, I do [I like them].	• Awo, des yïluñal.	አዎ፡ ደስ ይሉኛል
No, I prefer these (pens).	• Ayluñïm, ïneñihn ïskriptoch ïmertellehu.	አይሉኝም፡ እነኚህን እስክሪፕቶች እመርጣለሁ

Numbers

0 zero	• 0 zéro	0 ዜሮ
1 one	• 1 and	1 አንድ
2 two	• 2 hulet	2 ሁለት
3 three	• 3 sost	3 ሦስት
4 four	• 4 arat	4 አራት
5 five	• 5 ammïst	5 አምስት
6 six	• 6 sïddïst	6 ስድስት
7 seven	• 7 sebat	7 ሰባት
8 eight	• 8 sïmmïnt	8 ስምንት
9 nine	• 9 zeṯeñ	9 ዘጠኝ
10 ten	• 10 asïr	10 አስር
11 eleven	• 11 asr'and	11 አስራ አንድ
12 twelve	• 12 asra hulet	12 አስራ ሁለት
13 thirteen	• 13 asra sost	13 አስራ ሦስት
14 fourteen	• 14 asr'arat	14 አስራ አራት
15 fifteen	• 15 asr'ammïst	15 አስራ አምስት
16 sixteen	• 16 asra sïddïst	16 አስራ ስድስት
17 seventeen	• 17 asra sebat	17 አስራ ሰባት
18 eighteen	• 18 asra sïmmïnt	18 አስራ ስምንት
19 nineteen	• 19 asra zeṯeñ	19 አስራ ዘጠኝ
20 twenty	• 20 haya	20 ሀያ
21 twenty-one	• 21 haya and	21 ሀያ አንድ
22 twenty-two	• 22 haya hulet	22 ሀያ ሁለት
23 twenty-three	• 23 haya sost	23 ሀያ ሦስት
24 twenty-four	• 24 haya arat	24 ሀያ አራት
25 twenty-five	• 25 haya ammïst	25 ሀያ አምስት
26 twenty-six	• 26 haya sïddïst	26 ሀያ ስድስት
27 twenty-seven	• 27 haya sebat	27 ሀያ ሰባት
28 twenty-eight	• 28 haya sïmmïnt	28 ሀያ ስምንት
29 twenty-nine	• 29 haya zeṯeñ	29 ሀያ ዘጥኝ
30 thirty	• 30 selasa	30 ሰላሳ
40 forty	• 40 arba	40 አርባ
50 fifty	• 50 hamsa (amsa)	50 ሃምሳ (አምሳ)
60 sixty	• 60 sïlsa	60 ስልሳ
70 seventy	• 70 seba	70 ሰባ
80 eighty	• 80 semanya	80 ሰማንያ
90 ninety	• 90 zeṯena	90 ዘጠና
100 a/one hundred	• 100 meto	100 መቶ
200 two hundred	• 200 hulet meto	200 ሁለት መቶ
1,000 a/one thousand	• 1,000 (and) shi	1,000 (አንድ) ሺ
1,000,000 a/one million	• 1,000,000 (and) milyon	1,000,000 (አንድ) ሚልዮን

Key phrases

Do you speak English?	• Ïnglizeña tnageralleh wey?	እንግሊዝኛ ትናገራለህ ወይ?
Not very well.	• Ïskezihm aydellem.	እስከዚህም አይደለም
Can you repeat?	• Ïbakwon ydgemulïñ?	እባክዎን ይድገሙልኝ
I don't understand.	• Algebañm.	አልገባኝም
How do you say ...?	• Mïn ybalal?	ምን ይባላል?
How do you write ...?	• Ïndét yïtsafal?	እንዴት ይጻፋል?
What does ... mean?	• Mïn mallet new?	ምን ማለት ነው?
Excuse me!	• Yqïrta adrïglïñ!	ይቅርታ አድርግልኝ
I'm sorry.	• Aznallehu.	አዝናለሁ
Please.	• Ïbakïhn/shïn.	እባክህን/ሽን
Thank you.	• Amesegnallehu.	አመሰግናለሁ
You're welcome	• Mïnïm aydellem.	ምንም አይደል
How are you?	• Ïndemn neh/nesh?	እንደምን ነህ/ነሽ?
Not bad.	• Dehna	ደህና
Very well, thank you. And you?	• Melkam, ïrswos?	መልካም፡ እርስዎስ?

Not too good ...	• **Bzu altemecheñïm?**	ብዙ አልተመቸኝም
Good morning.	• **Ïndemn adderu?**	እንደምን አደሩ
Good evening.	• **Ïndemn ameshu?**	እንደምን አመሹ
Good night.	• **Melkam lélit.**	መልካም ሌሊት
Good-bye	• **Dehna hunu.**	ደህና ሁኑ
Hello/Bye/See you!	• **Ṯéna ystïlïñ/dehna hunu/ bedehna yagenañen!**	ጤና ይስጥልኝ፡ ደህና ሁኑ፡ በደህና ያገናኘን
See you tomorrow.	• **Nege ïngenañ.**	ነገ እንገናኝ
This is Mary.	• **Yïchi Miryam nat.**	ይቺ ሚርያም ናት
May I introduce Mr. Keith Willis?	• **Ke'ato Keith Willis gar lastewawqïh wey?**	ከአቶ ከይዝ ዊልስ ጋር ላስተዋውቅህ ወይ?
How do you do?	• **Ïndemn newot?**	እንደምን ነዎት?
Pleased to meet you.	• **Melkam twïwïq yadrgïln.**	መልካም ትውውቅ ያድርግልን

Family

How many are you in your family?	• **Yebéte-sebachuh abalat sïnt nachew?**	የቤተ ሰባችሁ ኣባላት ስንት ናቸው?
Are there many of you in your family?	• **Bebéte-sebachuh sïnt nachïh?**	በቤተ ሰባችሁ ስንት ናችሁ?
There are four of us.	• **Arat nen.**	አራት ነን
What's your father's name?	• **Ye'abbatïh/sh sïm man ybalal?**	የአባትህ/ሽ ስም ማን ይባላል? (m/f)
What is your grandfather's name?	• **Ye'ayatïh/sh sïm man ybalal?**	የአያትህ/ሽ ስም ማን ይባላል?
What is your brother's name?	• **Ye'wendïmh/sh sïm man ybalal?**	የወንድምህ/ሽ ስም ማን ይባላል?
What is your uncle's name?	• **Ye'aggotïh/sh sïm man ybalal?**	የአጎትህ/ሽ ስም ማን ይባላል?
What is your cousin's name?	• **Yaggotïh/sh lïdj man ybalal?**	ያጎትህ/ሽ ልጅ ማን ይባላል?
	- **Ye'akstïh lïdj man ybalal?**	የአክስትህ ልጅ ማን ይባላል?
What is your son's name?	• **Yelïdjïh/sh sïm man ybalal?**	የልጅህ/ሽ ስም ማን ይባላል?
What is your husband's name?	• **Yeballebétïsh sïm man ybalal?**	የባለቤትሽ ስም ማን ይባላል?
What is your brother-in-law's name?	• **Yeïhïtïh/sh bal man ybalal?**	የእህትህ/ሽ ባል ማን ይባላል?
What is your nephew's name?	• **Yeïhïtïh/sh lïdj man ybalal?**	የእህትህ/ሽ ልጅ ማን ይባላል?
	• **Yewendïmh/sh lïdj man ybalal?**	የወንድምህ/ሽ ልጅ ማን ይባላል?
What is your father-in-law called?	• **Ye'amachïh/sh sïm man ybalal?**	የአማችህ/ሽ ስም ማን ይባላል?
(His name is) Charles.	• **Charles ybalal?**	ቻርለስ ይባላል
What's your mother's name?	• **Ïnnatïh/sh man ybalallu?**	እናትህ/ሽ ማን ይባላሉ?
What is your grandmother's name?	• **Ayatïh/sh man ybalallu?**	አያትህ/ሽ ማን ይባላሉ?
What is your sister's name?	• **Ïhïtïh/sh man ybalallu?**	እህትህ/ሽ ማን ትባላለች?
What is your aunt's name?	• **Akstïh/sh man ybalallu?**	አክስትህ/ሽ ማን ይባላሉ?
What is your cousin's name?	• **Yewendïmh/sh lïdj man ybalal?**	የወንድምህ/ሽ ልጅ ማን ይባላል?
	- **Yeïhïtïh/sh lïdj man ybalal?**	-የእህትህ/ሽ ልጅ ማን ይባላል?

What's your daughter's name?	• Lïdjïh/sh man tbalallech?	ልጅህ/ሽ ማን ትባላለች?
What is your wife's name?	• Balebétïh man tbalallech?	ባለቤትህ ማን ትባላለች?
What is your sister-in-law's name?	• Yewendïmh/sh mist man tbalallech?	የወንድምህ/ሽ ሚስት ማን ትባላለች?
What is your niece's name?	• Ye'aggotïh/sh lïdj man tbalallech? • Ye'akïstïh/sh lïdj man tbalallech?	የአጎትህ/ሽ ልጅ ማን ትባላለች? - የአክስትህ/ሽ ልጅ ማን ትባላለች?
What is your mother-in-law called?	• Amachïh/sh man ybalallu?	አማችህ/ሽ ማን ይባላሉ?
(Her name is) Mary.	• Miryam ybalallu?	ሚርያም ይባላሉ
Are you an only child?	• Lennatïh/sh and neh/sh wey?	ለናትህ/ሽ አንድ ነህ/ሽ ወይ?
No, I have two sisters.	• Aydelehum, hulet ïhïtoch alluñ.	አይደለሁም፡ ሁለት እህቶች አሉኝ
No, I have an older brother.	• Aydelehum, tallaq wendïm alleñ.	አይደለሁም፡ ታላቅ ወንድም አለኝ
No, I have a twin sister.	• Aydelehum, mentaya ïhiït allechïñ.	አይደለሁም፡ መንታያ እህት አለችኝ
What job does your father do?	• Abbatïh/sh mïn yserallu?	አባትህ/ሽ ምን ይሰራሉ?
What job does your mother do?	• Ïnnatïh/sh mïn yserallu?	እናትህ/ሽ ምን ይሰራሉ?
He/She works in an office.	• Biro wist yseral/tïserallech.	ቢሮ ውስጥ ይሰራል/ትሰራለች
He/She works in a factory.	• Fabrika wist yseral/tïserallech.	ፋብሪካ ውስጥ ይሰራል/ትሰራለች
He/She works in a shop.	• Suq wist yseral/tïserallech.	ሱቅ ውስጥ ይሰራል/ትሰራለች
He/She is an office worker.	• Yebiro serateña new/nat.	የቢሮ ሰራተኛ ነው/ናት
He/She is a labourer.	• Yeqen serateña new/nat.	የቀን ሰራተኛ ነው/ናት
He/She is a (primary) teacher.	• Astemari new/nat.	አስተማሪ ነው/ናት
He/She is unemployed.	• Sïra yelewm/yelatm.	ስራ የለውም/የላትም

House and Home

Where ...?

Where do you live?	• Yet tnoralleh/tnoryallesh?	የት ትኖራለህ/ትኖርያለሽ?
I live in the town-centre.	• Ketema wïst ïnorallehu.	ከተማ ውስጥ እኖራለሁ
I live in the suburbs.	• Keketema wïch ïnorallehu.	ከከተማ ውጭ እኖራለሁ
I live in a flat.	• Apartama wïst ïnorallehu.	አፓርታማ ውስጥ እኖራለሁ
I live in a block of flats.	• Band foq wïst ïnorallehu.	ባንድ ፎቅ ውስጥ እኖራለሁ
I live in a villa.	• Band villa wïst ïnorallehu.	ባንድ ቪላ ውስጥ እኖራለሁ

Is there a ...?

Is there a garage?	• Yemekina maqomya allew wey?	የመኪና ማቆምያ አለው ወይ?
Is there a garden?	• Ye'atkïlt bota allew wey?	የአትክልት ቦታ አለው ወይ?
Is there central heating?	• Yewïha mamoqya allew wey?	የውኃ ማሞቅያ አለው ወይ?
Is there a lift ?	• Lift allew wey?	ሊፍት አለው ወይ?
Yes, there is.	• Awo, allew.	አዎ፡ አለው
No, there isn't.	• Yellewm.	የለውም

Can I help?

Can I give you a hand?	• Lïrdah/sh wey?	ልርዳህ/ሽ ወይ?
Can I be of any help?	• Ltebaber wey?	ልተባበር ወይ?

Can I do something?	• **And neger lïsra wey?**	አንድ ነገር ልስራ ወይ?
Can I lay the table ?	• **Mïgïb laqrïb wey?**	ምግብ ላቅርብ ወይ?
Can I clear the table ?	• **Mïgbun lansaw wey?**	ምግቡን ላንሳው ወይ?
Can I wash the dishes?	• **Ïqawochun lïtebachew wey?**	እቃዎቹን ልጠባቸው ወይ?
Can I make something to eat?	• **Yemibela neger laqrïb wey?**	የሚበላ ነገር ላቅርብ ወይ?
Can I do the dusting?	• **Bétun latsedadaw wey?**	ቤቱን ላጸዳዳው ወይ?
Can I do the ironing?	• **Lïtekus wey?**	ልተኩስ ወይ?
No thank you, there is no need.	• **Dehna, amesegnallehu, ayasfelïgm.**	ደህና፡ አመሰግናለሁ፡ አያስፈልግም
(No, leave it!) I can manage.	• **Tewew/teyiw rasé adergewallehu.**	ተወው/ተዪው፡ እኔ ራሴ አደርገዋለሁ
Yes, thank you ...	• **Ïshi, amesegnallehu.**	እሺ፡ አመሰግናለሁ

Where is ...?

Where's the bathroom?	• **Yegela metatebyaw yet new?**	የገላ መታጠብያው የት ነው?
Where's the toilet?	• **Shïnt bét yet new?**	ሽንት ቤት የት ነው?
Where's the fridge?	• **Maqezqeja yet new?**	ማቀዝቀዣ የት ነው?
Where's the garage?	• **Yemekina maqomya yet new?**	የመኪና ማቆምያ የት ነው?
It's opposite ...	• **Ke ... fit lefit.**	ከ ... ፊት ለፊት
It's at the end of ...	• **Ke ... mecheresha.**	ከ ... መጨረሻ
It's next to ...	• **Ke ... qetlo.**	ከ ... ቀጥሎ
It's in front of ...	• **Ke ... fit lefit.**	ከ ... ፊት ለፊት
Where's the pillow?	• **Tras yet alle?**	ትራስ የት አለ?
Where's the blanket?	• **Bïrd lïbs yet alle?**	ብርድ ልብስ የት አለ?
Where's the cutlery?	• **Mankiyawochïna bilawoch yet allu?**	ማንኪያዎችና ቢላዎች የት አሉ?
Where are the plates?	• **Sehanoch yet allu?**	ሰሃኖች የት አሉ?
Here it is.	• **Yhew?**	ይኸው
Here they are.	• **Ïñiwlïh?**	እኚውልህ

Do you need ...?

Do you need any soap?	• **Samuna yasfelgïhal/shal wey?**	ሳሙና ያስፈልግሃል/ሻል ወይ?
Do you need any toothpaste?	• **Yetïrs samuna yasfelgïhal/shal wey?**	የጥርስ ሳሙና ያስፈልግሃል/ሻል ወይ?
Do you need a towel?	• **Fota yasfelgïhal/shal wey ?**	ፎጣ ያስፈልግሃል/ሻል ወይ?
Do you need an alarm clock?	• **Yemiqeseqes se'at yasfelgïhal/shal wey?**	የሚቀሰቅስ ሰዓት ያስፈልግሃል/ሻል ወይ?
Do you need anything?	• **Léla yemiyasfelgïh/sh neger alle wey?**	ሌላ የሚያስፈልግህ/ሽ ነገር አለ ወይ?
Yes, I need some/a ...	• **Awo,... yasfelgeñal.**	አዎ፡... ያስፈልገኛል

May I ...?

May I come in?	• **Lïgba?**	ልግባ?
May I?	• **Yfeqedal wey?**	ይፈቀዳል ወይ?
Am I interrupting?	• **Rebeshkawachuh wey?**	ረበሽኳችሁ ወይ?
Come in!	• **Gba/Gbi!**	ግባ/ግቢ!

Make yourself comfortable!	• **Qwïch bel/bey!**	ቍጭ በል/በይ
Not at all/(Please) come in!	• **Ygbu!**	ይግቡ

Thank you

Thank you for your hospitality!	• **Letederegelñ aqebabel amesegnallehu!**	ለተደረገልኝ አቀባበል አመሰግናለሁ
You have (all) been so kind!	• **Mïsgana yggebachïhwal!**	ምስጋና ይገባችኋል
I hope I can do the same for you soon!	• **Wleta melash yadrïgeñ!**	ውለታ መላሽ ያድርገኝ

Daily Routine

(At) what time ...?

What time do you wake up?	• **Besïnt se'at tneqalleh/ tneqyallesh?**	በስንት ሰዓት ትነቃለህ/ ትነቅያለሽ?
What time do you get up?	• **Besïnt se'at tnessalleh/ tneshyallesh?**	በስንት ሰዓት ትነሳለህ/ ትነሽያለሽ?
What time do you have breakfast?	• **Besïnt se'at qwïrsïhn tbelalleh/tbeyallesh?**	በስንት ሰዓት ቍርስህን ትበላለህ/ትበያለሽ?
What time do you have lunch?	• **Besïnt se'at mïsahn tbelalleh/tbeyallesh?**	በስንት ሰዓት ምሳህን ትበላለህ/ትበያለሽ?
What time do you have dinner?	• **Besïnt se'at ïratïhn tbelalleh/tbeyallesh?**	በስንት ሰዓት እራትህን ትበላለህ/ትበያለሽ?
What time do you go to bed?	• **Besïnt se'at tggaddemalleh/ tggaddemyallesh?**	በስንት ሰዓት ትጋደማለህ/ ትጋደምያለሽ?
What time do (you go to) sleep?	• **Besïnt se'at tïteñalleh/ tïteñiyallesh?**	በስንት ሰዓት ትተኛለህ/ ትተኚያለሽ?
I wake up at ...	• **Be ...se'at ïneqallehu.**	በ ... ሰዓት እነቃለሁ
I get up at ...	• **Be ...se'at ïnessallehu.**	በ ... ሰዓት እነሳለሁ
I have breakfast at ...	• **Be ...se'at qwïrsén ïbelallehu.**	በ ... ሰዓት ቍርሴን እበላለሁ
I have lunch at ...	• **Be ...se'at mïsayen ïbelallehu.**	በ ... ሰዓት ምሳየን እበላለሁ
I have dinner at ...	• **Be ...se'at ïratén ïbelallehu.**	በ ... ሰዓት እራቴን እበላለሁ
I go to bed at ...	• **Be ...se'at ïggaddemallehu.**	በ ... ሰዓት እጋደማለሁ
I (go to) sleep at ...	• **Be ...se'at ïteñallehu.**	በ ... ሰዓት እተኛለሁ

Work

Have you found a job?	• **Sïra ageñeh/sh wey?**	ስራ አገኘህ/ሽ ወይ?
Is it tiring?	• **Adkami new wey?**	አድካሚ ነው ወይ?
Is it demanding?	• **Gulbet yteyqal wey?**	ጉልበት ይጠይቃል ወይ?
How many hours do you work?	• **Sïnt se'at tïseralleh/ tïseryallesh?**	ስንት ሰዓት ትሰራለህ/ ትሰርያለሽ?
How much do you earn?	• **Sïnt ageñalleh/ tageñyallesh?**	ስንት ታገኛለህ/ታገኝያለሽ?
Do you earn a lot?	• **Bzu tageñalleh/ tageñyallesh wey?**	ብዙ ታገኛለህ/ታገኝያለሽ ወይ?
Yes, I work in a bar.	• **Awo, and bunna-bét wïst ïserallehu.**	አዎ፡ አንድ ቡና ቤት ውስጥ እሰራለሁ
I give English lessons.	• **Ïnglizïña astemrallehu.**	እንግሊዝኛ አስተምራለሁ
No, not really.	• **Ïskezihm aydellem.**	እስከዚህም አይደለም
Yes, but I like it.	• **Awo, neger gïn ïweddewallehu.**	አዎ፡ ነገር ግን እወደዋለሁ
I work 8 hours a day.	• **Beqen 8 se'at ïserallehu.**	በቀን 8 ሰዓት እሰራለሁ
I earn ... an hour.	• **Bese'at ... bïr ageñallehu.**	በሰዓት ... ብር አገኛለሁ
I earn ... a month.	• **Bewer ... bïr ageñallehu.**	በወር ... ብር አገኛለሁ

Geographical Surroundings

Where ...?

Where do you live?	• **Yet ager new yemïtnorew/yemïtnoriw?**	የት አገር ነው የምትኖረው/የምትኖሪው? (m/f)
I live in Ethiopia.	• **Ityop̱ya wïsṯ ïnorallehu.**	ኢትዮጵያ ውስጥ እኖራለሁ
I live in Italy.	• **Ṯalyan ager ïnorallehu.**	ጣልያን አገር እኖራለሁ
I live in England.	• **Ïngliz ager ïnorallehu.**	እንግሊዝ አገር እኖራለሁ
I live in Rome.	• **Roma wïsṯ ïnorallehu.**	ሮማ ውስጥ እኖራለሁ
I live in London.	• **London wïsṯ ïnorallehu.**	ለንደን ውስጥ እኖራለሁ
I live in Chicago.	• **Chicago wïsṯ ïnorallehu.**	ቺካጎ ውስጥ እኖራለሁ
Where are you from?	• **Keyet akebabi neh/nesh?**	ከየት አከባቢ ነህ/ነሽ?
I'm from Addis Ababa.	• **Ye Addis Abeba lïdj neñ.**	የአዲስ አበባ ልጅ ነኝ
I'm from Turin.	• **Ye Torino lïdj neñ.**	የቶሪኖ ልጅ ነኝ
Where is it?	• **Yet yggeñal/tggeñallech?**	የት ይገኛል/ትገኛለች?
It's in northern Italy.	• **Beseménawi ye Ṯalyan ager kïfil yggeñal/tggeñallech.**	በሰሜናዊ የጣልያን አገር ክፍል ይገኛል/ትገኛለች
It's in central Italy.	• **Mahel Ṯalyan yggeñal/tgeñallech.**	ማሐል ጣልያን አገር ይገኛል/ትገኛለች
It's in southern Italy.	• **Bedebubawi ye Ṯalyan ager kïfil yggeñal/tggeñallech.**	በደቡባዊ የጣልያን አገር ክፍል ይገኛል/ትገኛለች
It's in the north of Italy.	• **Besemén Ṯalyan ager yggeñal/tggeñallech.**	በሰሜን ጣልያን አገር ይገኛል/ትገኛለች
It's in the south of Italy.	• **Bedebub Ṯalyan ager yggeñal/tggeñallech.**	በደቡብ ጣልያን አገር ይገኛል/ትገኛለች
Is it a large city?	• **Ketemaw tïlïq newn?**	ከተማው ትልቅ ነውን?
No, it is a village in the mountains.	• **Bekwerebta lay yemtïgeñ tïnïsh mender nat.**	በኰረብታ ላይ የምትገኝ ትንሽ መንደር ናት
No, it is a village on a hill.	• **Aydellem, amba lay yeteqwereqwerech tïnïsh mender nat.**	አይደለም አምባ ላይ የተቈረቈረች ትንሽ መንደር ናት
No, it is a village by the sea.	• **Bahr dar yemtïgeñ tïnïsh mender nat.**	ባሕር ዳር የምትገኝ ትንሽ መንደር ናት
No, it is a village on a river.	• **Wenz dar yemtïgeñ tïnïsh mender nat.**	ወንዝ ዳር የምትገኝ ትንሽ መንደር ናት
No, it is a village on a lake.	• **Hayq dar yemtïgeñ tïnïsh mender nat.**	ሃይቅ ዳር የምትገኝ ትንሽ መንደር ናት
Which is the nearest city?	• **Be'aqrabiya yemtïgeñew ketema yetïñaw nat?**	በአቅራቢያ የምትገኘው ከተማ የትኛዋ ናት?
(It's near) Turin.	• **Torino nat.**	ቶሪኖ ናት
(It's near) Naples.	• **Napoli nat.**	ናፖሊ ናት
(It's near) Addis Ababa.	• **Addis Abeba nat.**	አዲስ አበባ ናት

What ...?

What's the country-side like?	• **Yemenderu akebabi mïn ymeslal?**	የመንደሩ አከባቢ ምን ይመስላል?

It's hilly.	• Beterara yetekebbebe new.	በተራራ የተከበበ ነው
It's enchanting.	• Maraki new.	ማራኪ ነው
It's monotonous.	• Asalchi new.	አሰልቺ ነው
It's picturesque.	• Asdenaqi new.	አስደናቂ ነው
It's wonderful.	• Asgerami new.	አስገራሚ ነው
Where do you live?	• Yet new yemïtnorew/ yemïtnoriw?	የት ነው የምትኖረው/ የምትኖሪው?
I live in the old part of town.	• Arogéw ketema akebabi ïnorallehu.	አሮጌው ከተማ አካባቢ እኖራለሁ
I live in the suburbs.	• Ketemaw dar akebabi ïnorallehu.	ከተማው ዳር አካባቢ እኖራለሁ

Is there ...?

Is there an airport?	• Érport allew wey?	ኤርፖርት አለው ወይ?
Is there a sports centre?	• Yesport ma'kel allew wey?	የስፖርት ማእከል አለው ወይ?
Is there a shopping centre?	• Yegebeya addarash allew wey?	የገበያ አዳራሽ አለው ወይ?
Is there a castle?	• Tarikawi gïnb allew wey?	ታሪካዊ ግንብ አለው ወይ?
Is there a cathedral?	• Bétekrïstyan allew wey?	ቤተክርስትያን አለው ወይ?
Yes, there is ...	• Awo ... allew.	አዎ፡ ... አለው
No, there isn't ...	• ... yellewm.	... የለውም

Are there ...?

Are there many monuments?	• Bzu haweltoch allu wey?	ብዙ ሓወልቶች አሉ ወይ?
Are there many shops?	• Bzu suqoch allu wey?	ብዙ ሱቆች አሉ ወይ?
Are there many gardens?	• Bzu ye'atkïlt botawoch allu wey	ብዙ የአትክልት ቦታዎች አሉ ወይ?
Are there many theatres?	• Bzu tyatroch bétoch allu wey?	ብዙ ትያትሮች ቤቶች አሉ ወይ?
Are there many avenues?	• Bzu mengedoch allu wey?	ብዙ መንገዶች አሉ ወይ?
Are there many discotheques?	• Bzu diskotékoch allu wey?	ብዙ ዲስኮቴኮች አሉ ወይ?
Are there many fountains?	• Bzu yewha mïnchoch allu wey?	ብዙ የውሃ ምንጮች አሉ ወይ?
Are there many industries?	• Bzu industriwoch allu wey?	ብዙ ኢንዱስትሪዎች አሉ ወይ?
Are there many factories?	• Bzu fabrikawoch allu wey?	ብዙ ፋብሪካዎች አሉ ወይ?
Yes, there are...	• Awo, ... allu.	አዎ፡ ... አሉ
No, there aren't..	• ... yellum.	... የሉም

Travel and Transport

How ...?

How do you get to school?	• Wede tmïhïrt-bét bemïn tïhédalleh?	ወደ ትምህርት ቤት በምን ትሔዳለህ?
How do you get to work?	• Wede sïra bemïn tïhédalleh?	ወደ ስራ በምን ትሔዳለህ?
By bus.	• Be'awtobus.	በአውቶቡስ
By car.	• Bemekina.	በመኪና
By train.	• Bebabur	በባቡር
By bicycle.	• Bebisiklet.	በቢሲክለት
By coach.	• Be'awtobus.	በአውቶቡስ
On foot.	• Be'ïgr.	በእግር
How long does it take?	• Sïnt se'at yfedjal?	ስንት ሰዓት ይፈጃል?
(About) 10 minutes.	• Asïr deqiqa yahl.	አስር ደቂቃ ያህል
(About) an hour	• And se'at yahl.	አንድ ሰዓት ያህል

Asking the way

Excuse me!	• **Yqïrta!**	ይቅርታ
Yes!	• **Ïshi, mïn nebber.**	እሺ ምን ነበር?
Where's the museum?	• **Béte mezekïru yet ïndehone lïtnegreñ tchïlalleh wey?**	ቤተ መዘክሩ የት እንደሆነ ልትነግረኝ ትችላለህ ወይ?
Where's the castle?	• **Yetïntu gïnb yet ïndehone lïtnegreñ tchïlalleh wey?**	የጥንቱ ግንብ የት እንደሆነ ልትነግረኝ ትችላለህ ወይ?
Where's the post office?	• **Posta bétu yet ïndemigeñ lïtnegreñ tchïlalleh wey?**	ፖስታ ቤቱ የት እንደሚገኝ ልትነግረኝ ትችላለህ ወይ?
Where's the information centre?	• **Yemastaweqya tsïhfet bét yet ïndehone lïtnegreñ tchïlalleh wey?**	የማስታወቅያ ጽሕፈት ቤት የት እንደሆነ ልትነግረኝ ትችላለህ ወይ?
Where's the church?	• **Bétekrïstyanu yet ïndehone lïtnegreñ tchïlalleh wey?**	ቤተ ክርስትያኑ የት እንደሆነ ልትነግረኝ ትችላለህ ወይ?
Where's the chemist?	• **Medhanit bétu yet ïndehone lïtnegreñ tchïlalleh wey?**	መድኃኒት ቤቱ የት እንደሆነ ልትነግረኝ ትችላለህ ወይ?
Where's the swimming pool?	• **Mewañaw yet ïndehone lïtnegreñ tchïlalleh wey?**	መዋኛው የት እንደሆነ ልትነግረኝ ትችላለህ ወይ?
Can you tell me the way to the police station?	• **Polis tabyaw yet ïndehone lïtnegreñ tchïlalleh wey?**	ፖሊስ ጣብያው የት እንደሆነ ልትነግረኝ ትችላለህ ወይ?
Can you tell me the way to the bus stop?	• **Fémataw yet ïndehone lïtnegreñ tchïlalleh wey?**	ፌርማታው የት እንደሆነ ልትነግረኝ ትችላለህ ወይ?
Can you tell me the way to the station?	• **Yebabur tabyaw yet ïndehone lïtnegreñ tchïlalleh wey?**	የባቡር ጣብያው የት እንደሆነ ልትነግረኝ ትችላለህ ወይ?

Directions

Take the first on the right.	• **Kemedjemeryaw metemzeja wede qeñ tatef/fi.**	ከመጀመርያው መጠምዘዣ ወደ ቀኝ ታጠፍ/ፊ
Take the second on the right.	• **Kehuleteñaw metemzeja wede gra tatef/fi.**	ከሁለተኛው መጠምዘዣ ወደ ግራ ታጠፍ/ፊ
Take the third on the right.	• **Kesosteñaw metemzeja wede qeñ tatef/fi.**	ከሦስተኛው መጠምዘዣ ወደ ቀኝ ታጠፍ/ፊ
Turn left.	• **Wede gra tatef/fi.**	ወደ ግራ ታጠፍ/ፊ
(Go) straight on.	• **Wede fit qetïl/y.**	ወደ ፊት ቀጥል/ይ
Go as far as the traffic lights.	• **Ïske trafik mebratu qetïl/y.**	እስከ ትራፊክ መብራቱ ቀጥል/ይ
Go as far as the cross-road.	• **Ïske mesqeleñaw menged qetïl/y**	እስከ መስቀለኛው መንገድ ቀጥል/ይ
Cross the road.	• **Mengedun teshager/ri.**	መንገዱን ተሻገር/ሪ
Cross the pedestrian crossing.	• **Benechu mesmer teshager/ri.**	በነጩ መስመር ተሻገር/ሪ
It's there, on your right.	• **Ïziya new beqeñ bekul.**	እዚያ ነው በቀኝ በኩል

Is there a ...?

Excuse me, is there a bank near here?	• **Yqïrta, ïzih akebabi bank alle wey?**	ይቅርታ እዚህ አከባቢ ባንክ አለ ወይ?
Excuse me, is there a restaurant near here?	• **Yqïrta, ïzih akebabi mïgïb bét alle wey?**	ይቅርታ እዚህ አከባቢ ምግብ ቤት አለ ወይ?
20 metres, on the left.	• **Haya métïr wede gra.**	ሀያ ሜትር ወደ ግራ
Opposite...	• **Fit lefit.**	ፊት ለፊት
Next to...	• **Ategeb, begwen.**	አጠገብ፡ በጐን
Near...	• **... ategeb, ga.**	... አጠገብ፡ ጋ
On the road parallel to this one.	• **Bezih menged akwaya.**	በዚህ መንገድ አኳያ

Is it far ...?

Is it very far from here?	• **Kezih betam yrïqal wey?**	ከዚህ በጣም ይርቃል ወይ?
No, (it's about) ten minutes walk.	• **Ayrïqm, be'ïgr asïr deqiqa yahl yfedjal.**	አይርቅም፡ በእግር አሥር ደቂቃ ያህል ይፈጃል
Yes, you'll have to take a taxi.	• **Awo, taxi mewsed yasfelgehal.**	አዎ፡ ታክሲ መውሰድ ያስፈልገሃል

I don't understand ...

Excuse me, what did you say?	• **Yqïrta, mïnd new yalkew?**	ይቅርታ፡ ምንድ ነው ያልከው?
I don't understand.	• **Algebañïm.**	አልገባኝም
Could you say it again, please?	• **Lidegmuliñ yïchlallu wey?**	ሊደግሙልኝ ይችላሉ ወይ?
Could you speak more slowly, please?	• **Qes bïlew linageru yïchlallu wey?**	ቀስ ብለው ሊናገሩ ይችላሉ ወይ?

Thank you!

Thank you!	• **Amesegnallehu!**	አመሰግናለሁ
Thank you very much!	• **Betam amesegnallehu!**	በጣም አመሰግናለሁ
Very kind of you!	• **Betam tedesïchallehu!**	በጣም ተደስቻለሁ

Public Transport

Is there ...?

Is there a coach to Florence?	• **Wede Florens yemihéd autobus alle wey?**	ወደ ፍሎረንስ የሚሔድ አውቶቡስ አለ ወይ?
Is there a bus to the station?	• **Wede leghar babur tabya yemihéd autobus alle wey?**	ወደ ለግሀር ባቡር ጣብያ የሚሔድ አውቶቡስ አለ ወይ?
I'm sorry, I don't know.	• **Yqïrta, alaweqkum.**	ይቅርታ፡ አላወቅኩም
(Yes,) number 20.	• **Awo, haya qwïtr.**	አዎ፡ ሀያ ቍጥር
Is there an express train for Bologna?	• **Wede Boloña yemihéd fetan autobus alle wey?**	ወደ ቦሎኛ የሚሔድ ፈጣን አውቶቡስ አለ ወይ?
Yes, there's one in half an hour.	• **Awo,kegïmash se'at behwala yemimeta alle.**	አዎ፡ ከግማሽ ሰዓት በኋላ የሚመጣ አለ
Yes, there's one at ten past seven.	• **Awo, besebat se'at kasr yemimeta alle.**	አዎ፡ በሰባት ሰዓት ካሥር የሚመጣ አለ

I would like ...

I'd like a single ticket.	• **Mehédja tikét ïfelgallehu.**	መሔጃ ቲኬት እፈልጋለሁ
I'd like a return ticket.	• **Memelesha tikét ïfelgallehu.**	መመለሻ ቲኬት እፈልጋለሁ
First class?	• **Andeña ma'reg?**	አንደኛ ማዕረግ?
Second class?	• **Huleteña ma'reg?**	ሁለተኛ ማዕረግ?

What time ...?

What time is the next train for Rome?	• **Baburu besïnt se'at new wede Roma yemihédew?**	ባቡሩ በስንት ሰዓት ነው ወደ ሮማ የሚሔደው?
What time is the next coach for Rome?	• **Autobusu besïnt se'at new wede Roma yemihédew?**	አውቶቡሱ በስንት ሰዓት ነው ወደ ሮማ የሚሔደው?
It leaves at 4.30 p.m.	• **Be 10.30 new yeminessaw.**	በ10:30 ነው የሚነሳው
What time does it leave Naples?	• **Besïnt se'at new keNapoli yeminessaw?**	በስንት ሰዓት ነው ከናፖሊ የሚነሳው?
What time does it get to London?	• **Besïnt se'at new wede London yemidersew.**	በስንት ሰዓት ነው ወደ ሎንዶን የሚደርሰው?
It leaves at 3.00 p.m	• **Be 9 se'at new yeminessaw.**	በ 9 ሰዓት ነው የሚነሳው
It gets in at 3.00 p.m.	• **Be 9 se'at new yemidersew.**	በ 9 ሰዓት ነው የሚደርሰው

Is this ...?

Excuse me, is this platform 3?	• **Yqïrta, hadidu 3 qwïtr new wey?**	ይቅርታ፡ ሐዲዱ 3 ቍጥር ነው ወይ?
Excuse me, is this the coach for ...?	• **Yqïrta, yïh wede ... yemihéd autobus new wey?**	ይቅርታ፡ ይህ ወደ ... የሚሔድ አውቶቡስ ነው ወይ?
Excuse me, is this the stop for ...?	• **Yqïrta, ... ïzih new yemiqomew?**	ይቅርታ፡ ... እዚህ ነው የሚቆመው?
Yes.	• **Awo.**	አዎ
No, it's that one over there.	• **Aydellem, ïziyaw new.**	አይደለም፡ እዚያው ነው

Which platform ...?

Which platform does the train for Genoa leave from?	• **Djenova yemihédew babur keyetñaw hadid new yeminessaw?**	ጀኖቫ የሚሔደው ባቡር ከየትኛው ሐዲድ ነው የሚነሳው?
It leaves from platform 3.	• **Kehadid 3 qwïtr new yeminessaw?**	ከሐዲድ 3 ቍጥር ነው የሚነሳው?

I would like ...

I'd like to reserve a seat.	• **Asqedmé wenber lemeyaz ïfelgallehu.**	አስቀድሜ ወንበር ለመያዝ እፈልጋለሁ
I'd like to reserve a couchette.	• **Asqedmé alga lemeyaz ïfelgallehu.**	አስቀድሜ አልጋ ለመያዝ እፈልጋለሁ

Asking the time

What's the time? What time is it?	• **Sïnt se'at new?**	ስንት ሰዓት ነው?
It's [It is] midnight. (24.00)	• **Ïkule lélit new.**	እኩለ ሌሊት ነው
It's midday/twelve o'clock.	• **Ïkule qen new.**	እኩለ ቀን ነው
It's one (o'clock)/one p.m.	• **Sebat se'at new.**	ሰባት ሰዓት ነው

It's two (o'clock)/two a.m.	• **Sïmmïnt se'at new.**	ስምንት ሰዓት ነው
It's three (o'clock)/three a.m.	• **Zeteñ se'at new.**	ዘጠኝ ሰዓት ነው
It's four (o'clock)/four a.m.	• **Asïr se'at new.**	አሥር ሰዓት ነው
It's five (o'clock)/five a.m.	• **Asr'and se'at new.**	አሥራ አንድ ሰዓት ነው
It's six (o'clock)/six a.m.	• **Asra hulet se'at new.**	አሥራ ሁለት ሰዓት ነው
It's seven (o'clock)/seven a.m.	• **And se'at new.**	አንድ ሰዓት ነው
It's eight (o'clock)/eight a.m.	• **Hulet se'at new.**	ሁለት ሰዓት ነው
It's nine (o'clock)/nine a.m.	• **Sost se'at new.**	ሦስት ሰዓት ነው
It's ten (o'clock)/ten a.m.	• **Arat se'at new.**	አራት ሰዓት ነው
It's eleven (o'clock)/eleven a.m.	• **Ammïst se'at new.**	አምስት ሰዓት ነው
It's twelve (o'clock)/twelve a.m.	• **Sïddïst se'at new.**	ስድስት ሰዓት ነው
It's one (o'clock)/one p.m.	• **Kemïshtu sebat se'at new.**	ከምሽቱ ሰባት ሰዓት ነው
It's two (o'clock)/two p.m.	• **Kemïshtu sïmmïnt se'at new.**	ከምሽቱ ስምንት ሰዓት ነው
It's three (o'clock)/three p.m.	• **Kemïshtu zeteñ se'at new.**	ከምሽቱ ዘጠኝ ሰዓት ነው
It's four (o'clock)/four p.m.	• **Kemïshtu asïr se'at new.**	ከምሽቱ አሥር ሰዓት ነው
It's five (o'clock)/five p.m.	• **Kemïshtu asr'and se'at new.**	ከምሽቱ አስራ አንድ ሰዓት ነው
...	...	...
It's five (minutes) past two.	• **Sïmmïnt kammïst.**	ስምንት ካምስት
It's ten (minutes) past two.	• **Sïmmïnt kasïr.**	ስምንት ካሥር
It's a quarter past two/two fifteen.	• **Sïmmïnt kerub.**	ስምንት ከሩብ
It's twenty (minutes) past two/ two twenty.	• **Sïmmïnt kehaya.**	ስምንት ከሀያ
It's half past two/two thirty.	• **Sïmmïnt se'at tekul.**	ስምንት ሰዓት ተኩል
It's twenty-five (minutes) to three.	• **Lezeteñ se'at ammïst gwïday.**	ለዘጠኝ ሰዓት ሀያ አምስት ጉዳይ
It's twenty (minutes) to three.	• **Lezeteñ se'at haya gwïday.**	ለዘጠኝ ሰዓት ሀያ ጉዳይ
It's a quarter to three/ two forty-five	• **Lezeteñ se'at rub gwïday.**	ለዘጠኝ ሰዓት ሩብ ጉዳይ

Travel by Air or Sea

Departure/Arrival

What time is the a flight for Venice?	• **Wede Venezia berera besïnt se'at new?**	ወደ ቬነስያ በረራ በስንት ሰዓት ነው?
What time does the boat leave for Genoa?	• **Wede Djenova yemihéd merkeb besïnt se'at new yeminessaw?**	ወደ ጀኖዋ የሚሔድ መርከብ በስንት ሰዓት ነው የሚነሳው?
What time does the ferry leave for Messina?	• **Wede Messina yemihédew merkeb besïnt se'at new yeminessaw?**	ወደ መሲና የሚሔደው መርከብ በስንት ሰዓት ነው የሚነሳው?
What time does the ferry arrive in Messina?	• **Merkebu besïnt se'at new wede Messina yemidersew?**	መርከቡ በስንት ሰዓት ነው ወደ መሲና የሚደርሰው?

I would like ...

I'd like a single ticket to Rome.	• **Wede Roma mehédja tikét ïfelgallehu?**	ወደ ሮማ መሔጃ ቲኬት እፈልጋለሁ
I'd like a return ticket.	• **Yederso mels tikét yasfelgeñal?**	የደርሶ መልስ ቲኬት ያስፈልገኛል
In tourist class.	• **Beturist ma'reg.**	በቱሪስት ማዕረግ

In first class.	• **Be'andeña ma'reg.**	በአንደኛ ማዕረግ
I'd like a seat next to the window.	• **Meskot ategeb meqemet ïfelgallehu.**	መስኮት አጠገብ መቀመጥ እፈልጋለሁ
I'd like a seat near the corridor.	• **Koridor ategeb meqemet ïfelgallehu.**	ኮሪዶር አጠገብ መቀመጥ እፈልጋለሁ
I'd like a seat in a (smoking) non-smoking compartment.	• **Sigara (bemichesïbet) bemaychesbet kïfïl lemeqemet ïfelgallehu.**	ሲጋራ (በሚጨስበት) በማይጨስበት ክፍል ለመቀመጥ እፈልጋለሁ

(At) what time ...?

(At) what time are you leaving?	• **Besïnt se'at tnessalleh?**	በስንት ሰዓት ትነሳለህ?
(At) what time is he leaving?	• **Besïnt se'at ynessal/ tnessallech?**	በስንት ሰዓት ይነሳል/ ትነሳለች? (m/f)
(At) what time are you leaving?	• **Besïnt se'at tnessallachuh?**	በስንት ሰዓት ትነሳላችሁ?
(At) what time are they leaving?	• **Besïnt se'at ynessallu?**	በስንት ሰዓት ይነሳሉ?
(At) what time are you arriving?	• **Besïnt se'at tdersalleh?**	በስንት ሰዓት ትደርሳለህ?
I'm leaving at six (o'clock).	• **Be 12 se'at ïnessallehu.**	በ 12 ሰዓት እነሳለሁ
He/she is leaving at seven.	• **Be 1 se'at ynessal/ tnessallech.**	በ 1 ሰዓት ይነሳል/ትነሳለች
We're leaving at eight.	• **Be 2 se'at ïnïnessallen.**	በ 2 ሰዓት እንነሳለን
They're leaving at nine.	• **Be 3 se'at ynessallu.**	በ 3 ሰዓት ይነሳሉ
I'm arriving at ten.	• **Be 4 se'at ïdersallehu.**	በ 4 ሰዓት እደርሳለሁ

Private Transport

Buying petrol

I'd like 20 pounds worth of (unleaded) petrol.	• **Led yelébebbet ye 240 bïr nedadj ïfelgallehu.**	ለድ የሌለበት የ240 ብር ነዳጅ እፈልጋለሁ
I'd like 60 pounds worth of diesel.	• **Ye 200 bïr nafta ïfelgallehu.**	የ 200 ብር ናፍታ እፈልጋለሁ
I'd like 20 litres of four star.	• **Haya litr forestar ïfelgallehu.**	ሀያ ሊትር ፎረስታር እፈልጋለሁ
Fill it up, please.	• **Benzin limolulïñ yïchlallu wey.**	በንዚን ሊሞሉልኝ ይችላሉ ወይ?

Can you check the ...?

Can you check the oil, please?	• **ïbakwon zeyt yïyulñ.**	እባክዎን ዘይት ይዩልኝ
Can you check the water, please?	• **ïbakwon wïhawun yïyulñ.**	እባክዎን ውኃዉን ይዩልኝ
Can you check the tyres, please?	• **ïbakwon gommawun yïyulñ.**	እባክዎን ጐማዉን ይዩልኝ
Can you check the tyre pressure, please?	• **ïbakwon yegommawun yayer gfit yïyulñ.**	እባክዎን የጐማዉን ያየር ግፊት ይዩልኝ

Is there a ...?

Is there a garage near here?	• Ïzih akebabi garaj alle wey?	እዚህ አከባቢ ጋራዥ አለ ወይ?
Is there a motorway near here?	• Ïzih akebabi yemekina menged alle wey?	እዚህ አከባቢ የመኪና መንገድ አለ ወይ?
Is there a car park near here?	• Ïzih akebabi yemekina maqomya alle wey?	እዚህ አከባቢ የመኪና ማቆምያ አለ ወይ?
Is there a car wash near here?	• Ïzih akebabi mekina yemitatebïbet garaj alle wey?	እዚህ አከባቢ መኪና የሚታጠብበት ጋራዥ አለ ወይ?

I need a ...

I need a mechanic.	• Mekanik yasfelgeñal.	መካኒክ ያስፈልገኛል
My car has broken down.	• Mekina tebellashebñ.	መኪና ተበላሸብኝ
I've [I have] got engine trouble.	• Moteré alseram ale.	ሞተሬ አልሰራም አለ
My battery is flat.	• Batriw mote.	ባትሪው ሞተ
I've run out of petrol.	• Benzin chereskuñ (alleqebñ).	በንዚን ጨረስኩኝ (አለቀብኝ)

A receipt

Can you give me a receipt, please?	• Faktur lisetuñ ychïlallu wey?	ፋክቱር ሊሰጡኝ ይችላሉ ወይ?
Here you are. Have a good journey!	• Yhew, melkam menged/ guzo.	ይኸው፡ መልካም መንገድ/ ጉዞ

Holidays

Where ...?

Where do you usually go on holiday ?	• Abzañawn gzé le'ireft yet tïhédalleh/tïhédjyallesh?	አብዛኛውን ግዜ ለዕረፍት የት ትሔዳለህ/ትሔጂያለሽ?
Where do you usually spend your holidays?	• Abzañawn gzé ye'ïreft gzéhïn/gzéshïn yet tasalfewalleh/tasalfiwallesh?	አብዛኛውን ግዜ የዕረፍት ግዜህን/ግዜሽን የት ታሳልፈዋለህ/ታሳልፊዋለሽ?
Where are you going on holiday this year?	• Zendro ye'ïreft gzéhn/ gzéshn lemasallef yet tïhédalleh/tïhédjallesh?	ዘንድሮ የዕረፍት ግዜህን/ ግዜሽን ለማሳለፍ የት ትሔዳለህ/ ትሔጂያለሽ?
Where is he/she going on holiday this summer?	• Yekremtun ïreft yet yasalfewal/tasalfewallech?	የክረምቱን ዕረፍት የት ያሳልፈዋል/ታሳልፈውአለች?
Where are you going on holiday this summer?	• Yekremt ïreftachïhun yet tasalfut'allachïhu?	የክረምት ዕረፍታችሁን የት ታሳልፉትአላችሁ?
Where are they going on holiday this summer?	• Yekremt ïreftachewn yet yasalfutal?	የክረምት ዕረፍታቸውን የት ያሳልፉታል?
Usually I go to Italy.	• Abzañawn gzé wede Talyan ager ïhédallehu.	አብዛኛውን ግዜ ወደ ጣልያን አገር እሔዳለሁ
Usually I go to the mountains.	• Abzañawn gzé beterara lay asalfewallehu.	አብዛኛውን ግዜ በተራራ ላይ አሳልፈዋለሁ

Sometimes I go to the seaside.	• **Andand gzé wede bahr darcha ïhédallehu .**	አንዳንድ ግዜ ወደ ባሕር ዳርቻ እሔዳለሁ
Often I go abroad.	• **Abzañawn gzé wïch ager ïhédallehu.**	አብዛኛውን ግዜ ውጭ አገር እሔዳለሁ
I'm going to Florence.	• **Wede Florens ïhédallehu.**	ወደ ፍሎረንሰ እሔዳለሁ
He/she is going to Florence.	• **Wede Florens yhédal/ tïhédallech.**	ወደ ፍሎረንሰ ይሔዳል/ ትሔዳለች
We're going to Florence.	• **Wede Florens ïnïhédallen.**	ወደ ፍሎረንሰ እንሔዳለን
They're going to Florence.	• **Wede Florens yhédallu.**	ወደ ፍሎረንሰ ይሔዳሉ
I'm staying in England.	• **Ïngliz ager ïqoyallehu.**	እንግሊዝ አገር እቆያለሁ

(For) how long .../ Where ...?

How long will you stay on holiday?	• **Be'ïreftïh gzé mïn yahl tqoyalleh/tqoyallesh?**	በዕረፍትህ ግዜ ምን ያህል ትቆያለህ/ ትቆያለሽ?
How long will you be on holiday?	• **Mïn yahl be'ïreft lay tqoyalleh/tqoyallesh?**	ምን ያህል በዕረፍት ላይ ትቆያለህ/ ትቆያለሽ?
Where would you like to go on holiday?	• **Le'ïreft yet btïhéd/ btïhédji tweddalleh/ twedjiyallesh?**	ለዕረፍት የት ብትሔድ/ ብትሔጂ ትወዳለህ/ ትወጂያለሽ?
Two weeks.	• **Lehulet samïnt.**	ለሁለት ሳምንት
About a fortnight.	• **Lehulet samïnt yahl.**	ለሁለት ሳምንት ያህል
I'd like to go to Italy.	• **Wede Talyan agher bhéd des yleñ nebber.**	ወደ ጣልያን አገር ብሔድ ደስ ይለኝ ነበር
I'd like to go to Addis Ababa.	• **Addis Abeba bhéd des yleñ nebber.**	አዲስ አበባ ብሔድ ደስ ይለኝ ነበር
I'd like to go to Axum.	• **Axum bhéd des yleñ nebber.**	አክሱም ብሔድ ደስ ይለኝ ነበር

What do you do ...?

What do you usually do on holiday ?	• **Abzañawn gzé be'ïreftïh/sh gzé mïn tadergalleh/tadergiyallesh?**	አብዛኛውን ግዜ በዕረፍትህ/ሽ ግዜ ምን ታደርጋለህ/ ታደርጊያለሽ?
What do you usually do during your holidays?	• **Abzañawn gzé be'ïreft gzé mïn tadergalleh/ tadergiyallesh?**	አብዛኛውን ግዜ በዕረፍት ግዜ ምን ታደርጋለህ/ ታደርጊያለሽ?
I go for walks.	• **Ïnsherasherallehu.**	እንሸራሸራለሁ
I do some sport.	• **Sport ïserallehu.**	ስፖርት እሰራለሁ
I go to the discotheque.	• **Wede diskotek ïhédallehu.**	ወደ ዲስኮተክ እሔዳለሁ
I go skiing.	• **Beberedo lay ïnsheratetallehu.**	በበረዶ ላይ እንሸራተታለሁ
I go to the seaside.	• **Wede bahïr dar ïhédallehu.**	ወደ ባሕር ዳር እሔዳለሁ

Who ... with?

Who are you spending your holidays with?	• **Ye'ïreft gzéhn/gzéshn keman gar tasalfewalleh/ tasalfiwallesh?**	የዕረፍት ግዜህን/ግዜሽን ከማን ጋር ታሳልፋዋለህ/ ታሳልፊዋለሽ?
Who are you going on holiday with?	• **Le'ïreft keman gar tïhédalleh/tïhédjiyallesh?**	ለዕረፍት ከማን ጋር ትሔዳለህ/ ትሔጂያለሽ?
(I'm going) with my friends.	• **Kegwaddeñoché gar ïhédallehu.**	ከጓደኞቼ ጋር እሔዳለሁ
(I'm going) with my parents.	• **Kebéteseboché gar ïhédallehu.**	ከቤተሰቦቼ ጋር እሔዳለሁ

Tourist Information

What ...?

What places of interest are there to see ... ?	• **Mïn yemitayu asdenaqi botawoch allu?**	ምን የሚታዩ አስደናቂ ቦታዎች አሉ?
What are the city's main attractions?	• **Yeketemaw wanna maraki negeroch yetïñoch nachew?**	የከተማው ዋና ማራኪ ነገሮች የትኞቹ ናቸው?
There's a museum.	• **Bétemezekr alle.**	ቤተመዘክር አለ
There's a sea-front promenade.	• **Yebahr darcha godena allew.**	የባሕር ዳርቻ ጎዳና አለው
There are a lot of tourist itineraries.	• **Bzu yegobñiwoc yeshrïshïr botawoch allut.**	ብዙ የጎብኚዎች የሽርሽር ቦታዎች አሉት
There are a lot of historical monuments.	• **Bzu yetarik qïrsa qïrs allut.**	ብዙ የታሪክ ቅርሳ ቅርስ አሉት

Do they organize ...?

Do they organize any tourist itineraries?	• **Yeturist gubïñt yazegadjallu wey?**	የቱሪስት ጉብኝት ያዘጋጃሉ ወይ?
Do they organize any excursions?	• **Gubïñt yïzzegadjal wey?**	ጉብኝት ይዘጋጃል ወይ?
Could you recommend some excursions?	• **Sïle gubïñt mïn tmekreñalleh?**	ስለ ጉብኝት ምን ትመክረኛለህ?
Could you recommend a guided tour?	• **Asqedmo sletezegage gubïñt mïn tmekreñalleh?**	አስቀድሞ ስለተዘጋጀ ጉብኝት ምን ትመክረኛለህ?

We could ...

We could go to the museum.	• **Wede bétemezekr lemehéd ïnchïlallen.**	ወደ ቤተመዘክር ለመሔድ እንችላለን
We could go to the cinema.	• **Wede sinema lemehéd ïnchïlallen.**	ወደ ሲነማ ለመሔድ እንችላለን
You could go to the theatre.	• **Wede tïyatr lemehéd ïnchïlallen.**	ወደ ትያትር ለመሔድ ትችላለህ/ትችያለሽ
Yes, that's a great idea.	• **Melkam hasab.**	መልካም ሐሳብ
No, I'm tired.	• **Aychalm, dekmoñal.**	አይቻልም፡ ደክሞኛል
No, I don't feel like it.	• **Des allalleñm.**	ደስ አላለኝም
No, I'm busy	• **Sïra beztobñal.**	ሥራ በዝቶብኛል

Hotel

Checking in

Good morning. Can I help you?	• **Ïndemn adderu, mïn lïtazez?**	እንደምን አደሩ፡ ምን ልታዘዝ?
Good morning, I'm Mr. Skelton.	• **Ïndemn adderu, ato Skelton.**	እንደምን አደሩ አቶ ስከልቶን
I booked a room.	• **And meñïta kïfïl asmezgbé nebber.**	አንድ መኝታ ክፍል አስመዝግቤ ነበር
I have a room booked.	• **And yetemezegebe meñïta kïfïl alleñ.**	አንድ የተመዘገበ መኝታ ክፍል አለኝ
I haven't booked.	• **Alasmezgebkum.**	አላስመዘገብኩም

Do you have a single room?	• **Land sew yemihon meñta kïfïl alachuh wey?**	ላንድ ሰው የሚሆን መኝታ ክፍል አላችሁ ወይ?
Do you have a double room?	• **Lehulet sew meñïta alachuh wey?**	ለሁለት ሰው መኝታ አላችሁ ወይ?
At the moment we're full.	• **Legizéw hullum teyzewal.**	ለጊዜው ሁሉም ተይዘዋል

For how long?

For how long?	• **Lesïnt gzé?**	ለስንት ግዜ?
For how many nights?	• **Lesïnt lélit?**	ለስንት ሌሊት?
From ... to ...	• **Ke ... ïske.**	ከ ... እስከ
For one night.	• **Land lélit.**	ላንድ ሌሊት
For two weeks.	• **Lehulet samïnt.**	ለሁለት ሳምንት

How much ...?

How much is it for one night ?	• **Le'and lélit wagaw sïnt new?**	ለአንድ ሌሊት ዋጋው ስንት ነው?
How much is it for one person?	• **Le'and sew wagaw sïnt new?**	ለአንድ ሰው ዋጋው ስንት ነው?
How much is it for one room?	• **Le'and meñïta kïfïl wagaw sïnt new?**	ለአንድ መኝታ ክፍል ዋጋው ስንት ነው?
How much is it for full board?	• **Lemulu mestengdo wagaw sïnt new?**	ለሙሉ መስተንግዶ ዋጋው ስንት ነው?
How much is it for half board?	• **Lekefil (gmash) mestengdo wagaw sïnt new?**	ለከፊል(ግማሽ) መስተንግዶ ዋጋው ስንት ነው?

Breakfast/meals

Is breakfast included?	• **Kïfyaw qwïrsn yïchemral wey?**	ክፍያው ቍርስን ይጨምራል ወይ?
Are meals included?	• **Kïfyaw mïgbïn yïchemral wey?**	ክፍያው ምግብን ይጨምራል ወይ?
Yes, it's all included.	• **Awo, hullunm yateqallïlal.**	አዎ፡ ሁሉንም ያጠቃልላል
No, they're not included in the price.	• **Aydellem, hullunm ayateqallïlm.**	አይደለም፡ ሁሉንም አያጠቃልልም

Checking out

(I would like) the bill, please.	• **Ïbakwon hisab yamtuluñ.**	እባክዎን ሒሳብ ያምጡልኝ
Could you prepare the bill, please?	• **Ïbakwon hisab yngeruñ.**	እባክዎን ሒሳብ ይንገሩኝ
Here you are, thank you.	• **Yhewlïh, amesegnallehu.**	ይኸውልህ፡ አመሰግናለሁ

Restaurant

Eating out

Hello, is that "Bologna" restaurant?	• **Halo, Boloña mïgïb bét new?**	ሀሎ፡ ቦሎኛ ምግብ ቤት ነው?
Yes, what can I do for you?	• **Awo, mïn lïtazez?**	አዎ፡ ምን ልታዘዝ?
I'd [I would] like (to book) a table for two (people).	• **Lehulet sew bota ïfelg nebber.**	ለሁለት ሰው ቦታ እፈልግ ነበር
I'd like (to book) a table for five.	• **Le'ammïst sew bota ïfelg nebber.**	ለአምስት ሰው ቦታ እፈልግ ነበር

For what time?	• **Lesïnt se'at?**	ለስንት ሰዓት?
For two o'clock.	• **Lesïmmïnt se'at.**	ለስምንት ሰዓት
Fine, what's your name?	• **Betam tru, man lïbel?**	በጣም ጥሩ፡ ማን ልበል?

Snacks

Waiter!	• **Asallafi!**	አሳላፊ!
Waitress!	• **Astenagaj!**	አስተናጋጅ!
Yes, what would you like?	• **Ïshi, mïn lïtazez ?**	እሺ፡ ምን ልታዘዝ?
I'd like a coffee.	• **Bunna alle?**	ቡና አለ?
I'd like a cappuccino.	• **Bunna bewetet alle (kapuchino alle)?**	ቡና በውተት አለ (ካፑቺኖ አለ)?
I'd like a sandwich.	• **Sandwich alle?**	ሳንድዊች አለ?
I'd like a cheese roll.	• **Yeformadjo sandwich alle?**	የፎርማጆ ሳንድዊች አለ?
I'd like a 'croissant'.	• **Brïyosh alle?**	ብርዮሽ አለ?
I'd like an orangeade.	• **Aranchiata alle?**	አራንቻታ አለ?
I'd like a small pizza.	• **Pissa alle?**	ፒሳ አለ?

Ordering

I'd like to see the menu.	• **Yemïgïb zïrzïr lemayet ïfelgallehu.**	የምግብ ዝርዝር ለማየት እፈልጋለሁ
(As a starter) I'd like ham and melon.	• **Beqïdmiya ye'asama sïgana melon btaqerblïñ.**	በቅድሚያ የአሳማ ስጋና መሎን ብታቀርብልኝ
(As a starter) I'd like Russian salad.	• **Beqïdmiya yeRussia selata btaqerblïñ.**	በቅድሚያ የሩስያ ሰላጣ ብታቀርብልኝ

First course

For first course I'd like (some) lasagna.	• **Medjemerya lasaña ïfelgallehu.**	መጀመርያ ላዛኛ እፈልጋለሁ
For first course I'd like (some) tagliatelle with tomato sauce.	• **Medjemerya talyateli ketimatim sïgo gar ïfelgallehu.**	መጀመርያ ታልያተሊ ከቲማቲም ስጎ ጋር እፈልጋለሁ
For first course I'd like (some) spaghetti.	• **Medjemerya spageti ïfelgallehu.**	መጀመርያ ስፓገቲ እፈልጋለሁ

Drinks

And what would you like to drink?	• **Mïn metetat yfelïgallu?**	ምን መጠጣት ይፈልጋሉ?
I'd like an orangeade.	• **Aranchiata ïfelïgallehu.**	አረንቻታ እፈልጋለሁ
I'd like a bottle of red/white wine.	• **Qey/nech weyn-tej ïfelgallehu.**	ቀይ/ነጭ ወይን ጠጅ እፈልጋለሁ
I'd like some fizzy/natural mineral water.	• **Gaz yallew/yelélew ambo wïha ïfelgallehu.**	ጋዝ ያለው/የሌለው አምቦ ውኃ እፈልጋለሁ

Second course

(For the second course) what do you recommend?	• **Sekondo mïn yshalleñal?**	ሰኮንዶ ምን ይሻለኛል?
I recommend the dish of the day.	• **Yeqenu mïgïb yshallewotal.**	የቀኑ ምግብ ይሻለዎታል
I recommend this (dish).	• **Yïh mïgïb yshallewotal.**	ይህ ምግብ ይሻለዎታል
I recommend the fried fish	• **Yetetebese asa yshallewotal.**	የተጠበሰ ዓሣ ይሻለዎታል

Side dishes

All right, I'll have this with mixed salad.	• Ïshi, kesu gar dïbïlq selata amtalñ.	እሺ፡ ከሱ ጋር ድብልቅ ሰላጣ አምጣልኝ
Thanks, but I prefer French fries.	• Amesegnallehu, honom yetetebese dïnïch yshalleñal.	አመሰግናለሁ፡ ሆኖም የተጠበሰ ድንች ይሻለኛል
Thanks, but I prefer cooked vegetables.	• Amesegnallehu, honom yetetebese atkïlt yshalleñal.	አመሰግናለሁ፡ ሆኖም የተጠበሰ አትክልት ይሻለኛል

Dessert

Do you have any sweet/cake?	• Kék alachuh wey?	ኬክ አላችሁ ወይ?
Do you have (any) ice-cream?	• Djelati alachuh wey?	ጀላቲ አላችሁ ወይ?
Do you have (any) cheese?	• Formadjo alachuh wey?	ፎርማጆ አላችሁ ወይ?
Do you have (any) fresh fruit?	• Adadis frafréwoch aluwachuh wey?	አዳዲስ ፍራፍሬዎች አሏችሁ ወይ?
I'm sorry, it's finished.	• Yqïrta, alqwal.	ይቅርታ፡ አልቋል

Compliments

It's all very nice.	• Hullum tafach new.	ሁሉም ጣፋጭ ነው
It's very nice.	• Betam tafach new.	በጣም ጣፋጭ ነው

Complaints

The soup is too salty/needs more salt.	• Yïh mereq chew beztobetal/yïh mereq chew yansewal.	ይህ መረቅ ጨው በዝቶበታል /ይህ መረቅ ጨው ያንሰዋል
The meat is over-cooked/ underdone.	• Sïgaw betam beslïwal/ sïgaw bzum albeselem	ስጋው በጣም በስሏል/ ስጋው ብዙም አልበሰለም
The pizza is burnt.	• Pissaw arrïwal.	ፒሳው አሯል
The plate/glass is dirty.	• Sahnu qoshïshwal/ bïrchïqow qoshïshwal.	ሳህኑ ቆሽሿል/ ብርጭቆው ቆሽሿል

The bill

Can I have the bill, please?	• Bilun biyaqerbulñ?	ቢሉን ቢያቀርቡልኝ

Shopping

At what time ...?

At what time do (clothes) shops open?	• Yelïbs suq besïnt se'at yïkkefetal?	የልብስ ሱቁ በስንት ሰዓት ይከፈታል?
They open at eight thirty.	• Behulet se'at tekul yïkkefetal.	በሁለት ሰዓት ተኩል ይከፈታል
At what time do (clothes) shops close?	• Yelïbs suq besïnt se'at yïzzegal?	የልብስ ሱቁ በስንት ሰዓት ይዘጋል?
They close at...	• Be ... yïzzegal.	በ ... ይዘጋል

Where is a ...?

Is there a supermarket?	• Ïzih akababi supermarkét alle wey?	እዚህ አካባቢ ሱፐርማርኬት አለ ወይ?
Where's the shopping centre?	• Yegebeya aderash yet new?	የገበያ አደራሽ የት ነው?
Where's the market?	• Gebeyaw yet new?	ገበያው የት ነው?

Where is a greengrocer's?	• **Ye'atkïltïna yefrafré gebeya yet new?**	የአትክልትና የፍራፍሬ ገበያ የት ነው?
Where is a bureau de change/ an exchange bureau?	• **Frank yemimenezerbet yet new?**	ፍራንክ የሚመነዘርበት ቦታ የት ነው?
Where is a chemist's?	• **Medhanit bét yet new?**	መድሓኒት ቤት የት ነው?
Where is a butcher's?	• **Yesïga meshecha bet yet new?**	የስጋ መሸጫ ቤት የት ነው?
Where is a baker's?	• **Dabbo bét yet new?**	ዳቦ ቤት የት ነው?
Where is a pastry shop?	• **Kék bét yet new?**	ኬክ ቤት የት ነው?
Where is a jeweller's?	• **Werq serri bét yet new?**	ወርቅ ሰሪ ቤት የት ነው?

Departments

Where's the food department?	• **Yememegebya kïfïl yet new?**	የመመገብያ ክፍል የት ነው?
Where's the clothing department?	• **Yelïbs meshecha kïfïl yet new?**	የልብስ መሸጫ ክፍል የት ነው?
Where's the book department?	• **Yemetsahïft meshecha kïfïl yet new?**	የመጻሕፍት መሸጫ ክፍል የት ነው?
Where's the electrical department?	• **Ye'élektrik ïqawoch meshecha yet new?**	የኤለክትሪክ ዕቃዎች መሸጫ ክፍል የት ነው?

I would like ...

I'd like a litre of milk.	• **And litr wetet ïfelgallehu.**	አንድ ሊትር ወተት እፈልጋለሁ
I'd like a kilo of bread.	• **And kilo dabbo ïfelgallehu.**	አንድ ኪሎ ዳቦ እፈልጋለሁ
I'd like a dozen eggs.	• **And derzen ïnqwïlal ïfelgallehu.**	አንድ ደርዘን እንቍላል እፈልጋለሁ
I'd like a plastic bag.	• **And yeplastik shanta ïfelgallehu.**	አንድ የፕላስቲክ ሻንጣ እፈልጋለሁ
I'd like a bottle of wine.	• **And termus yeweyn tej ïfelgallehu.**	አንድ ጠርሙስ የወይን ጠጅ እፈልጋለሁ
I'd like a pullover.	• **And shurab ïfelgallehu.**	አንድ ሹራብ እፈልጋለሁ
I'd like a raincoat.	• **And yeznam kaport ïfelgallehu.**	አንድ የዝናም ካፖርት እፈልጋለሁ
I'd like an umbrella.	• **And djantïla ïfelgallehu.**	አንድ ጃንጥላ እፈልጋለሁ
I'd like a bag.	• **And ye'ïj shanta ïfelgallehu.**	አንድ የእጅ ሻንጣ እፈልጋለሁ
I'd like a jacket.	• **And djaket ïfelgallehu.**	አንድ ጃኬት እፈልጋለሁ
I'd like a coat.	• **And kot ïfelgallehu.**	አንድ ኮት እፈልጋለሁ
I'd like a pair of shoes.	• **Chamma ïfelgallehu.**	ጫማ እፈልጋለሁ

Made of ...

Made of nylon.	• **Kenaylon yeteserra.**	ከናይሎን የተሰራ
Made of leather.	• **Keqoda yeteserra.**	ከቆዳ የተሰራ
Made of plastic.	• **Keplastik yeteserra.**	ከፕላስቲክ የተሰራ
Made of silk.	• **Kehar yeteserra.**	ከሀር የተሰራ
Made of cotton.	• **Ketït yeteserra.**	ከጥጥ የተሰራ

Paying

How much (is it)?	•**Yïh, wagaw sïnt new?**	ይህ፡ ዋጋው ስንት ነው?
Can I pay by cheque?	• **Chék mekfel ychalal wey?**	ቼክ መክፈል ይቻላል ወይ?
Can I pay by credit card?	• **Bekredit kard mekfel ychalal wey**	በክረዲት ካርድ መክፈል ይቻላል ወይ?

Post Office

Where is a ...?

Excuse me, where is a post office?	• **Yqïrta, posta bét yet new?**	ይቅርታ፡ ፖስታ ቤት የት ነው?
Excuse me, where is a tobacconist's?	• **Yqïrta, sigara yemishetbet suq bét yet new?**	ይቅርታ፡ ሲጋራ የሚሸጥበት ሱቅ ቤት የት ነው?
Excuse me, where is a post box?	• **Yqïrta, yeposta satn yet new?**	ይቅርታ፡ የፖስታ ሣጥን የት ነው?
It's there, near the bank.	• **Ïziyaw, banku ategeb new.**	እዚያው፡ ባንኩ አጠገብ ነው
It's down there, on the right.	• **Ïtach, wede qeñ new.**	እታች፡ ወደ ቀኝ ነው
I'm sorry, I don't know.	• **Yqïrta, allawqewm.**	ይቅርታ፡ አላውቀውም

At what time ...?

At what time does the post office open?	• **Posta bétu besïnt se'at yïkkefetal?**	ፖስታ ቤቱ በስንት ሰዓት ይከፈታል?
At what time does the post office close?	• **Posta bétu besïnt se'at yïzzegal?**	ፖስታ ቤቱ በስንት ሰዓት ይዘጋል?
It opens at eight fifteen.	• **Behulet se'at kerub yïkkefetal .**	በሁለት ሰዓት ከሩብ ይከፈታል
It closes at 2.00 pm.	• **Besïmmïnt s'at kemïshïtu yïzzegal.**	በስምንት ሰዓት ከምሽቱ ይዘጋል

How much ...?

How much is it to send a letter to Germany?	• **Debdabé wede Djermen ager lemelak wagaw sïnt ydersal?**	ደብዳቤ ወደ ጀርመን አገር ለመላክ ዋጋው ስንት ይደርሳል?
How much is it to send a card to Belgium?	• **Post kard wede Beldjum ager lemelak wagaw sïnt ydersal?**	ፖስት ካርድ ወደ በልጂዩም አገር ለመላክ ዋጋው ስንት ይደርሳል?
How much is it to send a parcel to Ireland?	• **And tïql wede Ireland lemelak wagaw sïnt ydersal?**	አንድ ጥቅል ወደ አየርላንድ ለመላክ ዋጋው ስንት ይደርሳል?
How much is it to send a greeting card?	• **Yeselamta kard lemelak wagaw sïnt ydersal?**	የሰላምታ ካርድ ለመላክ ዋጋው ስንት ይደርሳል?

Stamps

Would you give me a stamp for Great Britain, please?	• **Ïbakwon leÏngliz ager témber ystuñ?**	እባክዎን ለእንግሊዝ አገር ቴምብር ይስጡኝ?
Would you give me a stamp for a letter, please?	• **Ïbakwon yedebdabé témber ystuñ?**	እባክዎን የደብዳቤ ቴምብር ይስጡኝ?
Would you give me a stamp for a card, please?	• **Ïbakwon yekard témber ystuñ?**	እባክዎን የካርድ ቴምብር ይስጡኝ?

I would like ...

I'd like to send this letter by air-mail to Holland.	• **Yïchïn debdabé wede Holland be'ayyer lemelak ïfelg nebber.**	ይችን ደብዳቤ ወደ ሆላንድ በአየር ለመላክ እፈልግ ነበር
I'd like to send this parcel to Denmark.	• **Yïchïn kard wede Denmark be'ayyer lemelak ïfelg nebber.**	ይችን ካርድ ወደ ዴንማርክ በአየር ለመላክ እፈልግ ነበር
I'd like to send a registered letter (with advice of receipt) to Australia.	• **Yadera debdabé wede Australia lemelak ïfelg nebber.**	ያደራ ደብዳቤ ወደ አውስትራልያ ለመላክ እፈልግ ነበር

Telephone

Where is ...?

Where's the nearest phone-box?	• **Yetéléfon satn yet new?**	የቴሌፎን ሣጥን የት ነው?
Where's the nearest public phone?	• **Yehïzb téléfon yet new?**	የህዝብ ቴሌፎን የት ነው?
In Piazza Dante, next to the newspaper kiosk.	• **Piyassa Dante yegazéta meshecha bét bestedjerba.**	ፒያሳ ዳንተ የጋዜጣ መሸጫ ቤት በስተጀርባ
A hundred metres on your right.	• **Meto métr besteqeñ.**	መቶ ሜትር በስተቀኝ

Could I ...?

Can I make a phone call to my parents?	• **Lebéteseboché lïdewl ïchlallehu wey?**	ለቤተሰቦቼ ልደውል እችላለሁ ወይ?
Could I make a phone call?	• **Medewel ïchlallehu wey?**	መደወል እችላለሁ ወይ?
Can I phone Sandra?	• **LeSandra lïdewlïlat?**	ለሳንድራ ልደውልላት?
Yes, of course!	• **Awo, ïndéta.**	አዎ፡ እንዴታ

Telephone number

What's your phone number?	• **Téléfon qwïtrïh sïnt new?**	ቴሌፎን ቍጥርህ ስንት ነው?
What is the code for Florence?	• **YeFlorens kod sïnt new?**	የፍሎረንስ ኮድ ስንት ነው?
What number do I have to dial for Great Britain?	• **Wede Ïngliz ager lemedewel yetïñawn qwïtr lïteqem?**	ወደ እንግሊዝ አገር ለመደወል የትኛውን ቍጥር ልጠቀም?
My number is (0184) 357136.	• **Yetéléfon qwïtré (0184) 357136 new.**	የተሌፎን ቍጥሬ [0184] 357136 ነው
The code for Florence is 055.	• **YeFlorens kod 055 new.**	የፍሎረንስ ኮድ 055 ነው

Speaking

Hello!	• **Halo!**	ሀሎ
Hello! Who's speaking?	• **Halo, man lïbel?**	ሀሎ፡ ማን ልበል?
This is Mr. Haile.	• **Ato Hayle ïballallehu.**	አቶ ኃይለ እባላለሁ
This is Anna.	• **Anna ïballallehu.**	አና እባላለሁ
Could I speak to Dr. Brandi?	• **Dokter Brandi lemanegager ïchlallehu wey?**	ዶክተር ብራንዲን ለማነጋገር እችላለሁ ወይ?
Is Sonia there?	• **Sonya ïziyaw allech wey?**	ሶኒያ እዚያው አለች ወይ?
I can't hear you, please speak louder!	• **Aysemam chiok yïbelu.**	አይሰማም፡ ጮክ ይበሉ
Yes, one moment!	• **Awo, andé.**	አዎ፡ አንዴ
Yes, it's me.	• **Awo, ïné neñ.**	አዎ፡ እኔ ነኝ
I'll [I will] call him for you.	• **Lïtralwot.**	ልጥራልዎት
I'll call her for you.	• **Lïtralwot.**	ልጥራልዎት
You've got the wrong number.	• **Tesastewal.**	ተሳስተዋል
I'm sorry, but he has just gone out.	• **Yqïrta, ahununu wetïtwal/ wettallech.**	ይቅርታ፡ አሁኑኑ ወጥትዋል/ ወጥታለች
Could you phone tonight?	• **Kemïshïtu lidewlu yïchlallu wey?**	ከምሽቱ ሊደውሉ ይችላሉ ወይ?

Could you call back later?	• Tinïsh qoytew lidewïlu yïchlallu wey?	ትንሽ ቆይተው ሊደውሉ ይችላሉ ወይ?
Could you call back in ten minutes?	• Ke'asïr deqiqa behwala lidewïlu yïchlallu wey?	ከአሥር ደቂቃ በኋላ ሊደውሉ ይችላሉ ወይ?

Bank

I would like ...

I'd like to change some travellers' cheques.	• Tqit yegwïzo chék lemeqeyer ïfelg nebber.	ጥቂት የጉዞ ቼክ ለመቀየር እፈልግ ነበር
I'd like to change ... dollars.	• Dollar lemeqeyer ïfelg nebber.	ዶላር ለመቀየር እፈልግ ነበር
I'd like to change ... lire.	• Lire lemeqeyer ïfelg nebber.	ሊረ ለመቀየር እፈልግ ነበር
I'd like to change ... pounds.	• Pound lemeqeyer ïfelg nebber.	ፓውንድ ለመቀየር እፈልግ ነበር

Identification

Have you any means of identification?	• Yemetaweqya wereqet allewot wey?	የመታወቅያ ወረቀት አለዎት ወይ?
Yes, I have my passport.	• Awo, pasport yjallehu.	አዎ፡ ፓስፖርት ይዣለሁ
Sign here, please!	• Ïbakwo ïzih ga yferïmu.	እባክዎ እዚህ ጋ ይፈርሙ

The exchange rate

What is the exchange rate for the Australian Dollar?	• YeAustralia genzeb sïnt ymenezeral?	የአውስትራልያ ገንዘብ ስንት ይመነዘራል?
What is the exchange rate for the Pound?	• And Pound sïnt ymenezeral?	አንድ ፓውንድ ስንት ይመነዘራል?
What is the exchange rate for the Yen?	• And Yen sïnt ymenezeral?	አንድ የን ስንት ይመነዘራል?

Could you give me ...?

Could you give me some ten thousand lire notes?	• Ye'asïr shi Lire tïqloch lisetuñ yïchlallu wey?	የአስር ሺ ሊረ ጥቅሎች ሊሰጡኝ ይችላሉ ወይ?
Could you give me two five thousand lire notes?	• Hulet ye'ammïst shi Lire tïqloch lisetuñ yïchlallu wey?	ሁለት የአምስት ሺ ሊረ ጥቅሎች ሊሰጡኝ ይችላሉ ወይ?
Could you give me some change?	• Tïqit mïnzari lisetuñ yïchlallu wey?	ጥቂት ምንዛሪ ሊሰጡኝ ይችላሉ ወይ?
And the change, how would you like it?	• Mïnzariwn bemn aynet new yemifelgut?	ምንዛሪውን በምን ዓይነት ነው የሚፈልጉት?
I would like it in thousand lire notes.	• Ye'and shi tïqloch ïfelg nebber.	የአንድ ሺ ጥቅሎች እፈልግ ነበር
It doesn't matter!	• Chïgr yellem.	ችግር የለም
As you like!	• Ïnde fellegu.	እንደ ፈለጉ

Health

How do you feel?

How are you?	• Ïnde mïn neh Ïnde mïn nesh	እንደ ምን ነህ ? (m) እንደ ምን ነሽ? (f)
How is it going?	• Hunétaw ïndét new?	ሁኔታው እንዴት ነው?
How do you feel?	• Mïn ysemahal? Mïn ysemashal?	ምን ይሰማሃል? (m) ምን ይሰማሻል? (f)
I am well/I'm fine.	• Deg, melkam [dehna neñ].	ደግ፡ መልካም [ደህና ነኝ]
I am not well/I don't feel well.	• Meṯfo ysemañal.	መጥፎ ይሰማኛል
I feel weak.	• Beṯam dïkam ysemañal.	በጣም ድካም ይሰማኛል
I feel better.	• Ahun yshalleñal.	አሁን ይሻለኛል

What's wrong ...?

What's wrong with you?	• Yemiyaschegrïh/ Yemiyaschgrïsh mïnd new?	የሚያስቸግርህ/የሚያስቸግርሽ ምንድ ነው?
What's wrong?	• Chïgru mïnd new?	ችግሩ ምንድ ነው?
Where does it hurt?	• Mnïhn/shïn yamhal/ yamshal?	ምንህን/ሽን ያምሃል/ያምሻል?
What symptoms do you have?	• Mïn ysemahal/ ysemashal?	ምን ይሰማሃል/ይሰማሻል?

Symptoms

I've got toothache.	• Ṯïrsén yameñal.	ጥርሴን ያመኛል
I've got a sore throat.	• Guroroyen yameñal.	ጉሮሮየን ያመኛል
I've got stomach-ache.	• Hodén yameñal.	ሆዴን ያመኛል
I've got backache.	• Wegebén yameñal.	ወገቤን ያመኛል
I've got a headache.	• Rasén yameñal.	ራሴን ያመኛል
My feet hurt.	• Ïgrén yameñal.	እግሬን ያመኛል
My eyes hurt.	• Aynén yameñal.	ዐይኔን ያመኛል
I'm hot.	• Muqet ysémañal.	ሙቀት ይሰማኛል
I'm cold.	• Bïrd ysémañal.	ብርድ ይሰማኛል
I'm hungry.	• Rboñal.	ርቦኛል
I'm thirsty.	• Ṯemtoñal.	ጠምቶኛል
I have a pain here.	• Ïzih lay hïmem ysemañal.	እዚህ ላይ ሕመም ይሰማኛል
I've got cramps.	• Qurṯmat ysemañal.	ቁርጥማት ይሰማኛል
I've got sun-stroke.	• Tsehay mettoñal.	ፀሐይ መትቶኛል
I've got diarrhoea.	• Teqmaṯ yzoñal.	ተቅማጥ ይዞኛል
I've vomited.	• Astawekeñ.	አስታወከኝ
I have a temperature.	• Tïkusat allebïñ.	ትኩሳት አለብኝ
I've got flu.	• Gunfan yzoñal.	ጉንፋን ይዞኛል
I've got high/low blood pressure.	• Yedem bïzat/yedem manes allebïñ.	የደም ብዛት/የደም ማነስ አለብኝ

Injury

I've burnt myself.	• Ïsat fedjeñ.	እሳት ፈጀኝ
I've hurt myself.	• Gudat dersobñal.	ጉዳት ደርሶብኛል
I've injured myself.	• Tegwedchiallehu.	ተጐድቻለሁ

I've pricked myself.	• **Tewegchiallehu.**	ተወግቻለሁ
I've cut myself.	• **Teqoretku.**	ተቆረጥኩ

At the chemist's

I would like some aspirin.	• **Asprin allachuh wey?**	አስፕሪን አላችሁ ወይ?
I would like some bandages.	• **Fasha allachuh wey?**	ፋሻ አላችሁ ወይ?
I would like some plasters.	• **Plaster allachuh wey?**	ፕላስተር አላችሁ ወይ?
I would like some tablets.	• **Kenin allachuh wey?**	ኪኒን አላችሁ ወይ?
I would like cotton-wool.	• **Tït allachuh wey?**	ጥጥ አላችሁ ወይ?
I would like a cough syrup.	• **Yesal shïrop allachuh wey?**	የሳል ሽሮፕ አላችሁ ወይ?
I would like something for a head-ache.	• **Yehone yeras mïtat medhanit allachuh wey?**	የሆነ የራስ ምታት መድኃኒት አላችሁ ወይ?
I would like something to treat a burn/scald.	• **Yehone yeqatelo medhanit allachuh wey?**	የሆነ የቃጠሎ መድኃኒት አላችሁ ወይ?
I would like something for an insect bite.	• **Yehone yetebayoch mekelakeya medhanit allachuh wey?**	የሆነ የተባዮች መከላከያ መድኃኒት አላችሁ ወይ?

Prescriptions

Take one spoonful of this medicine twice a day.	• **Kezihu medhanit and mankiya beqen hulet gzé ywsedu.**	ከዚሁ መድኃኒት አንድ ማንኪያ በቀን ሁለት ግዜ ይውሰዱ
Take three drops ... every two hours.	• **Sost tebta beyehulet se'at ywsedu.**	ሦስት ጠብታ በየሁለት ሰዓት ይውሰዱ
Take one tablet before each meal.	• **Kememegebwo befït and kinin ywsedu.**	ከመመገብዎ በፊት አንድ ኪኒን ይውሰዱ
Take half a dose ... in the evening.	• **Mata gmash doz ... ywsedu.**	ማታ ግማሽ ዶዝ ... ይውሰዱ

Free Time

Hobbies/Free time

What is your favourite hobby?	• **Betam yemimarkïh yegzé masallefya yetñaw new?**	በጣም የሚማርክህ የግዜ ማሳለፍያ የትኛው ነው?
How do you spend your free time?	• **Tïrf gzéhïn ïndét tasalfewalleh?**	ትርፍ ግዜህን እንዴት ታሳልፈዋለህ?
What do you do in your free time?	• **Betïrf gzéh mïn tadergalleh?**	በትርፍ ግዜህ ምን ታደርጋለህ?

I like ...

(I like) collecting stamps.	• **Témber mesebseb des yleñal.**	ቴምብር መሰብሰብ ደስ ይለኛል
(I like) collecting post cards.	• **Postkardoch mesebseb des yleñal.**	ፖስትካርዶች መሰብሰብ ደስ ይለኛል
(I like) playing draughts.	• **Dama mechawet des yleñal.**	ዳማ መጫወት ደስ ይለኛል
(I like) playing chess.	• **Ces mechawet des yleñal.**	ቸስ መጫወት ደስ ይለኛል
(I like) playing cards.	• **Karta mechawet des yleñal.**	ካርታ መጫወት ደስ ይለኛል
(I like) playing billiards.	• **Kerenbula mechawet des yleñal.**	ከረንቡላ መጫወት ደስ ይለኛል

(I like) photography.	• **Fotograf mansat des yleñal.**	ፎቶግራፍ ማንሳት ደስ ይለኛል
(I like) model making.	• **Sïne-tïbeb des yleñal.**	ስነ-ጥበብ ደስ ይለኛል
(I like) computers.	• **Kompyuter des yleñal.**	ኮምፒዩተር ደስ ይለኛል
(I like) football.	• **Yegïr kwas des yleñal.**	የግር ኳስ ደስ ይለኛል
(I like) music.	• **Musiqa des yleñal.**	ሙዚቃ ደስ ይለኛል
(I like) playing the guitar.	• **Gitar mechawet des yleñal.**	ጊታር መጫወት ደስ ይለኛል
(I like) ballet.	• **Klasikal dans des yleñal.**	ክላሲካል ዳንስ ደስ ይለኛል
(I like) walking.	• **Be'ïgr megwaz des yleñal.**	በእግር መጓዝ ደስ ይለኛል

Sports

Do you do any sport?	• **Sport tïseralleh wey?**	ስፖርት ትሰራለህ ወይ?
Yes, I go cross-country running.	• **Awo, ager aqwarach rucha ïrotallehu.**	አዎ፡ አገር አቋራጭ ሩጫ እሮጣለሁ
Yes, I do high-jumps.	• **Awo, ïzelallehu.**	አዎ፡ እዘላለሁ
Yes, I go swimming.	• **Awo, ïwañallehu.**	አዎ፡ እዋኛለሁ
Yes, I go cycling.	• **Awo, bebisiklet wdïdïr ïsatefallehu.**	አዎ፡ በቢሲክለት ውድድር እሳተፋለሁ
Yes, I play football.	• **Awo, yegïr kwas ïchawetallehu.**	አዎ፡ የግር ኳስ እጫወታለሁ
Yes, I play tennis.	• **Awo, ténis ïchawetallehu.**	አዎ፡ ቴንስ እጫወታለሁ
Yes, I play basketball.	• **Awo, yemereb kwas ïchawetallehu.**	አዎ፡ የመረብ ኳስ እጫወታለሁ
Yes, I play handball.	• **Awo, ye'ïdj kwas ïchawetallehu.**	አዎ፡ የእጅ ኳስ እጫወታለሁ
Yes, I play rugby.	• **Awo, rugby ïchawetallehu.**	አዎ፡ ራግቢ እጫወታለሁ

What do you do ...?

What do you usually do in the evening?	• **Abzañawn gzé mata mïn tïseralleh?**	አብዛኛውን ግዜ ማታ ምን ትሰራለህ?
How do you spend your evenings?	• **Mata ïndét tasalfewalleh?**	ማታ እንዴት ታሳልፈዋለህ?
I watch television.	• **Télevijn ayallehu.**	ቴለቪዥን አያለሁ
I listen to music.	• **Muziqa adamtallehu.**	ሙዚቃ አዳምጣለሁ
I go out with my friends.	• **Kegwaddeñoché gar ïwetallehu.**	ከጓደኞቼ ጋር እወጣለሁ
I read a book.	• **Metshaf anebballehu.**	መጽሐፍ አነባለሁ
I play cards.	• **Karta ïchawetallehu.**	ካርታ እጫወታለሁ
Nothing in particular.	• **Mïnm lyu neger alseram.**	ምንም ልዩ ነገር አልሰራም

What do you like...?

What do you like to read?	• **Mïn manbeb des ylehal?**	ምን ማንበብ ደስ ይለሃል?
I like adventure books.	• **Ye'advéncher metsahïft des yïluñal.**	የአድቬንቸር መጻሕፍት ደስ ይሉኛል
I like science fiction books	• **Yesayns lboledoch des yïluñal.**	የሳይንስ ልቦለዶች ደስ ይሉኛል
I like sports papers.	• **Yesport gazétoch des yïluñal.**	የስፖርት ጋዜጦች ደስ ይሉኛል

I like comics.	• **Kartun manbeb des yïluñal.**	ካርቱን ማንበብ ደስ ይሉኛል
I like fashion magazines.	• **Yefashïn metsïhétoch des yïluñal.**	የፋሽን መጽሔቶች ደስ ይሉኛል
I like music magazines.	• **Yemuziqa metsïhétoch des yïluñal.**	የሙዚቃ መጽሔቶች ደስ ይሉኛል

What do you do ...?

What do you do at weekends ?	• **Qdaména ïhud mïn tadergalleh?**	ቅዳሜና እሁድ ምን ታደርጋለህ?
What do you do during the holidays?	• **Be'ïreft gzéh mïn tadergalleh?**	በዕረፍት ግዜህ ምን ታደርጋለህ?
I sometimes go horse-riding.	• **Andandé beferes ïnsherasherallehu.**	አንዳንዴ በፈረስ እንሸራሸራለሁ
I often go to play ...	• **Abzañawn gzé lemechawet ... ïhédallehu.**	አብዛኛውን ግዜ ለመጫወት ... እሔዳለሁ
I usually go dancing.	• **Abzañawn gzé ledans ïwetallehu.**	አብዛኛውን ግዜ ለዳንስ እወጣለሁ
I usually go fishing.	• **Abzañawn gzé asa lematmed ïhédallehu.**	አብዛኛውን ግዜ ዓሣ ለማጥመድ እሔዳለሁ
I usually go to the theatre.	• **Abzañawn gzé tïyatr ïhédallehu.**	አብዛኛውን ግዜ ትያትር እሔዳለሁ
I usually go to see friends.	• **Abzañawn gzé gwadeñochén lemagïñet ïwetallehu.**	አብዛኛውን ግዜ ጓደኞቼን ለማግኘት እወጣለሁ
I usually go to the cinema.	• **Abzañawn gzé sinema bét ïhédallehu.**	አብዛኛውን ግዜ ሲነማ ቤት እሔዳለሁ
I usually go to the sports club.	• **Abzañawn gzé sport kleb ïhédallehu.**	አብዛኛውን ግዜ ስፖርት ክለብ እሔዳለሁ
I usually go to concerts.	• **Abzañawn gzé konsert ïhédallehu.**	አብዛኛውን ግዜ ኮንሰርት እሔዳለሁ
I usually go to discos.	• **Abzañawn gzé disko bét ïhédallehu.**	አብዛኛውን ግዜ ዲስኮ ቤት እሔዳለሁ

Television

Which television programmes do you prefer?	• **Yetñawn yetélévijn program tmertalleh?**	የትኛውን የቴለቪዥን ፕሮግራም ትመርጣለህ?
Which are your favourite programmes?	• **Yetñawn yetélévijn program new des yemilh?**	የትኛውን የቴለቪዥን ፕሮግራም ነው ደስ የሚልህ?
I like cartoons.	• **Kartun film des yleñal.**	ካርቱን ፊልም ደስ ይለኛል
I like musical programmes.	• **Yemuziqa program des yleñal.**	የሙዚቃ ፕሮግራም ደስ ይለኛል
I like plays.	• **Drama des yleñal.**	ድራማ ደስ ይለኛል
I like documentaries on nature.	• **Dokuméntari film des yleñal.**	ደኩሜንታሪ ፊልም ደስ ይለኛል
I like sports programmes.	• **Yesport program des yleñal.**	የስፖርት ፕሮግራም ደስ ይለኛል
I like current affairs programmes.	• **Yezéna program des yleñal.**	የዜና ፕሮግራም ደስ ይለኛል
I like serials.	• **Yefïqr film des yleñal.**	የፍቅር ፊልም ደስ ይለኛል

Cinema

Which kind of films do you like?	• **Mïn aynet film des ylïhal?**	ምን ዓይነት ፊልም ደስ ይልሃል?
What kind of films do you like?	• **Mïn aynet film des ylïshal?**	ምን ዓይነት ፊልም ደስ ይልሻል?
I like comedies.	• **Asqiñ film des yleñal.**	አስቂኝ ፊልም ደስ ይለኛል
I like westerns.	• **YeTexas film des yleñal.**	የቴክሳስ ፊልም ደስ ይለኛል
I like dramas.	• **Drama des yleñal.**	ድራማ ደስ ይለኛል
I like adventure films.	• **Ye'advéncher film des yleñal.**	የአድቬንቸር ፊልም ደስ ይለኛል
I like romantic films.	• **Yefïqr film des yleñal.**	የፍቅር ፊልም ደስ ይለኛል
I like historical films.	• **Yetarik film des yleñal.**	የታሪክ ፊልም ደስ ይለኛል
I like horror films	• **Yemiyasfera film des yleñal.**	የሚያስፈራ ፊልም ደስ ይለኛል
Why?	• **Lemïn?**	ለምን?
Because they make me laugh.	• **Sïlemiyasïqeñ.**	ስለሚያስቀኝ
Because they amuse me.	• **Sïlemiyaznanañ.**	ስለሚያዝናናኝ
Did you like Fellini's film?	• **YeFellini film weddedkew wey?**	የፈሊኒን ፊልም ወደድከው ወይ?
Did he like Goldoni's play?	• **YeGoldoni film weddedew wey?**	የጎልዶኒን ፊልም ወደደው ወይ?
Did she like the cartoons?	• **Yekartunun film weddedechïw?**	የካርቱኑን ፊልም ወደደችው ወይ?
Did you like the songs ...?	• **... zefenochun weddedachïhwachew wey?**	... ዘፈኖቹን ወደዳችኋቸው ወይ?
I did/didn't like it.	• **Weddedkut/alwededkutm.**	ወደድኩት/አልወደድኩትም
He did/didn't like it.	• **Weddedew/alwededewm.**	ወደደው/አልወደደውም
She did/didn't like them.	• **Weddedechïw/ alweddedechïwm.**	ወደደችው/አልወደደችውም
We did/didn't like them.	• **Weddednachew/ alweddednachewm.**	ወደድናቸው/ አልወደድናቸውም

At what time ...?

(At) what time does the next show start?	• **Yemiqeṯlew tïr'it besïnt se'at ydjemral?**	የሚቀጥለው ትርኢት በስንት ሰዓት ይጀምራል?
(At) what time does the next show finish?	• **Yemiqeṯlew tïr'it besïnt se'at yalqal?**	የሚቀጥለው ትርኢት በስንት ሰዓት ያልቃል?
It starts at eight.	• **Behulet se'at ydjemral.**	በሁለት ሰዓት ይጀምራል
It finishes at half past nine.	• **Besost se'at yalqal.**	በሦስት ሰዓት ተኩል ያልቃል

Education

School/Class

What school do you attend?	• **Yet tmaralleh?**	የት ትማራለህ?
I attend the ...	• **... ïmarallehu?**	... እማራለሁ
What year are you in?	• **Yesïnteña amet temari neh?**	የስንተኛ ዓመት ተማሪ ነህ?
The first (year).	• **Andeña (amet).**	አንደኛ (ዓመት)
The second (year).	• **Huleteña (amet).**	ሁለተኛ (ዓመት)
What class are you in?	• **Sïnteña kïfïl tmaralleh?**	ስንተኛ ክፍል ትማራለህ?
The third.	• **Sosteña.**	ሦስተኛ
The fourth.	• **Arateña.**	አራተኛ
Where is your school?	• **Tmïhïrt-bétïh yet new?**	ትምህርት ቤትህ የት ነው?
It's in Rome Square.	• **BeRom adebabay.**	በሮም አደባባይ
It's in the centre.	• **Mahel ketema).**	ማሐል ከተማ
Is your school big?	• **Tmïhïrt-bétïh tïliq new wey?**	ትምህርት ቤትህ ትልቅ ነው ወይ?
Is your school small?	• **Tmïhïrt-bétïh tïnïsh new wey?**	ትምህርት ቤትህ ትንሽ ነው ወይ?
It's quite large.	• **Bemetenu tïlïq new.**	በመጠኑ ትልቅ ነው
Are the classes large?	• **Bzu temariwoch allut wey?**	ብዙ ተማሪዎች አሉት ወይ?
No, there are usually about twenty of us.	• **Yellutm, abzañawn gzé wede haya gedema nen.**	የሉትም፡ አብዛኛውን ግዜ ወደ ሀያ ገደማ ነን
Is it a good school?	• **Tiru tmïhïrt-bét new wey?**	ጥሩ ትምህርት ቤት ነው ወይ?
Yes, the teachers are very good.	• **Awo, astemariwoch betam gwebezoch nachew.**	አዎ፡ አስተማሪዎቹ በጣም ጉበዞች ናቸው
No, it is lacking in facilities.	• **Aydellem, yemesaryawoch ïtret allew.**	አይደለም፡ የመሳሪያዎች እጥረት አለው

Facilities

Are there many sports facilities?	• **Bzu yesport mesariyawoch allut wey?**	ብዙ የስፖርት መሳሪያዎች አሉት ወይ?
There's a gymnasium.	• **And yesport kïfïl allew.**	አንድ የስፖርት ክፍል አለው
There's a swimming pool.	• **And mewaña allew.**	አንድ መዋኛ አለው
There's a tennis court.	• **And yetenis méda allew.**	አንድ የተኒስ ሜዳ አለው
There's a volleyball court.	• **And yemereb kwas mechawecha allew.**	አንድ የመረብ ኳስ መጫወቻ አለው
There's a basketball court.	• **And yeqïrchat kwas mechawecha allew.**	አንድ የቅርጫት ኳስ መጫወቻ አለው

Lessons

At what time do the lessons start?	• **Tmïhïrtu besïnt se'at ydjemral?**	ትምህርቱ በስንት ሰዓት ይጀምራል?

At what time do the lessons finish?	• **Tmïhïrtu besïnt se‘at yalïqal?**	ትምህርቱ በስንት ሰዓት ያልቃል?
(They start) at eight.	• **Behulet se‘at ydjemral.**	በሁለት ሰዓት ይጀመራል
(They finish) at one.	• **Be‘and se‘at yalïqal.**	በአንድ ሰዓት ያልቃል
How many hours (of lessons) do you have?	• **Mïn yahl yetmïhïrt se‘atoch alluwachuh?**	ምን ያህል የትምህርት ሰዓቶች አሉዋችሁ?
(Usually) five hours.	• **Abzañawn gzé ammïst se‘atoch.**	አብዛኛውን ግዜ አምስት ሰዓቶች
How long does a lesson last?	• **And kïfïle gzé mïn yahl deqiqa new?**	አንድ ክፍለ ግዜ ምን ያህል ደቂቃ ነው?
One hour.	• **And se‘at.**	አንድ ሰዓት
Fifty minutes.	• **Amsa deqiqa.**	አምሣ ደቂቃ
Are you given much class-work?	• **Bzu yekïfïl sïra ysetuhal wey?**	ብዙ የክፍል ሥራ ይሰጡሃል ወይ?
Are you given much homework?	• **Bzu yebét sïra ysetuhal wey?**	ብዙ የቤት ሥራ ይሰጡሃል ወይ?
Too much!	• **Betam bzu!**	በጣም ብዙ
Quite a lot!	• **Bemetenu!**	በመጠኑ
Yes, mostly Mathematics, ...	• **Awo, beteley hisabïn bemimeleket.**	አዎ፡ በተለይ ሂሳብን በሚመለከት

Subjects

What subjects do you study?	• **Mïn aynet tmïhïrt tmaralleh?**	ምን ዓይነት ትምህርት ትማራለህ?
(I study) Italian and French.	• **Talyaniñana Ferensayña (ïmarallehu).**	ጣልያንኛና ፈረንሳይኛ (እማራለሁ)
(I study) English and Amharic .	• **Ïnglizñana Amarïña (ïmarallehu).**	እንግሊዝኛና አማርኛ (እማራለሁ)
(I study) German and Arabic.	• **Djermeniñana Arebïña (ïmarallehu).**	ጀርመንኛና ዓረብኛ (እማራለሁ)
(I study) Maths.	• **Hisab (ïmarallehu).**	ሂሳብ(እማራለሁ)
(I study) Science.	• **Sayns (ïmarallehu).**	ሳይንስ (እማራለሁ)
(I study) History.	• **Tarik (ïmarallehu).**	ታሪክ (እማራለሁ)
(I study) Geography.	• **Djiograf (ïmarallehu).**	ጂኦግራፊ (እማራለሁ)
(I study) Art.	• **Sï‘ïl (ïmarallehu).**	ስዕል (እማራለሁ)
(I study) P.E.	• **Sport (ïmarallehu).**	ስፖርት (እማራለሁ)
(I study) Music.	• **Muziqa (ïmarallehu).**	ሙዚቃ (እማራለሁ)
What's your favourite subject?	• **Yetñaw yetmïhïrt aynet des ylehal?**	የትኛው የትምህርት ዓይነት ደስ ይልሃል?
Which are your favourite subjects?	• **Yetñochu yetmïhïrt aynetoch des yluhal?**	የትኞቹ የትምህርት ዓይነቶች ደስ ይሉሃል?
Do you like Mathematics?	• **Hisab tweddalleh wey?**	ሂሳብ ትወዳለህ ወይ?
Do you like Literature?	• **Sïnetsïhuf tweddalleh wey?**	ስነጽሑፍ ትወዳለህ ወይ?
Yes, I do/I like it.	• **Awo, des yleñal.**	አዎ፡ ደስ ይለኛል
No, I don't (like it).	• **Alwedm, des ayleñïm.**	አልወድም፡ ደስ አይለኝም

Plans for the future

What are your plans for the future?	• **Yewedefit ïqïdochïh mïnd nachew?**	የወደፊት እቅዶችህ ምንድ ናቸው?
I am going to university.	• **Yuniversiti lememmar new.**	ዩኒቨርሲቲ ለመማር ነው
I am going to work.	• **Sïra lemedjemer new.**	ሥራ ለመጀመር ነው
What will you do when you have finished school?	• **Tmïhïrt kecheresk behwala mïn tadergalleh?**	ትምህርት ከጨረስክ በኋላ ምን ታደርጋለህ?
I will look for a job.	• **Sïra lïfelïg new.**	ሥራ ልፈልግ ነው
I am going to France for a year.	• **Leand amet Ferensay ager lïhéd new.**	ለአንድ ዓመት ፈረንሳይ አገር ልሔድ ነው
(I don't know) we'll see ...	• **(Alaweqkum) ïnayewallen.**	(አላወቅኩም) እናየዋለን

I would like to be ...

What kind of work would you like to do?	• **Mïn aynet sïra mesrat des ylïhal?**	ምን ዓይነት ሥራ መስራት ደስ ይልሃል?
I would like to be an architect.	• **Anati mehon des yleñ nebber.**	አናጢ መሆን ደስ ይለኝ ነበር
I would like to be a journalist.	• **Gazéteña mehon des yleñ nebber.**	ጋዜጠኛ መሆን ደስ ይለኝ ነበር
I would like to be a hairdresser.	• **Tegwïr astekakay mehon des yleñ nebber.**	ጠጕር አስተካካይ መሆን ደስ ይለኝ ነበር
I would like to be a mechanic.	• **Mekanik mehon des yleñ nebber.**	መካኒክ መሆን ደስ ይለኝ ነበር
I would like to be a teacher.	• **Astemari mehon des yleñ nebber.**	አስተማሪ መሆን ደስ ይለኝ ነበር

Functions

Greeting People

Hello!, Hi.	• **Selam!/Téna'stïlñ!**	ሰላም/ጤና'ስጥልኝ
Good morning!	• **Ïndemn adderu!**	እንደምን አደሩ
Good afternoon!	• **Ïndemn walu!**	እንደምን ዋሉ
Good morning, Mr./Mrs/Miss ...	• **Ïndemn adderu ato/ weyzero/weyzerit ...**	እንደምን አደሩ አቶ/ወይዘሮ/ወይዘሪት
Good evening ...	• **Ïndemn ameshu ...**	እንደምን አመሹ

Introducing Someone And Being Introduced

This is ...	• **Yïh ...**	ይህ ... (m)
	• **Yïchi ...**	ይቺ ... (f)
This is Mr...	• **Ato ... yïbbalallu.**	አቶ ... ይባላሉ
May I introduce Mr... (to you?)	• **Ke'ato ... lastewaweqïh.**	ከአቶ ... ላስተዋውቅህ
My name is ...	• **Sïmé ... ybalal.**	ስሜ ... ይባላል
Hello! (I am Carla).	• **Téna'stïlñ (Karla ïbbalallehu)**	ጤና'ስጥልኝ (ካርላ እባላለሁ)
How do you do?	• **Ïndemn neh?**	እንደምን ነህ? (m)
	• **Ïndemn nesh?**	እንደምን ነሽ? (f)
Pleased to meet you!	• **Melkam twïwq yadrïglïn!**	መልካም ትውውቅ ያድርግልን

Taking Leave

Bye!	• **Dehna hun!**	ደህና ሁን (m)
	• **Dehna huñi!**	ደህና ሁኚ (f)
See you soon!	• **Bedehna yagenañen!**	በደህና ያገናኘን
Goodbye!	• **Dehna hun/huñi!**	ደህና ሁን/ሁኚ (m/f)
Good night!	• **Dehna ïdder/ïdderi!**	ደህና እደር/እደሪ (m/f)
See you later!	• **Ïngenañallen!**	እንገናኛለን
See you tomorrow!	• **Nege ïngenañallen!**	ነገ እንገናኛለን

Attracting Attention

Excuse me ...	• **Yqïrta ...**	ይቅርታ
Excuse me, please ...	• **Yqïrta adrïgliñ!**	ይቅርታ አድርግልኝ

Congratulating

Well done!	• **Gosh!**	ጎሽ
Congratulations!	• **Ïnkwan des alleh!**	እንኳን ደስ አለህ
You've done very well!	• **Asdesetken!**	አስደሰትከን (m)
	Asdesetshïn!	አስደሰትሽን (f)

Expressing Good Wishes

Best wishes!	• **Melkam mñot!**	መልካም ምኞት
All the best!	• **Melkam ïddïl!**	መልካም ዕድል
I wish you ...	• **... ïmeñlïhallehu!**	... እመኝልሀለሁ
Merry Christmas!	• **Melkam yeGenna be'al!.**	መልካም የገና በዓል
Happy New Year!	• **Melkam Addis Amet!**	መልካም አዲስ ዓመት
Happy Easter!	• **Melkam Fasika!**	መልካም ፋሲካ
Happy Birthday!	• **Melkam yeLïdet be'al!**	መልካም የልደት በዓል
Have a good holiday!	• **Melkam ïreft!**	መልካም ዕረፍት
Have a good trip!	• **Melkam guzo!**	መልካም ጉዞ

Expressing And Responding To Thanks

Thanks!	• **Ïgzihér ystïlñ!**	እግዚሄር ይስጥልኝ
Thanks a lot/ thank you very much!	• **Betam amesegnallehu!**	በጣም አመሰግናለሁ
Thank you for ...	• **Le ... amesegnallehu.**	ለ ... አመሰግናለሁ
Thank you!	• **Amesegnallehu!**	አመሰግናለሁ
I don't know how to thank you!	• **Ïndét ïndemamesegïnh/sh allawqïm!**	እንዴት እንደማመሰግንህ/ሽ አላውቅም

Don't mention it!	• **Mnïm aydellem!**	ምንም አይደለም
It's all right!	• **Mnïm aydellem!**	ምንም አይደለም
It has been a pleasure!	• **Betam des bloñal!**	በጣም ደስ ብሎኛል

Expressing Lack Of Understanding

Pardon?	• **Yqïrta!**	ይቅርታ
(I beg your) pardon?	• **Mïn alu, yqïrta?**	ምን አሉ፡ ይቅርታ
I don't understand.	• **Yqïrta, algebañïm.**	ይቅርታ፡አልገባኝም
I haven't understood.	• **Alteredañïm.**	አልተረዳኝም
Would you repeat it, please?	• **Ïbakwon ïndegena ydgemulñ.**	እባክዎን እንደገና ይድገሙልኝ
What does it mean?	• **Mïn malet new?**	ምን ማለት ነው
Can you repeat it, please?	• **Lïtdegmew tchïlalleh wey?**	ልትደግመው ትችላለህ ወይ?
It is not clear.	• **Gïlts aydellem.**	ግልፅ አይደለም

Expressing Agreement And Disagreement

I agree.	• **Ïsmamallehu.**	እስማማለሁ
You're right!	• **Lïk neh/nesh!**	ልክ ነህ/ነሽ (m/f)
Of course!	• **Gïlts new!**	ግልፅ ነው
Right!	• **Tkïkïl!**	ትክክል
I don't agree!	• **Alsmamam!**	አልስማማም
You are wrong!	• **Tesastehal/shal!**	ተሳስተሃል/ሻል (m/f)
It's not true!	• **Wushet!**	ውሸት
Not at all!	• **Befïtsum!**	በፍጹም

Expressing Surprise

What a surprise!	• **Ygermal!**	ይገርማል
What a nice surprise!	• **Yemïsrach!**	የምስራች
This is a real surprise!	• **Betam yemigerm new!**	በጣም የሚገርም ነው
No kidding?	• **Mïn tqeldalleh?**	ምን ትቀልዳለህ
I can't believe it!	• **Alamïnm!**	አላምንም
No!	• **Ayhonm!**	አይሆንም

Expressing Hope

Let's hope so!	• **Tesfa ïnadergallen!**	ተስፋ እናደርጋለን
I hope so!	• **Bale mulu tesfa neñ!**	ባለ ሙሉ ተስፋ ነኝ
If only!	• **Biyadergïln!**	ቢያደርግልን
I hope you'll be better.	• **Dehna ïndemïthon/ñi tesfa alleñ.**	ደህና እንደምትሆን/ኚ ተስፋ አለኝ

Expressing Satisfaction

Wonderful!	• **Grum new!**	ግሩም ነው
How lovely!	• **Abét siyamr!**	አቤት ሲያምር
I'm very happy/satisfied ...	• **... des bloñal/rekkahu!**	... ደስ ብሎኛል/.ረካሁ
It's just what I wanted.	• **.... fïllagotén ageñehu.**	... ፍላጎቴን አገኘሁ
It's lovely!	• **Abét des sil!**	አቤት ደስ ሲል

Expressing Gratitude

I am very grateful to you ...	• **Letederegelñ betam amesegnallehu.**	ለተደረገልኝ በጣም አመሰግናለሁ
You've been very kind ...	• **Betam deg sew newot.**	በጣም ደግ ሰው ነዎት
Thank you!	• **Amesegnallehu!**	አመሰግናለሁ
Thanks for everything!	• **Lehullum neger amesgnallehu!**	ለሁሉም ነገር አመሰግናለሁ

Apologizing

Sorry!	• **Yqïrta!**	ይቅርታ
I am so sorry!	• **Betam aznallehu!**	በጣም አዝናለሁ
I apologize for ...	• **... yqïrta ïteyqallehu.**	... ይቅርታ እጠይቃለሁ
I am sorry!	• **Aznallehu!**	አዝናለሁ

Expressing Indifference

I don't care!	• **Denta yeleñm!**	ደንታ የለኝም
It's all the same to me.	• **Lené hullum and new!**	ለኔ ሁሉም አንድ ነው
Do as you like!	• **Ïnde felegïk adrïg!**	እንደ ፈለግክ አድርግ

Suggesting A Course Of Action (Including The Speaker)

Shall we go ...?	• **... bnïhéds?**	... ብንሔድስ
We could ...	• **... ïnchïl nebber.**	... እንችል ነበር
Will you come with us ...?	• **Keña gar tmetalleh wey?**	ከኛ ጋር ትመጣለህ ወይ?
Would you like to ...?	• **... des ylïh nebber wey? ... twed nebber wey?**	... ደስ ይልህ ነበር ወይ? ... ትወድ ነበር ወይ?

Requesting Others To Do Something

Could you ...?	• **... tchïlalleh/tchïyallesh?**	... ትችላለህ/ትችያለሽ (m/f)
Would you mind ...?	• **Ïbakïhn/ïbakïshn?**	እባክህን/እባክሽን ... (m/f)
I would be very grateful if you could ...	• **... betam des yleñ nebber.**	... በጣም ደስ ይለኝ ነበር

Asking For Advice

What do you think of ...?	• **Mïn ymeslehal?**	ምን ይመስለሃል?
Any ideas?	• **Mïn addis hasab alleh?**	ምን አዲስ ሐሳብ አለህ?
What would you do (in my situation?)	• **Bené bota bïthon/bithoñi noro mïn taderg/tadergi nebber?**	በኔ ቦታ ብትሆን/ብትሆኚ ኖሮ ምን ታደርግ/ታደርጊ ነበር?
What do you suggest?	• **Mïn hasab taqerblïñalleh/ taqerbilñallesh?**	ምን ሐሳብ ታቀርብልኛለህ/ ታቀርቢልኛለሽ?
What would you suggest?	• **Mïn tmekreñalleh/ tmekriñallesh?**	ምን ትመክረኛለህ/ ትመክሪኛለሽ?

QUESTIONS		
WHEN?	• Meché?	መቼ?
WHERE?	• Wedét?	ወዴት?
WHY?	• Lemïn?	ለምን?
WHO?	• Man?	ማን?
WHAT?	• Mïn?	ምን?
WHICH?	• Yetïñaw?	የትኛው?
HOW?	• Ïndét?	እንዴት?
HOW MUCH?	• Sïnt?	ስንት?

LENGTH OF TIME		
DAY	• Qen	ቀን
WEEK	• Samïnt	ሳምንት
MONTH	• Wer	ወር
SEASONS	• Weqt	ወቅት
YEAR	• Amet	ዓመት
YESTERDAY	• Tnant	ትናንት
TOMORROW	• Nege	ነገ
TODAY	• Zaré	ዛሬ

DAYS OF THE WEEK		
MONDAY	• Seño	ሰኞ
TUESDAY	• Makseño	ማክሰኞ
WEDNESDAY	• Rob	ሮብ
THURSDAY	• Hamus	ሐሙስ
FRIDAY	• Arb	ዓርብ
SATURDAY	• Qdamé	ቅዳሜ
SUNDAY	• Ïhud	እሁድ

MONTHS		
JANUARY	• T̲ïr	ጥር
FEBRUARY	• Yekatit	የካቲት
MARCH	• Megabit	መጋቢት
APRIL	• Miyazya	ሚያዝያ
MAY	• Gïnbot	ግንቦት
JUNE	• Sené	ሰኔ
JULY	• Hamlé	ሓምሌ
AUGUST	• Nehasé	ነሐሴ
SEPTEMBER	• Meskerem	መስከረም
OCTOBER	• T̲qïmt	ጥቅምት
NOVEMBER	• H̄dar	ኅዳር?
DECEMBER	• Tahsas	ታህሳስ

HOW OFTEN?		
HOW OFTEN	• Beyesïnt gzé	በየስንት ግዜ
ALWAYS	• Hulgzé	ሁልግዜ
SOMETIMES	• Andand gzé	አንዳንድ ግዜ
NEVER	• Befïtsum, bec̲h̲rash	በፍጹም፡ በጭራሽ
TWICE	• Hulet gzé	ሁለት ግዜ
OFTEN	• Zewetïr	ዘወትር
ONCE	• Andé	አንዴ
SELDOM	• Andandé	አንዳንዴ
USUALLY	• Abzañawn	አብዛኛውን ግዜ

DANGEROUS		
HELP!	• Ïrduñ!	እርዱኝ!
FIRE!	• Ïsat!	እሳት!
IT'S DANGEROUS!	• Kadega tet̲enqequ!	ካደጋ ተጠንቀቁ!
DON'T TOUCH!	• Atïnka!	አትንካ!
BE CAREFUL!	• Tet̲enqeq/raq bel!	ተጠንቀቅ/ራቅ በል!